NETWORK RESOURCE PLANNING
FOR SAP R/3, BAAN IV, AND PEOPLESOFT

THE MCGRAW-HILL SERIES ON COMPUTER COMMUNICATIONS (SELECTED TITLES)

Network Resource Planning for SAP R/3, BAAN IV, and PeopleSoft

A Guide to Planning Enterprise Applications

Annette Clewett
Dana Franklin
Ann McCown

McGraw-Hill
New York San Francisco Washington, D.C.
Auckland Bogotá Caracas Lisbon London
Madrid Mexico City Milan Montreal New Delhi
San Juan Singapore Sydney Tokyo Toronto

Library of Congress Cataloging-in-Publication Data

Clewett, Annette.
    Network resource planning for SAP R/3, BAAN IV, and Peoplesoft : a
guide to planning enterprise applications / Annette
Clewett, Dana Franklin, Ann McCown.
        p.   cm.
    Includes index.
    ISBN 0-07-913647-8
    1. Business enterprises—Computer networks—Management.   2. SAP
R/3.   3. Baan IV.   4. PeopleSoft Financials.   I. Franklin, Dana.
II. McCown, Ann.   III. Title.
HD30.37.C58   1998
658'.05468—dc21   98-21011
                                                                              CIP

McGraw-Hill

A Division of The McGraw·Hill Companies

    234567890   DOC/DOC   90321098

ISBN 0-07-913647-8

*The sponsoring editor for this book was Steven Elliot and the production supervisor was
Tina Cameron. It was set in Vendome by Publication Services.*

Printed and bound by R. R. Donnelley & Sons Company.

McGraw-Hill books are available at special quantity discounts to use as
premiums and sales promotions, or for use in corporate training programs.
For more information, please write to Director of Special Sales, McGraw-Hill,
11 West 19th Street, New York, NY 10011. Or contact your local bookstore.

This book is printed on recycled, acid-free paper containing a minimum of 50%
recycled de-inked fiber.

NRP is a trademark or registered trademark of Make Systems, Inc. in the United States
and other countries. McGraw-Hill is independent of Make Systems, Inc.

CONTENTS

Contents

Contents

PREFACE

This book is intended as a guide for network planners, both technical staff and managers, who are responsible for ensuring that an enterprise's wide area network infrastructure can support mission-critical enterprise application deployments. For the experienced network manager, the book describes how to implement Network Resource Planning (NRP) methodologies, with examples using specific performance management software tools available today. However, NRP is very much a matter of process rather than specific tools. For an experienced network manager, the mechanics of using a software tool to collect data on network performance is not problematic—rather, the questions are what data to collect and how to interpret the meaning of that data in terms of overall network planning objectives. This book is thus focused on the processes of NRP: setting objectives, determining what data to collect, making assumptions about the deployment of a new enterprise application, assessing the validity of the data that is collected, and evaluating the results in light of the assumptions that are required in order to predict network performance under conditions that may not yet exist in reality.

While the focus of this book is on analyzing a network's ability to support deployment of a new Enterprise Resource Planning (ERP) application such as SAP R/3, BAAN IV, or PeopleSoft, its techniques are applicable to many other types of client/server applications. It can also be used to provide valuable insights into how the enterprise network is supporting existing applications and to help diagnose conditions within the enterprise network that may be contributing to application performance problems.

This book should provide valuable insights for several types of readers:

■ *Network planners and designers* need to determine the effect of new applications introduced on their networks such as SAP R/3, BAAN IV, PeopleSoft, or other enterprise applications and to find support for decisions concerning the adequacy of each segment of the network. This book will provide them with practical information on the tools and processes available to help them with this task as well as techniques for carrying out those processes.

■ *Information Technology managers* at all levels need to be able to present a solid, business-oriented rationale for the growth or upgrades of their corporate networks, including network enhancements necessary to support applications such as SAP R/3, BAAN IV, or PeopleSoft. This book will provide them with the practical knowledge to help them quantify and document a network's current and projected performance in order to provide the justification for proposed network improvements.

■ *Senior nontechnical managers* (CEOs, Finance, Procurement, Operations), who as part of their need for an overview of their organization's present or proposed network, want to understand how the network's use is to be measured, and how its costs are identified and controlled.

Although some of the book's material is technical, we hope that the majority of the book will prove to be readable and valuable to nontechnical readers. We hope the reader will finish this book with an understanding of the following:

■ How to set focused, bounded, achievable objectives for a network resource planning project

■ How to collect relevant, valid data on current network performance and to understand the limitations of that data in terms of providing a current baseline for network planning purposes

■ How to collect valid data on the traffic demands made by specific client/server applications (specifically, applications not yet deployed on the enterprise network) and to develop valid assumptions about how the application will be used when it is deployed

■ How to determine the criteria for evaluating the performance of the network under various capacity planning ("what-if") scenarios

■ How to set up capacity planning scenarios, run the models or simulations, and evaluate the results of the scenarios in light of both the performance criteria and the assumptions made when setting up the scenarios

■ How to use the results of capacity planning activities to redesign a network to meet performance objectives

■ The limitations of NRP techniques, given today's data collection and performance management tools and methodologies—what sorts of NRP objectives cannot realistically be supported with any validity as of today

■ How NRP processes and tools will evolve in the future both to reduce the limitations of the current NRP techniques and to support emerging networking technologies

Organization of the Book

This book is organized in two parts. Part One explains the methodologies of network resource planning and issues involved in the implementation of those methodologies. Part Two presents case studies showing how Network Resource Planning methodologies are being used in three organizations.

Part 1, "Network Resource Planning":

- Chapter 1, "Network Resource Planning Overview," provides the motivation for NRP. It explains why NRP techniques are becoming critical for any organization looking at deploying mission-critical client/server applications within an enterprise network.

- Chapter 2, "The Network Resource Planning Process," provides a high-level overview of NRP processes and tools.

- Chapter 3, "Getting Started," covers the planning that is needed and the issues that must be addressed up front to help ensure a successful NRP project.

- Chapter 4, "Baselining the Network," covers the specific processes, methodologies, and issues involved in analyzing the current performance of an existing enterprise network.

- Chapter 5, "Application Planning," covers the processes, methodologies, and issues involved in assessing the demands made on the network by a specific application. It also discusses how to define assumptions about how the application will be used on the network and how to determine quality-of-service criteria for evaluating whether the network will provide acceptable support for the application after deployment.

- Chapter 6, "Capacity Planning," discusses how to build a valid network model to use for testing "what-if" scenarios to evaluate the network's ability to support a new enterprise application and how to test certain types of network redesign scenarios.

- Chapter 7, "The Future of Network Resource Planning," discusses the evolution of NRP techniques and tools to support the emergence of new networking technologies and to address some of today's NRP limitations.

Part 2, "Case Studies":

- Chapter 8, "Lucent Technologies," describes an NRP project that looked at the performance of a portion of the existing global network, and modeled future performance after deployment of a PeopleSoft (version 6) Human Resources application.

- Chapter 9, "3M Company," describes an NRP project that looked at the deployment of several PeopleSoft (version 6) modules across portions of the domestic enterprise network.

- Chapter 10, "AlliedSignal," describes how the organization uses baselining techniques to monitor and solve performance problems on its existing enterprise network.

ACKNOWLEDGMENTS

Many people have contributed to and supported the development of this book, and our heartfelt thanks go to all of them. There are a number of these who deserve special mention.

The authors would like first to thank Walt Brown and Bill Schaffer, both formerly of Make Systems, Inc., for the original inspiration and support that led to this project. In addition, we would like to thank Stephen Howard and Beverly Dygert at Make Systems, Inc., for their continual support and encouragement, and Dr. Richard Tibbs, at Make Labs, for sharing his knowledge and expertise in network modeling theory and implementations.

We would also like to thank Lucent Technologies, the 3M Company, and AlliedSignal for their willing cooperation in allowing us to share their NRP projects and experiences. Specifically, we would like to thank Kerry Field and Joe Huehne at the 3M Company and Dan Tulledge at AlliedSignal for their patience and perseverance in helping us put together the case studies in Part Two of this book.

Dan Macagney, Sandon Joren, Dan Tulledge, and Janis Bishop all deserve our gratitude for their thoughtful and timely reviews of the material in the book.

In addition, we would like to thank a number of others who have chosen to remain anonymous, but who nevertheless should be acknowledged for providing us with invaluable insights into the NRP process through their involvement with various NRP consulting projects. You know who you are, and we thank you.

Finally, and most importantly, we would like to acknowledge Linda Hamilton, Melisa Tse, and Phillip, Paige, and Rebecca Franklin for their enormous contributions to this project. Without the support and patience they gave regularly throughout the creation of this book, this accomplishment would not have been possible.

INTRODUCTION

SAP R/3, BAAN IV, and PeopleSoft are all examples of client/server applications designed to run in a distributed computing environment. In order to meet the objectives inherent in their implementation, an enterprise network infrastructure that adequately supports the application's functionality is required. This book focuses on that network infrastructure.

The goal of this book is to help the reader plan for an implementation of SAP R/3, BAAN IV, PeopleSoft, or another enterprise client/server application from the point of view of the network infrastructure required to support that implementation. This book will address how a network manager can assess the performance and capacity of an existing network, how to plan changes to the network to increase capacity, and how to "test" those changes to determine whether they will actually produce the desired results under the proposed new application load before physically implementing the changes.

In today's enterprise networks, planning is essential. As organizations continue to migrate to distributed computing and client/server applications and to establish remote connectivity for outlying plants and offices, the performance of wide area networking resources becomes business-critical. As the demands for wide area connectivity and capacity increase, organizations need to be able to anticipate and plan for adequate capacity.

At its ITxpo/97 symposium, the GartnerGroup made the following predictions:

- Enterprise WAN usage will increase by up to 300 percent and WAN costs will double in the next five years.

- Eighty percent of user applications will rely on network computing architectures by 2002; however, unless major reengineering efforts are undertaken by 2000, 80% of today's WANs will not be "network computing–ready."

- By 2000, 20 percent of major network-centric applications will experience severe performance problems because of users' failure to understand network/application interactions.

- By 2000, no network design process will be successful without the characterization of applications—a process that will consume 30 percent of the overall project.

- Without completion of a thorough and comprehensive network baseline, efforts to create a network design simulation model will fail.

- The need to supply quality of service to networked applications and establish SLAs for network performance will render the bandwidth overprovision approach ineffective and eliminate "back of the envelope" planning.

This book will help you address these issues. The goal of this book is to explain the methodologies for using data collection and performance management software tools available today to automate the network planning process as much as possible. The use of NRP techniques can provide the following benefits for a large client/server application deployment project:

- Shorter time to full deployment, by avoiding delays due to network infrastructure problems

- More effective implementation, because of having accurately predicted the demands a new application will make on the network

- Higher probability of quality of service being met for the new application, due to being able to anticipate and provision for the added demand on the network that the application will create.

This book will help you set realistic, achievable objectives for your NRP project; collect relevant, valid data to use in your performance analyses; and provide you with methods for determining whether or not you have met your goals. This book focuses on real-world tools and solutions and is based on actual consulting projects undertaken by the authors.

Limitations on the Scope of This Book

There are some limitations in the scope of this book that should be addressed up front. First, many of the critical challenges in implementing an ERP system such as SAP R/3, BAAN IV, or PeopleSoft are in the areas of business process reengineering. These challenges go far beyond technical implementation issues; they affect how the company functions and how employees do their jobs. These types of issues are not covered in this book. Neither are details on the implementation of the

ERP application itself. These are covered very well in other publications such as *Implementing SAP R/3* by Nancy Bancroft for SAP R/3. This book focuses on the specific challenge of determining how to use NRP techniques to ensure that the network on which the SAP R/3, BAAN IV, or PeopleSoft application depends is adequate to the task.

The second caveat is that this book focuses strictly on the performance of the enterprise network and its effects on application performance. Actual application performance, and quality of service as perceived by the user, may be affected by other factors in addition to network performance, such as the design of the application, the capacity and performance of the client and server systems, and database performance (which may in turn be affected by other, competing database applications). These are all beyond the scope of this book. However, the techniques discussed here may still provide valuable insights into the actual cause of an application performance problem by ruling out the network component of performance problems in some cases.

Examples

Examples are used throughout this book to illustrate how organizations can make use of the techniques presented here. In almost all cases, these examples are based on actual projects undertaken by the authors of this book as part of their experience as consultants. In many cases, however, the names and specifics have been changed to preserve the anonymity of organizations, who understandably do not want details of their network operations made public. In other cases, examples have been created by combining issues and situations from several actual projects to make the examples easier to follow, more to the point, or more complete.

It should be noted that most of the examples in this book are based on consulting projects the authors did under the sponsorship of Make Systems, Inc., using their NetMaker XA product. However, as we have noted throughout the book, there are other tools from other vendors that can also be used to implement the processes described in this book. While we believe that the Make Systems suite of tools is a good choice for implementing most NRP projects, tools from other vendors can be used with equal success, based on the needs and objectives of an individual project.

NETWORK RESOURCE PLANNING
FOR SAP R/3, BAAN IV, AND PEOPLESOFT

Network Resource Planning

CHAPTER 1

Network Resource Planning Overview

Network Resource Planning (NRP^{TM}) is a set of well-defined, software-supported processes that ensure that distributed applications achieve an acceptable quality of service at minimum network cost.

In order to meet the objectives inherent in an application's implementation, the organization's network infrastructure must adequately support the application's functionality. If the network cannot process transactions or respond to users fast enough, users will be unhappy and productivity will suffer, with a negative impact on the entire business. Even worse, if the network is so overloaded that it fails, the corporation may be unable to proceed with business. Enterprise applications such as SAP R/3, BAAN IV, and PeopleSoft implement mission-critical business functions and depend on reliable, high-performance networks.

NRP addresses one of the challenges inherent in implementing any major distributed client/server application: how to ensure that the application will perform up to expectations when it is deployed onto a corporation's production network.

Why Enterprise Applications Need Network Resource Planning

Enterprise applications are large-scale business applications that organizations use to manage their processes. Enterprise Resource Planning (ERP) applications are the applications used by industrial manufacturing firms to build and execute global manufacturing plans (Smith Barney Research, 1997). Products from the vendors SAP AG, BAAN, and PeopleSoft are currently among the best known and most widely implemented ERP applications. These applications promise to integrate an entire corporation's business processes, enabling the corporation to become more flexible, efficient, and competitive.

SAP AG has quite successfully introduced SAP R/3 into the manufacturing market in Europe and North America, including process manufacturers, automobile manufacturers, and high-tech companies. It is also making inroads into financial services, health care, utility, and nonprofit industries. The BAAN IV product suite supports the entire business processes of an industrial organization and is designed to handle multinational and multisite organizations. The BAAN IV product family is widely recognized for its ease of use and implementation. PeopleSoft products are designed to offer users superior ease of use, flexibility, and scalability. The product line that currently represents the core of PeopleSoft's revenue is PeopleSoft HRMS, which addresses human-resources functions such as personnel and salary administration, recruiting, position management, and training.

The objective for enterprise applications is typically to provide enterprisewide access to integrated information and business processes. This implies access to a common set of business data from anywhere within the enterprise, which in turn implies a distributed network infrastructure that enables access from anywhere, typically including access over the wide area network. Figure 1-1 shows an information infrastructure that would support a typical enterprise application.

Figure 1-1
Diagram illustrating a
shared information
infrastructure.

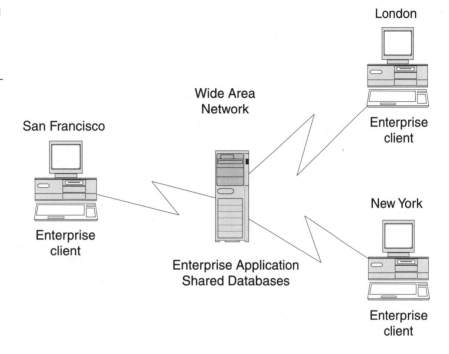

Enterprise applications usually support clients that communicate over a wide area network (WAN) to access data from a centralized database resource.

Businesses implement an enterprise application to improve information access and to create such competitive advantages as

- Increased responsiveness to customers, to increase customer satisfaction
- Better availability of information to employees, to help individual employees be more productive and to facilitate team-oriented work environments
- Better availability of needed information anywhere within the global enterprise, regardless of the actual location of that information, to facilitate better business decisions and business management

SAP R/3, BAAN, and PeopleSoft products promise streamlined, simplified processes that are efficient and effective, for higher productivity and increased responsiveness. They make corporate data available to those who need it, regardless of the physical location of that data.

The Evolution of Enterprise Computing

In the "old days," major business applications were mainframe based, with control of the application and its resources residing in the "glass house." Figure 1-2 illustrates the type of mainframe environment that was common prior to the growth of client/server computing. All application processing, including the user interface, occurred centrally on the mainframe. The user devices were "dumb terminals" with display memory but virtually no processing power.

In this type of environment it was relatively straightforward to predict the performance characteristics of an application. The number of possible users and the characteristics of those user sessions were well-defined, and the number of applications competing for mainframe resources was also well-defined. All computing resources were under the centralized control of the Management Information System (MIS) department (commonly known today as information technology [IT] or information systems [IS]).

With the move to distributed computing and client/server applications, the orderly, centralized nature of applications disappeared. The advent of powerful desktop computers and local area networks (LANs) meant that applications could be implemented completely outside the domain of the traditional mainframe environment, and data became decentralized. As shown in Fig. 1-3, departmental computing environments emerged with local processing power (personal computers) at each user's desk, with a local server for shared services such as file and

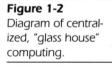

Figure 1-2

Diagram of centralized, "glass house" computing.

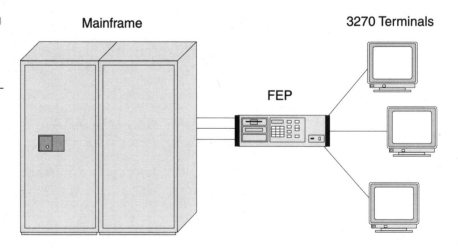

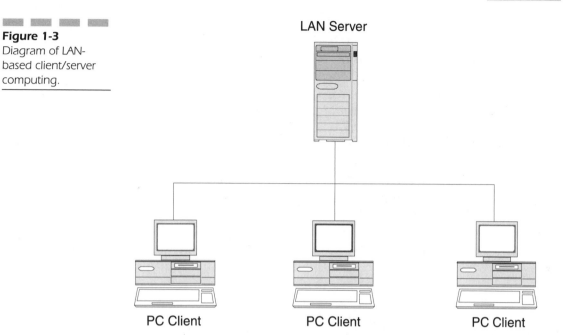

Figure 1-3

Diagram of LAN-based client/server computing.

LAN Server

PC Client   PC Client   PC Client

print sharing. For the most part, client/server applications ran in these local environments.

The benefits of local computing over mainframe computing were many: dedicated resources meant much better response times, and local control of those resources meant that departments could select or develop applications that best met their needs, independently of other corporate needs or priorities. These applications were isolated from, and often invisible to, the rest of the corporation, so an application running in one part of the company would not affect operations in another part. The downside was that each local group developed its own processes and data, thus making it difficult to share those resources with other parts of the corporation.

Enterprise applications change all that. They are designed to run in a widely dispersed distributed computing environment. Data and application logic are typically centralized, but users are spread throughout the organization—all over the world in a multinational organization (as shown in Figure 1-1). Enterprise applications are implemented to eliminate the problems inherent in having many isolated, localized applications handling basic business functions. The corporation is typically trying to move to an integrated set of processes that span the corporation as a whole. For that purpose, access to the necessary corporate resources is centralized and users must communicate via the wide area network (WAN) to run the applications and access corporate data.

This type of client/server application combines the best of both the "glass house" and the departmental computing paradigms (as shown in Fig. 1-2 and 1-3). Centralizing the information resources allows more effective sharing of information throughout the corporation, but processing power is still controlled locally to allow local groups the flexibility to meet their unique computing needs.

Client/server computing is implemented in multiple tiers to allow separation of the computing tasks, so that processing for a given task is performed close to the resources required for that task, minimizing the amount of network communication required. Tasks are usually split into presentation tasks, application tasks, and database tasks. Figure 1-4 shows a three-tier application architecture that includes a database server, an application server, and multiple clients, which use the application-provided graphical user interface (GUI). Each tier is physically located on separate workstations. In a three-tier architecture, clients communicate across the network to the application server to

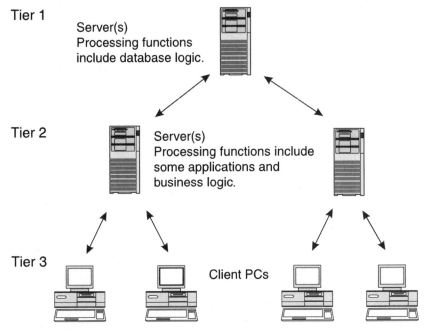

Figure 1-4
Three-tier client/
server application
architecture.

Tier 1   Server(s)
          Processing functions
          include database logic.

Tier 2   Server(s)
          Processing functions include
          some applications and
          business logic.

Tier 3   Client PCs

Processing functions include some application and business logic,
all presentation (GUI) logic.

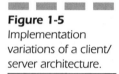

Figure 1-5
Implementation
variations of a client/
server architecture.

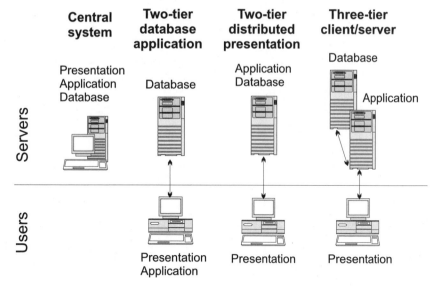

request and receive data in support of whatever task or process the user is performing. The application server in turn communicates with the database server to retrieve or store data in the database. In order to meet application quality-of-service goals, the underlying network must facilitate this communication, making it efficient and reliable.

Figure 1-5 shows the variations possible in implementing client/server applications. In a two-tier application architecture two of the tiers are collapsed: either database server and application server reside on the same physical workstation, or the application GUI (presentation) and application server reside on the client workstation. In a small enterprise application implementation, clients and servers may reside on a single LAN, but in the more typical implementation, clients and even servers may be distributed over the wide area enterprise network. Applications such as SAP R/3, BAAN, and PeopleSoft can be implemented as two-tier or three-tier client/server applications.

The Reality of Distributed Enterprise Computing

An application such as SAP R/3, BAAN IV, or PeopleSoft is not normally deployed as the first application on a brand-new network. Rather, it is added as yet another application onto an existing network infrastructure that is already handling some level of application load. The catch is that most corporate networks today are a far cry from the very tightly controlled glass houses of the past.

Because it is now relatively inexpensive and easy to implement applications locally given powerful desktop PCs and relatively inexpensive LAN technology, corporate networks have grown up unexpectedly, like weeds, sometimes without the approval or even knowledge of those responsible for corporate IT. In the experience of the authors, many organizations literally do not know what their networks actually look like, much less have any idea of the usage of those networks.

Implementing an application such as SAP R/3, BAAN IV, or People-Soft HRMS may replace selected applications, but typically there are many other applications that will continue to make demands on the network. In addition, the accessibility and popularity of the Internet, and the associated move to capitalize on that technology through corporate intranets and browser-based interfaces to applications, increase the demands on wide area networks daily. In the real world, the new enterprise application competes with other network uses for a finite amount of resources, leading to situations where the performance of the network may not support the quality-of-service goals required for the new enterprise application users.

Deploying a major, mission-critical application in the relatively wild environment of a wide area network is definitely a challenge, and requires careful planning. Network Resource Planning techniques help the network manager to determine whether the network is up to the task. NRP techniques can also provide guidance on how to make changes to the network to ensure that the network can support the new application load. In addition, NRP provides a methodology that helps the network management staff manage the ongoing application lifecycle of enterprise applications and other client/server applications.

Network Resource Planning is important to applications such as SAP R/3, BAAN IV, and the suite of products from PeopleSoft for a variety of reasons (Make Systems, 1997):

■ High quality of service is a business requirement. Mission-critical applications affect an organization's fundamental ability to do business.

■ Problem avoidance early in the application implementation process can yield substantial financial and operational efficiencies.

■ A high level of coordination is needed between application developers/implementers and network managers. IT staff needs sufficient lead time to be able to implement any changes in the network that may be required to support the new application deployment.

■ An ongoing network planning methodology is required to support multiyear application rollouts and the evolution of applications and networks.

Because SAP AG, BAAN, and PeopleSoft are currently among the market leaders in the realm of packaged enterprise application software, they are used in this book as the application focus to which NRP techniques are applied. However, the techniques discussed are equally applicable to virtually any client/server application, including other enterprise application packages, such as those from Oracle; user-developed client/server applications supporting the same processes as the packaged enterprise application software; applications such as Microsoft Exchange, Lotus Notes, and Microsoft SMS; and the whole range of emerging browser-based applications running on corporate intranets.

Network Resource Planning Methodology

Network Resource Planning consists of techniques for measuring and modeling network performance, analyzing the demands various applications make on network resources (including the projected demands of applications not yet deployed), and using the information about the existing network as the basis for planning for the future. These techniques can be used to determine the capacity of a corporate network before a major client/server application is deployed, potentially heading off major (and very costly) problems.

The Basic Network Resource Planning Processes

Network Resource Planning methodology makes use of performance management tools such as those mentioned in the next section. The processes of NRP depend on the data provided by the data collection tools and are implemented using the performance management software tools for analysis and modeling.

The three basic processes of NRP are baselining, application planning, and capacity planning.

■ Baselining is the process of collecting and documenting the physical configuration and traffic utilization of an existing network. Baselining is the basis for creating a model of an existing network for capacity planning purposes. Additional demand for network resources, caused by new applications, can then be "added" to the baseline model to predict how the network will function with the changes in place. Baselining techniques can also provide information about the existing applications that use the network, including how they contribute to the current utilization levels.

■ Application planning involves analyzing individual applications to determine the demands they make on the network. This information can be used to create "profiles" of applications not yet deployed and to project how those applications will affect the network when they are deployed. In addition, application planning techniques can be used to determine quality-of-service goals that can guide capacity planning efforts.

■ Capacity planning methodologies use the results of baselining and application planning to analyze and manipulate models of the network and see the effects of various changes. Models can be modified iteratively to simulate adding a new application, increasing bandwidth, changing circuit types, relocating resources such as application or database servers, and so on. These techniques allow a network planner to "test" changes to the network and analyze the results for performance bottlenecks without having to actually implement the changes.

The NRP processes—baselining, application planning, and capacity planning—are discussed in much greater detail in the later chapters of this book.

The Tools Used for Network Resource Planning

The network tools available to aid in NRP are of two basic types: those that collect data from the network and those that analyze the data.

The first type consists of network tools that aid in the collection of data about the behavior of a network or an application. Simple Network Management Protocol (SNMP) agents are small programs that reside in network devices such as routers and gather network configuration information, statistics on various measures of throughput, error rates, and the like. Data collection devices, such as the various Network General (now Network Associates) Sniffer traffic analyzers, HP NetMetrix RMON2 (Remote Monitoring) probes, or NetScout RMON2 probes, can provide more detailed information about traffic on the network, such as source and destination (host addresses), the application that initiated the transfer, and so on. This type of information, when imported into performance management tools, is important for creating traffic profiles of applications or analyzing end-to-end traffic patterns.

The second type of network tools consists of performance management software to analyze and model network performance, using the information collected from SNMP agents and traffic probes. Within the class of performance management tools there are two distinct approaches to analyzing network performance. The first approach uses mathematical techniques to model network behavior based on sample data. These analytical modeling tools include products such as NetMaker XA from Make Systems, Inc., the NETSYS Service Manager Suite from Cisco Systems, and ComNet Predictor from CACI Products Company. The second approach is discrete event simulation. Network tools that use event simulation techniques to model network behavior include the Optimal tools from Optimal Networks, ComNet III from CACI Products Company, and the OpNet tools from MIL3. Both analytical modeling and discrete event simulation techniques, with their benefits and drawbacks, will be discussed in some detail in Chapter 2, "The Network Resource Planning Process," and in Chapter 6, "Capacity Planning," for readers interested in a further discussion of these topics.

The Consequences of Not Using Network Resource Planning

Of course, major enterprise client/server applications such as SAP R/3, BAAN IV, and the suite of products from PeopleSoft are being deployed all the time without the aid of NRP processes. However, these application development projects frequently overrun their budgets and slip their schedules as well. NRP can help avoid many of the major problems that arise in projects of this type.

First, because of the way networks have been able to expand outside of any centralized control, many organizations do not know what their networks look like or how the resources are being used. Even when there is an attempt to maintain central control and management, today's network technology makes it easy for individual workgroups to add users and applications and generally make changes that will not be visible to the rest of the organization. Thus, when the corporation is ready to roll out a major application, its managers may discover that the network is not in the condition they expected. In particular, with the advent of the Internet and Web technology used internally for corporate intranets, an organization may find that the network resources are already much more heavily used than expected, so that what was assumed to be adequate capacity for new network application traffic is in fact already used up.

Compounding this problem is the wide chasm that exists in many organizations between application developers and the IT professionals who are responsible for the network infrastructure. If an application is developed without involvement of the network management organization, there may not be sufficient lead time to do the required planning and infrastructure upgrades to meet the targeted rollout schedule. Upgrading the network after the fact to support the new enterprise application can impose significant unanticipated costs as well as delaying the application rollout. If network infrastructure improvements are ignored or are inadequate, the new application implementation will not perform as expected, hampering productivity and aggravating users, who have to suffer poor response time and long delays in accessing information. If the enterprise application rollout is at all controversial within the organization, application usage problems due to the network may reinforce the attitudes of those who opposed its implementation.

The Varied Causes of Poor Application Performance

Applications such as SAP R/3, BAAN IV, and PeopleSoft HRMS are commonly implemented and tested by application developers who are separated both functionally and organizationally from the IT professionals who are responsible for managing the corporate network infrastructure. Thus, the application may be developed and tested in an environment that does not reflect the production network environment of the corporation. Often the pilot implementation of a new application exists on a single LAN segment, and the application will not be properly tuned for wide area network usage.

When such an application is rolled out onto the production enterprise network, the realities of the network infrastructure may be such that the application performs far below expectations. For example, instead of subsecond response times, users may experience multiple-minute delays. When this happens, the typical and intuitive reaction is to assume that bandwidth across the WAN is inadequate, and that more should be added. For example, an organization may decide to upgrade everywhere to T1 circuits (or larger) to ensure that there is plenty of capacity.

This, however, is an area where intuition does not always serve the network manager well. While inadequate bandwidth may indeed be the problem, there are several other possible causes for poor response time:

- Insufficient server capacity can cause degraded server performance. This can cause the server to be slow in processing client requests. It can also mean that the server cannot process incoming traffic fast enough, resulting in a high rate of dropped packets and retransmissions.

- Inefficient use of networking protocols can contribute to network congestion and lowered throughput. For example, although TCP/IP is basically an efficient protocol, large numbers of small packets and no use of windowing (meaning that every packet must be acknowledged) can lead to poor overall application performance.

- Poor application design can be responsible for the inefficient use of network resources. For example, an application that does a lot of Structured Query Language (SQL) operations over a wide area network may not perform well, because SQL is a relatively "chatty" protocol, sending many small packets with high overhead.

- Even in a prepackaged application such as SAP R/3, the design of individual client GUIs can have a large effect on performance. For example, the more data items the user interface accesses and displays for a given transaction, the more demand each transaction will put on the network.

■ Other design issues that will affect performance are how application functionality is split and how communication is handled between servers in a multitier client/server application. These effects can be further compounded by the physical location of the server tiers relative to each other.

The Importance of Identifying the Real Problem

Because adding bandwidth can be an expensive proposition and typically requires a substantial lead time (especially for international circuits), it is advantageous to be certain that insufficient bandwidth is the real cause of performance problems before upgrading capacity.

A large Midwestern manufacturing company found this out the expensive way. This particular company was having significant performance problems with a new enterprise application. The application linked client users in business units and sales offices throughout the United States with servers in a centralized data center. Without doing any network performance analysis, they assumed that inadequate bandwidth was the cause of the poor application performance. To improve response times, they replaced several existing 56Kbps circuits between selected business units and the data center with T1 circuits, planning to upgrade all circuits. Much to their surprise, application performance to the targeted business unit did not improve and, in some cases, actually seemed to degrade further.

The IT group then had a performance analysis project conducted on their network using NRP techniques. They discovered that bandwidth utilization on their circuits was in the 1–2% range, even on the 56Kbps links. The actual problem was server capacity. The existing servers were already unable to handle the amount of traffic over the slower links, so increasing the bandwidth caused the servers to drop even more packets, with a resulting increase in packet retransmissions. Inefficient use of the networking protocols compounded the problem—transactions consisted of many small packets, and because no windowing was used, every individual packet required an acknowledgment.

The solution to their performance problems was to upgrade their servers and to redesign the application to make better use of the TCP/IP protocol. Had they used NRP techniques earlier in their application deployment cycle, they could have saved the considerable expense and delays involved in installing unneeded T1 circuits.

The timely use of NRP processes can help you avoid these types of costly and time-consuming problems when you deploy large client/server applications onto your enterprise network. Even if you cannot undertake a full-blown NRP project, doing some of the activities can be extremely beneficial. Network Resource Planning is a little like dieting—doing it even a little is better than not doing it at all.

The remainder of this book will cover how to use the various data collection tools, performance management tools, and NRP processes to realize the benefits of NRP within any organization facing deployment of a client/server application over a wide-area network. Although the deployment of an enterprise application such as SAP R/3, BAAN IV, or a PeopleSoft application may be the catalyst for developing an NRP strategy, once you do so, you will find that you will use these processes again and again as your network grows and evolves.

References

Make Systems, Inc. (1997). *Network Resource Planning, a Whitepaper.*

Smith Barney Research (1997). *Enterprise Software* (special report).

CHAPTER 2

The Network Resource Planning Process

Network Resource Planning (NRP) is a software-supported set of processes that ensure that distributed applications achieve an acceptable quality of service at minimum network cost. These processes include

- Documenting the current network topology and configuration
- Creating a baseline of current network utilization and application distribution
- Testing network behavior to assess the quality of service for specific applications
- Profiling the traffic demands to document the behaviors of existing and future applications
- Modeling network behavior to predict performance under specified conditions, such as worst-case traffic loads generated by business cycle phases (end of month or end of year, for example)

■ Redesigning the network to resolve problems

A number of performance management software tools, such as those from Make Systems, Optimal Networks, CACI, and Cisco Systems Inc.'s NETSYS Technologies Group, have been developed to automate and support these processes.

The reengineering of business processes involving enterprise applications such as SAP R/3 often causes significant changes in the behavior of a corporation's network environment. The rapid rate of these changes has forced many IT managers into a cycle of reactive, day-to-day management. However, for mission-critical applications such as SAP R/3, BAAN IV, and PeopleSoft, it is important to be proactive in managing the enterprise network—anticipating problems before they occur and resolving problems in "real time"—rather than reactive. In this type of environment, Network Resource Planning can play a critical role in gaining control of network management issues and moving from a reactive mode to a mode in which managers can anticipate problems and plan ahead for change.

The value of NRP in deploying a mission-critical enterprise application environment depends on many factors:

■ The nature of both the application architecture and the network architecture

■ The current usage of the existing network and projected usage of new applications

■ Quality-of-service requirements for network users

■ The probability of substantial changes—physical changes such as an upgrade to ATM, changes to network usage patterns, or both— being introduced into the network during the application deployment period, which may span many months or years

Factors affecting application performance in a given network environment may exist in one or more of these categories. Table 2-1 illustrates many of these factors. When any of these factors are present, NRP can produce measurable benefits.

Factors in Determining the Benefits of Network Resource Planning

The value of NRP within an organization is a function of the issues related to application and network architecture, network and applica-

	Category	Factors
TABLE 2.1	**Application/network architecture**	Enterprise-wide distributed network/application requiring a wide area network (WAN)
NRP Decision Factors (© Make Systems, 1997)		Multitier client/server application architecture
		Potential for distributing or replicating databases over multiple servers
	Network usage	Large numbers of users, either currently or planned
		Application is the first enterprise-wide mission-critical client/server application on the network
		Internet access provided/allowed for users
		Intranet projects planned or underway
	Quality of service	Complaints about network performance already exist
		Need to guarantee service levels
		24×7 availability required
	Network environment changes	Changes anticipated for network-based applications (new applications, adding users, server relocations)
		Changes anticipated for network infrastructure (topology redesign, technology upgrades)
		Lengthy application deployment timelines (more than six months)

tion usage, quality-of-service requirements, and the degree of change anticipated during the application rollout. Figure 2-1 shows the target environments that can benefit the most from NRP as a function of these factors.

Organizations with large distributed networks that are undertaking a complex client/server application deployment effort with stringent quality-of-service requirements are ideal candidates for using NRP processes. The more complex the environment, and the more significant the degree of change involved, the more valuable NRP becomes.

Organizations with small, relatively stable, well-documented network environments may be able to predict the effects of a new application deployment with a relatively simple planning effort. These organizations are effectively already using NRP-like processes at some level, although those processes may not be automated. The time and expense involved in purchasing additional performance management tools and learning to use them may not be justified in such cases. However, any organization deploying an enterprisewide application such as SAP R/3, BAAN IV, or PeopleSoft is *not* likely to fall into this category. These types of client/server applications almost always require complex

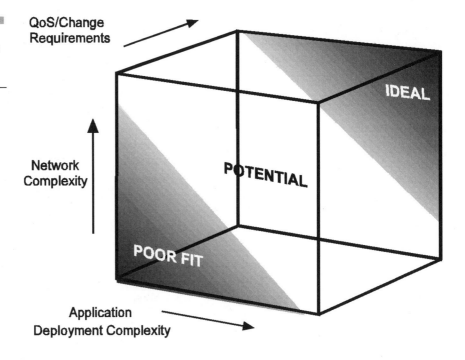

Figure 2-1
Target environments
for NRP (© Make
Systems, 1997).

deployment cycles involving a high degree of change over a long period of time.

The following sections discuss factors that influence the need for NRP.

Application/Network Architecture

Both the architecture of the specific client/server application and the architecture of the underlying network infrastructure are significant factors that affect the performance of the application. If application users are distributed throughout the enterprise and access the application servers over a WAN connection, the application is a logical candidate for NRP.

SAP R/3, BAAN IV, and PeopleSoft version 7 are logically three-tier client/server applications, with separate systems running the presentation modules, application server, and database server. The PeopleSoft version 6 applications are two-tiered, with presentation and application functionality combined on the client, which communicates with a database server.

Physically, a variety of configurations are possible, including having all three functions coresident on one system. Typically, however, the presentation function is done on systems close to the users (usually on their desktops), whereas the application server and database server functions are handled on centrally located corporate servers, which users access over the enterprise WAN. It is usually recommended in enterprise application deployments that the application server(s) and database server(s) are colocated on the same local area network (LAN) because of the very high volume of interactions between them.

The centralization of key application and database servers can represent a significant change to the daily usage patterns that exist in many corporations today. However, even if remote access to centralized resources is an already established pattern, the additional demands due to a new distributed application may stress the WAN resources. Further, if the application will involve communication from user groups that have previously been autonomous and have not used the WAN in any significant way, the network in its existing state may not be adequate to support the new application. NRP techniques can help determine how well the existing network will support the new application with acceptable quality of service, and can provide guidance as to the kinds of adjustments that may be required to provide adequate support.

Network Usage

Another factor in assessing how well an enterprise network will support a major enterprise client/server application deployment is the existing and projected usage of the network that will support the application. If the network already supports a large number of users, it is important to determine and understand the current usage and traffic patterns on the network. There may be single points of failure (without redundancy to handle a failure condition) or bandwidth bottlenecks (saturation on WAN or LAN segments) that have not been identified and resolved. This is frequently the case when the new application is the first mission-critical, enterprise-wide client/server application to be deployed and thus stresses the WAN in ways not previously encountered.

The centralization of application and database servers can have a dramatic impact on the daily usage patterns that exist within the corporation, affecting not only the quality of service of the new application but also the performance of the existing applications and services. Bandwidth that seems adequate in the first phases of an application rollout may cease to be adequate as network demands increase, not just because of the new application but also from other, competing network uses and users.

If the number of users is expected to increase over the application deployment time period, NRP processes are critical. If a large number of users will access the application servers or database servers over the enterprise WAN, the application is a logical candidate for NRP. For a mission-critical application, user interactions with the network are critical to meeting quality-of-service goals.

If the network is or will be supporting bandwidth-intensive browser activity over an intranet or the Internet, database queries over the wide area, or multimedia applications, then NRP will provide substantial benefits. Many companies involved in large-scale enterprise application deployment are also pursuing intranet projects that will contend for bandwidth and that will affect the reliability of the client/server connections required by the new application. Internet/intranet applications are a particularly important issue, as they tend to encourage a higher volume of use by a broader group of users than may have been true in the past.

Quality of Service

If a network is already failing to meet its quality-of-service objectives, as indicated by existing user performance complaints, there is every reason to believe that the network will also fail to support a new application's quality-of-service requirements. Using NRP in the early phases of an application deployment can help network managers project network utilization demands, anticipate performance problems, and proactively prepare to address and resolve those problems prior to application deployment.

With the emergence of new carrier services and new network technologies such as ATM, IT managers and carriers are increasingly being required to provide Service-Level Agreements (SLAs) for network users. If service-level guarantees are needed for applications on a shared network, NRP can be of substantial benefit by providing detailed quantitative information about application and network behavior. It also provides a methodology for continuing to monitor the SLA.

In cases in which applications are used around the clock, NRP processes can help provide an understanding of time-of-day behavior and performance.

Network Environment Changes

The final category of factors affecting the value of and need for NRP relate to the changes that are likely to occur on the network over the rollout life cycle that may affect the client/server application deployment.

The application rollout itself, of course, represents a significant source of changes. At a minimum it represents additional transactions (network conversation) traversing the network. Typically, this type of application deployment involves new application and database servers. It may also mean additional users, or global access for users who were previously restricted to local access. Not only will these users add to the overall network load, but they may have high application performance expectations based on their experience running applications over relatively high-performance LANs.

The deployment of an enterprise client/server application such as SAP R/3, BAAN IV, or PeopleSoft is often undertaken as part of an overall reengineering of organizational processes. In concert with application deployment, the corporation may be making significant changes in communications patterns as well as enhancements to the communications infrastructure. These changes can have a major impact on application behavior and performance. If an organization anticipates these types of changes concurrently with a mission-critical application deployment, NRP can provide significant benefits. By projecting the effects of the anticipated changes, NRP processes enable network managers to plan effectively for the capacity required to provide acceptable application performance.

In most cases, a major enterprise application such as SAP R/3, BAAN IV, or PeopleSoft will be deployed in phases over time (1 to 5 years). Thus, changes related to other applications or to the network infrastructure itself may affect the application at some point before the rollout is completed. Database servers may need to be relocated closer to the user communities they serve. A corporate merger or reorganization may significantly modify underlying traffic. Deployment of new networking technology such as LAN switches, Frame Relay, or ATM will have a major impact. As a result, the plans and projections that were valid at the beginning of a project may have to be redone to take into account the changing network environment. This is why NRP needs to be an ongoing process, providing updated information over time to enable network planners to reevaluate their designs and decisions as conditions change within the enterprise network environment.

The Techniques of NRP

The techniques of NRP represent an approach to systematic network planning that is organized around three basic operations:

- Baselining
- Application planning
- Capacity planning

Baselining provides a comprehensive understanding of how the network is currently configured and used; it provides the foundation on which all other network planning activities are built. Application planning addresses the deployment of new enterprise applications on an existing network. By creating a statistical representation of a new application and its usage, application planning makes it possible to anticipate the demands the application will make on the network and the resulting requirements for supporting the application effectively. Capacity planning analyzes baselined network data and application data to provide basic answers about predicted network utilization and the ability of the network to meet quality-of-service objectives; it facilitates the development and validation of optimal settings for the network environment.

Figure 2-2 shows the relationship between these three basic functions, with the tasks that are involved in each area. NRP projects can involve all three functions but do not always need to include all three. Baselining, however, is the fundamental operation on which the other two are built, so any NRP project will almost always include baselining activities.

The Cyclical Nature of NRP

A key aspect of the NRP cycle of activities is the cyclical nature of the entire process as well as each of the components. To be truly effective,

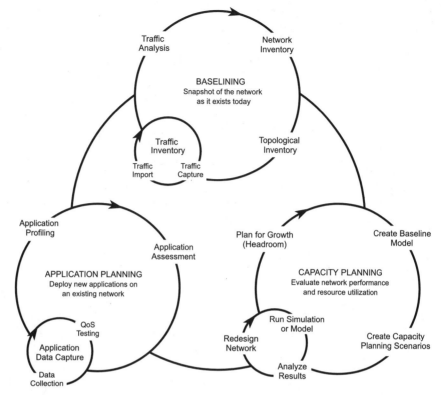

Figure 2-2
NRP cycle of activities.

NRP is not a one-time effort. To gain the maximum benefit, NRP activities should be repeated periodically to update the information about the network and to identify and characterize the changes that are inevitable over time.

Baselining

The goal of baselining is to produce an accurate understanding of the network as it currently exists. Baselining is the process of documenting the current network in order to understand what is available and how it is typically being used. This includes an accurate rendering (topology map) and characterization of the network infrastructure, as well as many snapshots of network activity or traffic flow.

Combining the topology information with information on network activity yields a great deal of information about the network design and the utilization of its WAN components as well as of its LANs.

Because it provides a picture of the "typical" use of the network, the baseline provides the foundation from which all further planning activities can be undertaken. While the baseline for any given network will change over time as the network evolves, for a given planning effort the baseline provides a "stake in the ground" or starting point against which the effects of proposed changes can be analyzed.

As illustrated in Figure 2-3, baselining activities include four basic tasks: network inventory, topological inventory, traffic inventory, and traffic analysis. To generate a baseline, the network topology must first be "discovered" by collecting inventory and connectivity information. Then, both usage-based and application-based network traffic data is collected. Both data sets must be analyzed and integrated to provide a workable, useful network data model. The diagram shows this as a cyclical process, because as a network changes, its managers will need to update the baseline components to identify and characterize the resulting changes in network behavior.

The steps in the baselining cycle of activities are the following:

■ The *network inventory* is a collection of all the known network elements (routers and their configurations, WAN circuits and circuit speeds, LANs) to be tracked and referenced throughout the network planning cycle. This includes a review of the available network documentation and discussions with knowledgeable network management staff.

Figure 2-3
Baselining cycle of activities.

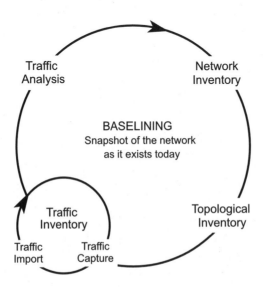

■ The *topological inventory* provides a visual representation (layout or network map) of the network built by importing topology data from routers into a performance management tool. The data includes all routers, LANs, and network connections. The resulting network model shows the logical position of network components relative to each other; some maps also show geographical position. This data can be collected using an SNMP discovery or from other sources such as Cisco router configuration files. The model must be validated by comparing it to the available network documentation before moving to the next step in the NRP process. This step often provides many surprises to the network management staff because of what they learn about their network.

■ The *traffic inventory* uses usage-based traffic data obtained from network routers and, if available, application-based data captured with RMON2 (Remote Monitoring)-compatible probes or traffic analyzers. This data is then imported into the appropriate performance management tools for analysis.

■ *Traffic analysis* uses the capabilities of the performance management tool to analyze usage-based data to determine network utilization and available capacity. Application-based data is also analyzed to generate a list of the major applications transiting the network, how they behave (throughput), and how they use network resources.

Application Planning

Application planning activities focus on characterizing the demands that new applications are likely to make on the network, or that existing applications will make as users are added or an application server is moved. When a new mission-critical application is introduced, such as SAP R/3, BAAN IV, or PeopleSoft, it is critical to determine whether or not the current network capacity is sufficient to handle the resulting traffic. Application planning methodologies provide a means to make such determinations quickly and efficiently by providing information about the network resources the application will need. With this information you can build upon the baseline model to predict how the network will support the application.

Application planning methodologies require that a representative set of application transactions be measured to determine what demands the application is likely to make upon the network. The application transactions can also be measured to create metrics for assessing how well the network will support the application's quality-of-service goals. These measurements are documented and analyzed to create a "profile" of the application, which can then be superimposed on the baseline model to simulate how the application load will affect the network. The three tasks that constitute an application planning activity, as shown in Figure 2-4, are application assessment, application data capture, and application profiling. As with baselining, application planning activities are also cyclical in nature and may need to be repeated to refine the information or to take changes in the network environment or application into account.

■ *Application assessment* is the process of identifying how an application will be used on the enterprise network. One part of this task is to determine how the application will be deployed on the network— that is, where users and servers will be located, how many users will be at each location, and how frequently these users will be expected to do various application tasks. Another step is to determine which transactions are representative of the way the application will be used by users (clients) on the network. These transactions (or a subset of them) will form a script, or benchmark, used to generate the traffic data that will become the basis for the application profiles. Finally, it is necessary to define and understand the network

Figure 2-4
Application planning
cycle of activities.

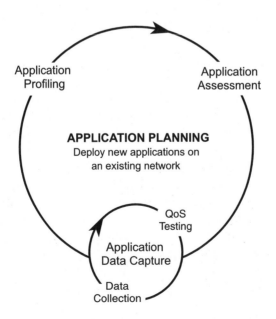

environment in which the application will run when it is deployed, including the existing application distribution and how the introduction of the new application may affect that distribution.

■ *Application data capture* is the process of collecting traffic data that corresponds to the target transactions that make up the application benchmark. The first part of this task is to identify a test environment where the application can be run and the data can be collected. It may also be desirable to test the application to quantify quality-of-service goals for application response time and throughput. The data capture itself is done using a traffic analyzer such as a Network General Sniffer to collect the appropriate data that corresponds to the application transactions in the benchmark, as executed by a knowledgeable user as part of the data collection process.

■ *Application profiling* is the process of creating a representative model (known as a profile) of the traffic characteristics of a set of application transactions based on the data captured during the data capture task. The profiles will be used to represent the "typical" load that an individual application user represents in terms of traffic demands.

Capacity Planning

The purpose of capacity planning as defined in this book is to analyze and predict how a network will perform, both under current conditions and under various scenarios for possible changes to traffic load (such as the introduction of new applications or users) or to network infrastructure. Capacity planning uses baseline network data and application profile data to provide basic answers about network usage and the ability of the network to meet service-level objectives. Capacity planning methodologies do not require the collection of network data beyond what was collected during the baselining and application planning stages of NRP.

The tasks in the capacity planning area, as shown in Figure 2-5, are to create a baseline model, to create capacity planning scenarios, to run the what-if scenarios, to analyze the results, to redesign the scenarios if necessary, and to plan for growth.

■ *Create the baseline model.* One or more baseline models will represent the existing usage on the enterprise network and will be the basis for the capacity planning scenarios. The baseline model starts with

the topology inventory and usage-based data sets from the baselining phase. The assumptions used in selecting the usage-based data
for the model are critical to determining how well the model
results will represent what will actually occur on the network when
a "what-if" scenario is implemented in reality.

- A *capacity planning scenario* is a description of the predicted usage of
  the network by an application (usually one expected to be added to
  the network) in terms of the locations of application users and
  application or database servers, the number of users at each location, and the frequency with which each user will execute the
  application transactions under study. The scenario is implemented
  on top of a network baseline model by adding network conversations typical of the new application's traffic based on the application profiles created during the application planning phase of the
  NRP project.

- *Run the model or simulation* using a performance management tool.

- *Analyze the results* in terms of whether the delays for target transactions meet the quality-of-service goals and in terms of circuit
  utilization, especially for circuits where quality-of-service goals are
  not met.

- *Redesign the network,* if needed, by identifying modifications to the
  network infrastructure that will have the desired effects on capacity and usage of the network's resources. A redesign can include

Figure 2-5
Capacity planning
cycle of activities.

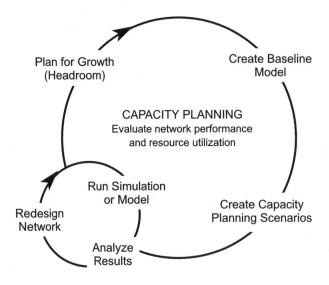

increasing or decreasing capacity, relocating application elements such as servers among existing network sites, or changing communications technology (e.g., moving from leased lines to Frame Relay circuits). The capacity planning scenarios are then modified to reflect these changes, and the simulation or model is rerun.

- *Plan for growth* to ensure that the network has sufficient headroom to accommodate increasing traffic demands due to new applications, new users, or increased frequency of use.

The Three Phases of NRP

Network Resource Planning processes can be used at any time during the life cycle of an enterprise application. There are three points in the application life cycle at which NRP techniques can provide particular benefit: during the preimplementation phase, during rollout validation, and during the ongoing life cycle management phases. The NRP activities within each phase are largely the same. However, the focus and objectives change according to the phase of application deployment.

Preimplementation Phase

The ideal time to begin NRP is before the implementation of a mission-critical enterprise application. A great deal can be accomplished before implementation to ensure that the network is ready to support the enterprise application. The results from NRP activities at this stage can help avoid expensive last-minute workarounds for problems or costly delays in the deployment schedule. During the preimplementation phase, NRP focuses on the following (Make Systems, 1997):

- Uncovering existing network issues and problems
- Identifying existing network utilization patterns
- Identifying issues related to the architecture (two-tier, three-tier, or multitier) of the application
- Assessing data collection instrumentation issues (availability and number of devices)
- Coordinating new application data collection activities with pilot and deployment schedules

- Identifying application transactions and creating benchmarks for the specific enterprise application modules to be installed

- Identifying the expected user community and their locations

In many organizations there is no systematic process defined for fully documenting the network topology, configuration, and usage. Furthermore, although data collection devices such as traffic analyzers or Remote Monitoring (RMON2)-compatible probes may be available, there is frequently no process or strategy in place for using these devices to collect data on application-level conversations on the network, especially to understand a specific application. The earlier these issues are addressed and processes are implemented for collecting data about the usage of the network, the better.

A strategy and process must also be created for collecting data about the new enterprise application under study. Pilot projects and application-testing activities are excellent sources of data about the new application. During the pilot stages of an application deployment project, you can use NRP techniques to "storyboard" possible "what-if" scenarios to determine how the current network will or will not support the new application. By identifying quantum changes in the general mix of applications and specific application modules to be deployed, testing with capacity planning "what-if" techniques can provide insight to the results of deployment prior to the actual deployment. The power of such an investigation is that it allows multiple avenues (multiple capacity planning scenarios) to be explored, possibly leading to a better implementation approach, that could not have been identified without this type of analysis.

Rollout Validation Phase

In nearly all major enterprise application deployments, the application is rolled out in a staged fashion. Some of the most common ways to stage an application deployment are:

- By functional application module

- By organizational structure (by departments or user domains)

- According to geographic boundaries

As with any project, it is critical to identify the priorities so that everyone involved can be working on the same goals in the agreed order of importance. The focus of the deployment validation phase (as the deployment project moves forward) is to determine whether the application is being supported by the network infrastructure sufficiently for the quality-of-service goals to be met.

By setting up a repeatable process of baselining, application planning, and capacity planning for each milestone, a stake in the ground can be identified and decisions can be formulated as to how the deployment is progressing. During an enterprise application rollout, many changes will typically occur on the network, related either to other enterprise applications or to the network infrastructure itself. For example, the company may be implementing a browser-based intranet in the same time frame as the enterprise application rollout. Or, as part of the deployment, the company may be switching WAN connections from private leased lines to Frame Relay PVCs.

During each stage of the rollout, production application transactions should be collected and their performance analyzed using capacity planning techniques. The results can be reviewed against the preliminary testing done in the preimplementation phase to determine whether the deployment is on track or whether further changes are needed to achieve the desired performance and quality-of-service goals for the new application. Even if NRP techniques were not used before implementation, the application deployment can be validated by measuring current behavior at each critical milestone of the rollout, which can still provide valuable feedback. NRP may make the difference between the project continuing or being completely derailed by unacceptable application performance.

Life Cycle Management Phase

Once the enterprise application reaches a critical mass of implementation (that is, most of the functional modules and users are operational), the emphasis of NRP shifts to monitoring. The focus now becomes measuring the network utilization and capturing application conversations in order to build historical behavior trends and to identify changes in network behavior and application behavior.

Two types of changes are important in this phase. The first type is the planned incremental change that occurs as a result of normal corporate growth, reorganizations, relocations, and mergers. Analyzing these changes with NRP essentially follows the same form as the rollout validation phase activities but usually on a limited scale.

The second type of change, which life cycle management addresses, is the underlying gradual change in application traffic behavior that may not correlate with the more noticeable planned and expected changes. Once a mission-critical client/server application reaches production status, its use evolves as the reliance on the application within the organization matures. These changes tend to be evolutionary and can go unnoticed. NRP focuses on tracking the evolution of network traffic, trending utilization, and actively identifying potential areas where network costs can be reduced or performance can be improved. Understanding these trends will in turn help to identify easily whether all application modules are functioning normally or whether there has been a shift in usage patterns that warrants further investigation.

Specifically, capacity planning techniques can continue to be used to predict the effects of moves, adds, and changes to the key enterprise application resources and user communities. Capacity planning provides a way to "test" the effects of increases or decreases in other application usage or to determine how changes to the network infrastructure will effect the enterprise system.

Network Tools That Are Available for NRP

The discussions that follow provide an introduction to the functionality provided by various types of network tools that can be used to facilitate the network planning cycle. These network tools are used to collect and report data, generate a traffic baseline description of a network, and model and analyze that network. Specific tools from selected vendors are discussed in more detail in Appendix B, "Network Resource Planning Tools."

Data Collection and Analysis Tools

Data collection and analysis tools are very important for collecting live data from networks for use by performance management tools. For most NRP projects, live data will be required, because it is literally impossible to know the traffic flow within a network well enough to enter it into a performance management tool. The data that is collected will be either usage-based data (utilization of WAN circuits or LANs) or application-based data (network conversations).

Data collection and analysis functionality is broken down into two areas: router MIB (Management Information Base) statistical collection tools, and traffic analyzers and RMON2-compatible probes. Router MIB statistical collection tools support the collection of usage-based data. Traffic analyzers and RMON2-compatible probes support the collection of application-based data.

Router MIB Statistical Collection Tools

Statistical collection tools extract router MIB data using the Simple Network Management Protocol (SNMP) to create a snapshot of the current traffic load or utilization on a segment. A byte count by interface of the traffic that transits through the internetworking device is collected by polling each router's MIB at designated time intervals (every five minutes, for example) over a number of hours. This is a quick and efficient, albeit gross, means for determining WAN usage. By focusing on busy hours or time periods of greatest WAN usage, maximum network loads can be identified. NetMaker XA WAN Baseliner from Make Systems, Inc., and Concord Network Health from Concord Communications are examples of tools that collect usage-based data.

Traffic Analyzers and RMON2-Compatible Probes

Usage-based data is limited in that it does not provide information about the application that generates the traffic, the source or destination addresses, volume or throughput per conversation, or other information needed to conduct application planning or capacity planning activities. Traffic analyzers and RMON2-compatible probes monitor network traffic and record detailed application-based data in the form of a series of network conversations. (A network conversation is a data exchange between two network endpoints—usually workstations or hosts.) A Network General Sniffer is an example of a popular traffic analyzer. NetScout probes are an example of popular RMON2-compatible probes.

Application-based data provides a substantially greater level of detail than usage-based data collected from router MIB statistics. This can include such information as the point of origin and destination of packets, packet and byte counts in both the forward and return directions, and an identifier for the type of application or protocol. However, application-based data is also limited, in that some traffic analyzers and RMON2 probes only capture a subset of the traffic transiting a LAN segment or a WAN circuit. While the data is more detailed than MIB statistical data, limitations within the analyzers or probes tend to cause some traffic to be ignored. Thus, a combination of application-based data and usage-based data is necessary to create the most accurate picture of existing network traffic and utilization.

Performance Management Tools

Performance management involves measuring and modeling the performance of network application traffic, network devices such as routers and switches and the network media (WAN circuits and LANs). Examples of measured or modeled activities are overall network application throughput (Kbps), utilization of WAN circuits and LANs, error rates, and user response time.

Performance management tool functionality is broken down into the following areas: visualization and reporting tools, topology acquisition tools, traffic import and consolidation tools, application profiling tools, and network modeling and simulation tools.

Visualization and Reporting Tools

Visualization (or layout) and reporting tools provide a means to view network resources and traffic either topologically or logically. Examples are the NetMaker XA Visualizer from Make Systems, Inc., which displays maps of a discovered network and provides both graphical and textual management reports, or NETSYS Connectivity Service Manager from Cisco Systems, which provides various topology "views" of a network.

Topology Acquisition Tools

Topology acquisition tools acquire information about the devices on a network in order to create a topological inventory of the network.

Network management platforms and other products such as Make Systems' NetMaker XA use an SNMP discovery process to do this. Network discovery tools use SNMP requests to extract information from the MIB maintained by a device's SNMP agent. Using this information, the tool can automate construction of a topological network inventory.

Depending on the capabilities and needs of the product, the discovery process may focus just on routers or may collect information about other network devices. Any network device that is running an SNMP agent can be discovered by this process. An entire global network can be discovered, or the discovery can be limited to just a portion of the network. For the purposes of creating a network topology, the discovery tool would query network routers to identify configuration assignments and connections within the network.

Some tools, such as NETSYS Connectivity Baseliner from Cisco Systems, import Cisco router configuration files to access the needed information instead of using an SNMP discovery process. This avoids the overhead of sending SNMP requests to all the routers over the network, but it limits the process to Cisco routers.

Traffic Import and Consolidation Tools

Traffic import tools import captured network data ("live data") from router MIB statistical tools, traffic analyzers, and RMON2-compatible probes into performance management tools for the purpose of baselining, application planning, and capacity planning. Depending on the traffic import tool, it will import application-based data only or both usage-based data and application-based data.

Traffic consolidation tools integrate multiple files of captured data that represent the same traffic seen by multiple RMON2-compatible probes or traffic analyzers. To gain a complete picture of application-based traffic, multiple network locations are usually sampled simultaneously, but doing so generates multiple data files with overlapping coverage or multiple occurrences of the same conversation. A consolidation tool purges duplicate, incomplete, or inadequate conversations from the captured data sets so that the resulting traffic data reflects the real traffic pattern of the network.

Examples of these types of tool are Make Systems' NetMaker XA Interpreter tool and Cisco Systems' NETSYS Performance Service Manager.

Application Profiling Tools

Application profiling is the process of creating a representative statistical model (a profile) of application transactions using application-based data. In order to use application-based data to create an application profile, the data collection device must be able to track the data by direction and to distinguish the data going from client to server from that going from server to client. Once application-based data has been captured for target application transactions, it must be imported into the performance management tool that will be used to create the profiles, which will be used to represent the "typical" load that an individual application user would place on the network with a specific application transaction.

Make Systems' NetMaker XA Interpreter tool and Cisco's NETSYS Performance Service Manager can both be used to create application profiles.

Network Modeling and Simulation Tools

Modeling and simulation tools are a useful approach for predicting the performance of enterprise networks. Modeling and simulation has traditionally been the job of mathematical experts who understand statistical theory and simulation languages. Now, new network modeling and simulation products are available that hide much of this complexity from the user. This allows modeling and simulation tools to be used to solve practical planning problems within networks in a timely fashion (Schaffer, 1997).

ANALYTICAL MODELING   There are two types of approaches within this new set of "canned" network modeling and simulation tools. The first approach, analytical modeling, uses a number of equations (such as router output queues and application traffic flows) that describe the enterprise network's performance. These equations are then solved for unknowns such as bandwidth utilization and packet latency. Analytical modeling has the benefit that it is computationally very fast, even for a large enterprise network (100 to over 1000 sites). The drawback is that analytical modeling may not be able to account for all the complex behaviors that applications and network devices exhibit.

The ability of analytical modeling to predict exact packet latencies accurately can be limited by the simplifying assumptions that are often made to make the mathematical analysis tractable. Despite this, analytical modeling is still a very viable approach for enterprise networks, because most networks are designed with some room for traffic growth, so approximations will yield very useful results (Shaffer, 1997). Further, most capacity planning scenarios in themselves are based on numerous assumptions about the existing usage of the network and the projected usage of new applications, so *any* results are at best an approximate prediction of future network behavior.

DISCRETE-EVENT SIMULATION The second approach, discrete-event simulation, uses a model in which the traffic is represented as a sequence of messages, packets, or frames. The movement of the traffic through the network is simulated by keeping track of the state of the network devices and traffic sources as they evolve (converge) over time. Discrete-event simulation uses a central clock that moves forward in time at distinct points during the simulation, such as when a packet is transmitted by a router. Discrete-event simulation requires a time profile of the creation of traffic. Traffic is often simulated using random arrival times because of the possible randomness of the traffic. Models of devices (bridges, routers, switches, and servers) simulate the queuing and processing of packets (Shaffer, 1997).

ANALYTICAL MODELING VS. DISCRETE-EVENT SIMULATION Each of the two approaches is valid, depending on the capacity planning problem and the size of the network system in question. Analytical modeling tools (NetMaker XA from Make Systems and the NETSYS Service Manager suite of tools from Cisco Systems) are very good for solving capacity planning problems for an entire enterprise network system. The size of the enterprise network could range from tens of sites to hundreds of sites.

Discrete-event simulation tools (such as ComNet III from CACI and OpNet Planner from MIL3) are very good for solving more discrete problems involving timing issues, protocol flow control impact, or other transit conditions that may happen in a network and are important to understand. However, the size of the network that can be handled using discrete-event simulation is much smaller (tens of sites or less), because of the length of time one simulation will take (each packet is an event that must be dealt with as it moves through the network).

A somewhat more detailed discussion of these two approaches to network simulation/modeling can be found in Chapter 6, "Capacity Planning."

Resources for Implementing an NRP Project

NRP can be applied to an application environment in at least three ways, depending on rollout schedules, budget limitations, and the condition of the network and its current operations.

The lowest level of commitment is simply to outsource one or more of the NRP processes. This can be appropriate if the planning process is conceived as a one-time event, such as the planning undertaken before a major physical redesign such as an upgrade to Frame Relay. Outsourcing can also be appropriate if the overall scope of the project is complex and the organization does not believe it can develop expertise in the methodology and tools in a sufficiently timely manner to meet its planning requirements. Organizations are available to do NRP projects, including performance management tool vendors (such as Make Systems, Inc., and CACI Products Company) as well as a variety of value-added resellers (VARs), system integrators, and independent consultants, often in partnership with the performance management tool vendors.

A second approach is for the organization to focus on a single process of special importance. This is appropriate when a component NRP process, such as baselining (acquiring and maintaining accurate usage-based and application-based data about the enterprise network), must be repeated periodically. This approach can be used in combination with outsourcing; for example, a consultant does the major initial analysis but also trains the organization's network management staff in the use of the performance management tools so that they can continue to do ongoing analyses of specific performance issues.

The third approach is the top-down or strategic approach, in which a complete NRP process is laid out and executed by the organization. This approach will lead to a superior system in the long run. Institutionalizing NRP within the organization can have immediate, positive impact and lasting strategic value. This approach can also be implemented with the aid of consultants, who can help the organization develop the NRP process for its network and train the organization's personnel in the use of the network tools and methodologies involved.

The rest of this book presents the procedures for developing and implementing a top-down, strategic NRP process based on the needs and objectives of an individual organization. The remaining chapters detail how to prepare for an NRP project, and then in detail how to work through the three NRP phases: baselining, application planning, and capacity planning.

References

Make Systems, Inc. (1997). *Network Resource Planning,* a White Paper.

Steve Schaffer (1997) "Effective Network Simulation," White Paper, pp. 1–2 (www.optimal.com).

CHAPTER 3

Getting Started

To achieve useful results from any planning activity, some preplanning is necessary. This chapter introduces the issues and decisions the network manager must address in order to carry out a Network Resource Planning (NRP) project. What are the objectives in doing an NRP exercise? What does the organization hope to learn from the project? What tools and resources (software, staff, instrumentation, consultants) are needed to implement a project that will meet the organization's objectives and answer its questions? What is the time frame for the NRP project: a one-time effort, or a repeated process throughout the rollout cycle? These questions must be answered before an effective NRP project can be undertaken that will provide useful, reliable results.

Most network planning efforts are highly interdependent processes. The underlying goals, objectives, assumptions, methods, and tools must mesh together well to achieve maximum benefit. As information is collected and analyzed, and as useful patterns and performance metrics emerge, processes may require redefinition or refinement. Preplanning activities must consider how best to target the needed results and how to ensure that the project activities stay on track toward achieving those results. A successful NRP effort must include

- A commitment to the planning effort
- Clear, succinctly stated objectives
- An identified methodology
- Resources, especially budget, people, and time
- Tools and the ability to use them

Commitment to the NRP process is the key requirement, because it is the ingredient that will make it possible to follow through on a specific project despite obstacles. NRP represents a shift in the general approach for managing an enterprise network. It does not replace network fault management as performed by network management platforms such as HP OpenView; rather, it provides a proactive way to continually determine how the network is meeting the needs of its customers—the network users in the organization—and to project whether it will continue to meet those needs in the future. For example, if a company implements NRP as an integral part of the way new applications are introduced onto the network, it can eliminate many of the problems that typically occur with new application deployments. This strategic shift in direction can make life much more manageable for the IT management responsible for application rollouts. Such a strategic shift requires support and commitment from higher levels in the organization in order for this process to survive and be used.

Formulate the Project Objectives

The first step in a successful NRP project is to define why there is a need for NRP. Is the organization facing specific network problems that must be solved, such as unacceptable network performance? Is a major application deployment project planned or in progress, and is there a concern as to how the current rollout plans will play out? Does IT management anticipate the need to redesign the network and want guidance on how to accomplish the project? The top-level objectives for the NRP process are driven by the business issues that the organization is facing rather than by purely technical issues.

The following examples show how different organizations set objectives for their NRP projects. These scenarios describe the organizational situations that led to the NRP projects. Based on each organization's issues, a set of objectives was identified to provide focus for the NRP efforts. These examples all involve client/server application deployments, which is the focus of this book.

Scenario 1: A Transportation Company

This organization planned to implement the BAAN IV suite of Enterprise Resource Planning (ERP) software. While this company had not had any performance problems with its network, it wanted to understand overall usage of its network resources, and specifically the mix of applications that were being used across the network, in preparation for implementing the new application. This company was supporting a network of approximately 70 Bay Networks routers, spread over domestic and international sites, with a large number of sites in Asia and Europe (see Figure 3-1). The WAN environment was made up of Frame Relay permanent virtual circuits (PVCs) and leased-line circuits. Two main network hub sites were located on the West Coast of the United States, and the network resources critical to the company were located at these two hub sites.

Figure 3-1

Diagram of the transportation company's network (Scenario 1).

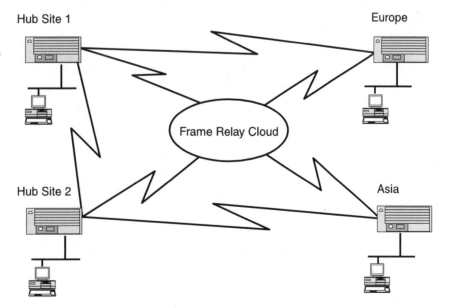

West Coast of the U.S.

This organization defined the following two objectives for its NRP project to help understand the usage of the network preparatory to implementing the BAAN IV application:

■ Characterize the traffic and bandwidth usage for the entire WAN, including all Frame Relay PVCs and all leased-line circuits.

■ Identify the applications and servers that generate significant volumes of data on the network (the top N hosts and applications).

Although this organization did not appear to be experiencing network performance problems, managers did not in fact have much of a feel for how their network was being used or was performing. The first objective enabled them to understand what sort of capacity demands the existing network usage was making, whether any of the WAN circuits was under- or overutilized, and if there were any existing bottlenecks in the network. That users do not complain about performance does not necessarily mean that there are no problems; it is possible that users are accepting poor performance as normal because it has always been that way. The second objective allowed the company to identify what applications were being used across the network, and it gave them an idea of what sorts of network activities might suffer an impact from a new application competing for bandwidth.

Scenario 2: A Manufacturing Company

This organization supported a global network environment divided into five major geographic regions. The NRP project undertaken by this corporation focused on one of these regions, Asia, shown in Figure 3-2. This company was in the process of developing a PeopleSoft HRMS application that it planned to roll out for use throughout the Asian region. The server(s) for the application would reside at a U.S. backbone site, with clients distributed throughout the corporation's sites in Asia. Before deploying the application, however, in light of current perceived performance problems on this portion of their network, the company wanted to study the performance of the existing network to determine how well it would support the quality-of-service goals of the new application.

The Asian portion of the network consisted of several factory sites, four of which were major sites of 300 or more employees. It also included several sales and business office sites with 10 to 100 employees each.

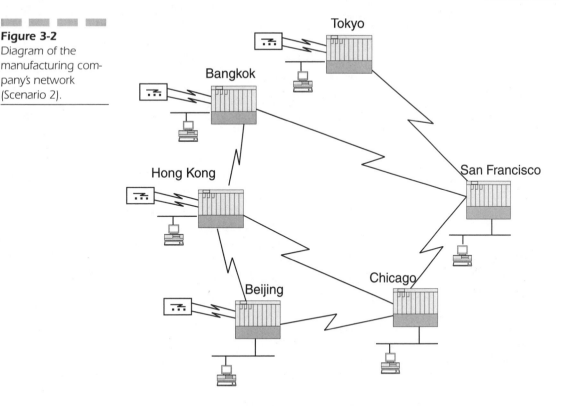

Figure 3-2
Diagram of the
manufacturing com-
pany's network
(Scenario 2).

The network was based primarily on Cisco routers in a spoke-and-wheel topology, using TCP/IP as the network protocol. Four main hub sites in Asia connected to the U.S. backbone through fractional T1 circuits. Three of the Asian hub sites were connected to one U.S. backbone site, and the fourth Asian hub site was connected to a second U.S. backbone site. Most of the remote sites within Asia connected directly to one of the four hubs in Asia using fractional T1 leased lines, although a few remote sites connected through another remote site to get to a hub site. Many of the applications used at the Asian sites were client applications communicating with servers located in U.S. data centers, and the same would also be the case with the PeopleSoft HRMS application under development.

The corporation identified the following objectives for its NRP study in preparation for implementing the PeopleSoft application:

■ To understand the utilization of the existing Asian network, both the traffic flow patterns within Asia and those between Asia and the United States

■ To understand the characteristics of the existing applications on the network, including what applications are being used, the through-put of those applications, the network conversations, and which servers the applications were using

■ To characterize the planned new PeopleSoft HRMS application to understand the demands it would make on the Asia network when it was deployed and whether the quality-of-service goals would be met

The first objective allowed the company to determine how much capacity was already being used and where any existing bottlenecks were located. The second objective allowed it to understand the nature of the usage observed as a result of the first objective and to under-stand what applications caused those usage patterns. The third objec-tive allowed the corporation to project how the new application would affect the existing network (or vice versa) and to determine what sort of performance it could expect from the new HRMS application. The results from this study were used to provide guidance in terms of both network design and application design to maximize performance of the application.

Scenario 3: A Service Company

This organization planned to upgrade its wide area network to incor-porate Frame Relay. Initially, the company planned to replace three of its existing leased-line connections with Frame Relay PVCs. Also, up to 14 remote sites were to be connected with Frame Relay PVCs, replacing dial-in access. The network environment consisted of six sites connected using leased lines (as shown in Figure 3-3). The pri-mary application of concern running over the network was SAP R/3. In addition, some of the remote sites used dial-in connections to run Lotus Notes.

This organization identified the following NRP objectives:

■ To characterize the bandwidth usage of the current network, espe-cially focusing on the initial three sites that would be moving to Frame Relay

■ To characterize the traffic demands due to the existing SAP R/3 application and those due to the Lotus Notes application for the remote sites that were switching from dial-in access to Frame Relay

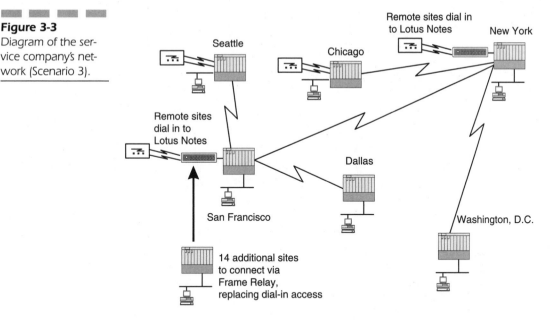

Figure 3-3
Diagram of the ser-
vice company's net-
work (Scenario 3).

■ Guarantee that acceptable quality of service will still be available for
SAP R/3 and Lotus Notes users after Frame Relay is deployed

The first objective allowed this organization to understand how much
capacity was currently being used in its network. The results of this
activity served as the baseline for the following objectives, which
involved projecting future performance based on changes to the network. In addition, these results helped the organization determine the
Frame Relay CIR (committed information rate) levels that would be
required for acceptable throughput. The second objective allowed the
organization to quantify the amount of traffic it could expect due to
SAP R/3 and Lotus Notes transactions. The third objective allowed the
organization to predict what capacity and CIR levels would be
required to support quality-of-service goals for SAP R/3 and Lotus
Notes users.

These three examples illustrate the types of objectives that organizations set for their NRP projects, based on the overall corporate goals for
their network.

Identify Methodologies and Strategies to Accomplish Project Goals

Once the objectives for an NRP project have been defined and agreed upon, the next step is to develop a simple, well-thought-out methodology to ensure that all tasks are addressed in a timely and correct manner. One of the best ways to accomplish this is to step through the entire project mentally, documenting along the way, identifying the tasks that need to be done (such as creating a network inventory) and the types of data that need to be collected to accomplish those tasks.

The next few sections discuss some of the issues the network planner needs to consider before starting the NRP tasks as described in the rest of this book. Preplanning will help set expectations correctly as to the timing and resources needed for the NRP project and can help avoid delays due to lack of timely availability of equipment or other resources.

Prioritize Network Planning Goals

The first step is to simplify as much as possible the set of goals and objectives that the NRP project is to achieve. What information is most important to meet the organization's planning objectives? Which areas of the network need the most attention and should therefore have priority?

It is important to start with realistic, manageable goals. In many cases the planning activities will have to be split into stages so that the scope of the tasks at any given point in the process is not too broad. It is also critical to understand the interrelationship of the various objectives—which of the objectives are the key, or driving, objectives and which are secondary objectives that support the main objectives.

For example, the key objective for the manufacturing organization discussed in Scenario 2 is to determine how a planned new application, PeopleSoft HRMS, is likely to perform when deployed onto a specific portion of its network. This is the third of its three objectives: "To characterize the planned new PeopleSoft HRMS application to understand the demands it would make on the Asia network when it is deployed, and whether the quality-of-service goals would be met."

Characterizing the traffic load that the new PeopleSoft HRMS traffic will create could be undertaken as one stand-alone objective. However, in order to achieve the broader objective (to determine and document the cumulative effect of adding that traffic to the current network), the first two objectives—understanding the existing traffic utilization of the Asia network and understanding the characteristics of the existing applications on the network—must also be completed.

Also note that in Scenario 2 the NRP effort has been defined to focus on only one portion of the manufacturing corporation's overall network. This makes the process of data collection and analysis much more manageable than attempting it for the entire global network. If the corporation subsequently decided to study other portions of the network, it could undertake those efforts as separate NRP projects.

Collect and Document What Is Already Known

The next step in collecting data about the network is to assess what is already known by finding as much information as possible from existing sources such as network maps, information from a network management platform, hardware inventory lists, and discussions with network management staff. This information can be extremely helpful in creating the NRP strategy and tactics. For example, basic information on the network topology can show how many traffic analyzers or RMON2-compatible probes will be required to collect the needed application traffic data.

Existing data can also be used to validate the results obtained from various planning activities. This data provides the basic metrics that make it possible to determine whether the results from an activity (such as a discovery or baselining) make sense, or whether there may be something wrong with the process. For example, lack of SNMP network access may mean that part of the network cannot be detected or queried by the performance management tools because of a firewall. That situation becomes apparent by comparing the results to an existing network map.

Defining Tasks That Support the Objectives

Once the objectives are clearly defined and ordered, the set of tasks required to accomplish those objectives can be defined. The planner should clearly identify the goal for each task. It is important that each task be focused on contributing to the overall planning objectives. Each task should be evaluated relative to the following questions:

- What must be accomplished with this task?
- How will the data from the task be used to support the main project objective?
- What decisions can be made as a result of this information?

These questions serve as a guide throughout the many steps of an NRP project. For example, the following list defines the tasks needed to analyze the proposed PeopleSoft deployment for the company described in Scenario 2, along with the objective of each task and how the results will be used:

- Build, discover, or import the topology information for the Asian portion of the network as well as the relevant portions of the U.S. network into a performance management tool. This task provides a model for the basic structure of the network, or at least the portion of it relevant to this NRP project.
- Validate the physical inventory of the network components within the network model, using existing network documentation. This task basically ensures that the model reflects the reality of the network.
- Collect usage-based data for the Asian network. This task provides the basic data on utilization of the network. This data will be used for the analysis of network utilization (the organization's first objective) and to create a baseline model of the network (showing "typical" network usage) for use in predicting the additional effects of the PeopleSoft application deployment.
- Collect application-based data using WAN Network General Distributed Server Sniffers (DSSs) installed on the U.S. side of the four circuits that connect the Asian network to the United States. This task provides the data about which applications are being used on the network and how they contribute to the overall traffic. This data will be used for the analysis of application usage on the existing network (the organization's second objective).
- Identify and document current network utilization. This task answers the organization's first objective, which was to understand the utilization of the current network.

- Identify and document the application mix, application through-put, and critical servers as observed through analysis of the Network General Sniffer data. This task provides the answers to the second objective.

- Create a benchmark for the PeopleSoft application that includes key transactions that users would typically perform with the application. In order to create a profile of the traffic associated with the various functions of the PeopleSoft application, those functions must be executed and collected. This benchmark provides a script for executing the functions that the organization considers typical or important in its deployment plans.

- Execute the benchmark and monitor the PeopleSoft application, using a Network General Sniffer to capture application traffic data. This step provides the data that will be used to create the traffic profiles of specific PeopleSoft activities or transactions.

- Create traffic profiles of the key PeopleSoft transactions. Analyze the data and create "typical" traffic profiles for the transactions that will be used in modeling the projected behavior of the PeopleSoft application when it is deployed. These profiles will be used to "load" the network baseline model to simulate the traffic demands made by the application. This answers part of the organization's third objective: to understand the characteristics of the traffic demands the new application will make on the network.

- Using a performance management tool, analyze the usage-based and application-based data running over the network, and build a baseline model of the network using an appropriate baseline model creation strategy. This model will be used as the basis of the "what-if" analysis of the PeopleSoft deployment.

- Using the baseline model, the PeopleSoft traffic profiles, and application usage projections, create a capacity planning scenario that incorporates the new PeopleSoft application traffic, as it reflects the organization's deployment strategy (number of users, locations, and transactions rates), to predict network operation under full application deployment.

- Run the "what-if" scenario and analyze the results to identify any network changes required to support the new network load. This task helps to answer the organization's third objective: to understand how the new application traffic will affect the existing network, and whether the application's quality-of-service goals can be met.

This step makes the recommendations as needed that will help the organization understand what will be required to solve any problems that are identified as a result of the answers to the three objectives.

- Make any changes necessary to the capacity planning scenario, such as changes in circuit type or circuit capacity; rerun the "what-if" scenario; and analyze the results to determine the effects of the simulated changes. This step has to be repeated more than once. This step helps to develop the recommendations for any changes to the network capacity to ensure that the application will meet its quality-of-service goals.

Once the tasks are laid out, with a clear understanding of why each one is needed, the next step is to determine how each task can be accomplished. This is particularly important in regard to collecting the data, which provides the basis for all the subsequent analysis tasks. Each of the prior tasks will be described in detail in the following three chapters ("Baselining the Network," "Application Planning," and "Capacity Planning").

Define a Data Collection Strategy

For any NRP project that proposes to look at application-based traffic, one or more collection devices are needed that can collect and identify key information about the applications that are traversing the network. Either RMON2-compatible probes or traffic analyzers can be used, and the appropriate number of these types of data collection devices must be available for the project. In order to determine how many devices will be needed, a data collection device placement strategy must be determined.

For example, one of the tasks required to accomplish the NRP objectives for the manufacturing organization described in Scenario 2 was to collect application-based data using Network General Distributed Sniffers installed on the U.S. side of the four circuits that connect the Asian region into the U.S. backbone. How was it determined that four Network General Sniffers were sufficient and that they should be placed on those specific circuits?

One data collection strategy would be to collect traffic from every segment in the network. Doing so would ensure that all the relevant data is captured, and nothing would be missed, but it would require placing a probe or traffic analyzer on every WAN circuit or LAN. This is rarely feasible and would be extremely costly. In addition, it is normally not necessary.

To create a focused and cost-effective data collection strategy, the network planner must thoroughly understand what data must be obtained from collection activities. This understanding will ensure that the data collection effort is on target to realize the project objectives. It will also help narrow the scope of the data collection strategy so as to collect only the data needed and not waste resources collecting data that is not relevant.

In order to determine a cost-effective data collection placement strategy, the following steps are necessary:

■ Identify the possible paths that the traffic of concern could take. Look at the existing network diagram to determine how many entry and exit points there are where data can be collected in order to capture as much of the relevant traffic as possible. In the example shown in Figure 3-4, there are four possible routes between Asia and the United States. Therefore, wherever in Asia the traffic of interest originates, it must eventually traverse one of these four circuits to reach critical servers in a U.S data center.

Figure 3-4
Data collection points
(key circuits) in
Scenario 2.

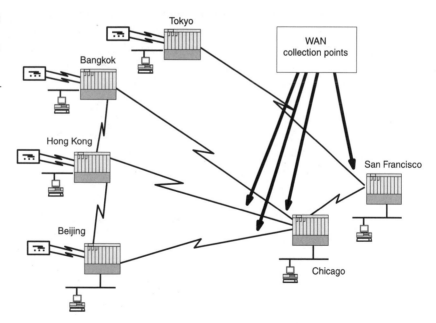

■ Identify where the primary network resources of interest are located. For example, in the manufacturing company's PeopleSoft deployment scenario (Figure 3-4), client users are spread throughout the Asia region, but most of the critical servers, as well as the Internet gateway, reside in the U.S. data centers. The PeopleSoft database servers will also be located in the U.S. data centers when the HRMS application is deployed. Identifying the location of the relevant resources may help reduce the number of data collection devices needed. For example, if the primary network resources in the example (Figure 3-4) are all in San Francisco, then only the two circuits from Tokyo to San Francisco and from Chicago to San Francisco would need to be monitored.

By determining where the key resources are located and the possible data paths to those resources, it is possible to significantly reduce the number of collection devices needed to collect the traffic of real interest. In Figure 3-4, application-based traffic will not be collected for the circuits within Asia, given the data collection strategy shown. However, based on the objectives for the NRP project, only usage-based data is needed for traffic patterns within Asia. Application-based data is needed only for the traffic to the critical application servers, which are located in the U.S. data centers. That application-based data can be adequately captured on the four circuits shown.

It is important to determine the data collection strategy early in the planning process, because if the organization does not already have these data collection devices on hand, they must be rented or purchased, and the resulting lead times must be taken into account.

Creating a list or chart to keep track of the data to be collected can be very helpful. This should include information on how the data will be used. In addition, the timing of data collection must be determined—both *when* the data needs to be collected (time of day, day of week, and so forth) and *how long* (how many hours or days for each type of data).

Determine Project Timing and Time Frame

The time needed to complete an NRP project will be affected by the nature of the objectives to be met, the size of the network being studied, and the methodologies and tools being used. It is important to be realistic in assessing the time required to complete all the activities.

An NRP project related to a major client/server application deployment, such as SAP R/3, PeopleSoft, or BAAN IV, may realistically extend over many months or years. The NRP project schedule may depend on other projects going on within the network, as well as the rollout schedule for the application deployment by user community.

In some cases the schedule for an NRP project may be very straightforward—that is, results must be obtained by a specific date, driven by a specific objective such as making a resource allocation decision within a budget cycle. The challenge in this case is to determine how to complete the tasks to deliver meaningful results in the necessary time frame.

In other cases, the timing may be determined by other network events—data collection may need to be scheduled before or after a system or network upgrade or change, depending on the objectives of the project. Data collection also may need to be correlated with business cycles (such as end of quarter) if the traffic patterns the cycle event creates need to be documented to accomplish the NRP objectives. Usually, the various phases of the NRP project have interdependent schedules, with the timing of one depending on the outcomes of preceding phases.

Create a Project Time Line

It is important to create a time line for the project. Whether on paper, in a spreadsheet, or using sophisticated project management software, it is extremely valuable to document how long each step is expected to take and any dependencies between the steps. For example, the documentation can help determine lead times required for ordering equipment (if necessary), as well as equipment setup and testing. It can help determine when to request the allocation of other people's time and resources, such as for creating and running application benchmarks, or setting up data collection at additional sites. Hidden time delays may become apparent through the scheduling exercise, making it possible to deal with at least some of them in advance. In addition, the time needed to massage and analyze the data needs to be taken into account, especially when an analysis needs to be completed before the next step can be undertaken.

Refine the Methodology

It is also important to realize that NRP objectives and methodologies may change along the way because of unanticipated results that occur in the earlier stages of the NRP activities, and those changes may necessitate changes to the schedule.

An NRP project is really an exercise in network sleuthing: confirming or disproving what is believed to be true about the network, and uncovering much that is unknown. For this reason, any NRP project should include periodic reviews of its goals and methods. As data is collected, it should be used to evaluate the appropriateness of the goals, objectives, and methodologies. The network planner should constantly question whether and how the data supports the project goals and adapt and modify the project, if necessary, to ensure that the best possible use of resources is being applied to gain the best possible information set. At all times it is critical to ensure that the project is on target to provide results that will meet the organization's overall objectives.

At the beginning of most NRP projects (especially those related to client/server application deployment), there is usually a major effort to baseline the network to gain an initial understanding of the network infrastructure and its performance characteristics. This first effort is usually completed in a bounded time frame (from a few days to a few weeks). However, networks change and evolve, and the initial NRP results become obsolete as the behavior of the network changes over time.

The manufacturing organization in Scenario 2 is an example of this situation. Its NRP project was a first-time effort to build a baseline model for network planning centered around the PeopleSoft HRMS application. However, as the network changes and evolves (whether because of the future PeopleSoft application rollout phases or because of other network changes), the baseline information will need to be updated. Continuing the baselining effort on a regular basis means that the organization will continue to benefit from its initial investment in data collection and performance management tools for collecting and analyzing the network data.

In an enterprise application deployment situation, such as with SAP R/3, in which multiple modules may be deployed over an extended rollout period, not only will new baseline data be needed over time, but new application planning activities may be needed to characterize new application modules, and new capacity planning activities may be required, or previous analyses may need to be revisited. If the application deployment project is a lengthy one, then the NRP time line must take into account the need to reexecute the NRP cycle of activities based on the phases of the application rollout as well as other network changes that may occur within the deployment time frame.

In some cases, it may not be possible to develop a plan for an entire NRP project initially. For example, depending on how much is already known about the network, it may be necessary to gather baseline data in certain areas before planners can determine how many traffic analyzers will be needed and where they must be placed. Or, one set of activities may provide results that lead to a change in the project objectives. The results of the earlier work may lead to a focus on different areas than initially planned.

For example, an analysis of which applications are using the network may show that the existing applications that use the largest amounts of bandwidth are not the ones expected. This may call for a change in which applications to focus on for the rest of the project. For example, suppose it had been planned to study the usage of electronic mail on the network for purposes of relocating or distributing mail servers, on the assumption that electronic mail is responsible for the bulk of the bandwidth usage. If it turns out that Internet and intranet usage is actually much higher than electronic mail, then the project might be changed to focus instead on the location of the Internet or intranet servers or proxy servers.

On the other hand, while unexpected results may indicate that additional analyses are needed, they may not change the focus of the current project. For example, if the goal of the project is to analyze electronic mail usage because of a planned changeover to a different electronic mail system, then finding out that Internet or intranet usage is much higher than expected would not change the need to analyze electronic mail usage. However, it might indicate the need for a second project to look at the usage of Internet and intranet applications.

Adopting a practice of continuously examining, evaluating, and refining the goals and methodologies based on the analysis of currently available data will ensure that the results of the planning effort will provide meaningful and useful information to the organization, even if those results turn out to be other than initially expected.

Ingredients for a Successful NRP Project

Some of the resources required for a successful NRP project, such as budget and network tools, are relatively simple to identify, and their availability is usually fairly obvious—they are available or they are not.

Within most organizations there are well-defined processes for obtaining those resources.

Other resources, such as commitment and time, are intangible and can be more difficult to pin down. For example, obtaining staff time can be a challenge, especially in a reactive network support organization in which the ability to predict time availability is impaired by the need to respond to the inevitable network crises. In addition, it may be necessary to get cooperation from other parts of the organization, such as knowledgeable staff who can place probes in various data centers or satellite locations. It may also be necessary to enlist the cooperation of an application development group in order to profile an application in development or to find a knowledgeable user who can create and execute a benchmark for an application under study. The coordination of such resources can create many challenges. Timing can affect the best-laid plans, so that when one set of resources becomes available, other needed resources may not be.

Commitment to the NRP process is included as a resource, because it is the ingredient that will make it possible to follow through on a specific project despite obstacles. Because NRP projects often require cooperation from different groups or departments within the IT organization, support and commitment from higher levels in the organization are necessary. If the NRP process is intended to become a long-term strategic shift in the way applications are deployed within the organization, then a high-level commitment within the organization is critical in order for this process to survive and be used.

Substantial progress can often be made without all possible desirable resources. Even if it is not possible to implement all the tasks of an NRP project from start to finish, completing some of the phases can provide valuable information. For example, even if it isn't possible to obtain the desired traffic analyzers or RMON2-compatible probes, a great deal can be learned just by collecting and analyzing usage-based data from the enterprise network. However, any NRP project must have some combination of commitment, people resources, budget, and the appropriate network tools in order to be successful.

People Resources

The first set of resources you must identify is the personnel needed to carry out the NRP activities. People's availability is a major consideration. Will all responsible IT personnel be able to deliver on their project commitments in a timely manner? This is particularly an issue if the same network management staff members involved in the NRP project are also responsible for the day-to-day operation of the network, where user needs and network problems may interfere with the staff members' ability to concentrate on the planning activities. Even when outside consultants are used, there will still be time commitments needed from internal network management personnel. In addition, if application planning is part of the NRP project, application developers, application vendor personnel, consultants, or knowledgeable users may be needed to assist with application planning activities.

There are two key considerations in looking at the people resources required:

■ *In-house staff.* Does the organization have sufficient expertise in-house to carry out the planning activities? Will the planner be able to dedicate sufficient time? Also, how difficult will it be to obtain resources from other parts of the organization, such as application developers or knowledgeable users who can create and execute benchmark scripts for application profiling activities?

■ *Consultants.* Will outside expertise be needed to help with the project or project planning? Consultants can provide the expertise that may not exist in-house, and they can also reduce (but not totally eliminate) the time commitments required on the part of in-house staff.

Even if the organization's long-term goals are to incorporate NRP principles into its network management practices, using consultants may still be a benefit in the beginning, especially if the in-house staff lacks expertise with performance management tools, and with NRP processes. The consulting engagement can be structured so that it also functions as a training project for the network management staff who will be responsible for the ongoing NRP efforts. Once they are trained, future cycles of baselining, application planning, and capacity planning can be accomplished with in-house network management staff and expertise.

Budget

The costs for conducting an NRP project can vary widely with the scope of the project and its objectives. Typically some budget dollars are always required, particularly if the organization has not yet purchased the network tools to be used or if there are plans to engage consultants to help with the NRP effort. Some equipment, such as Network General Sniffers, can be rented, although if NRP is envisioned as an ongoing effort, it may make better economic sense in the long run to purchase the appropriate data collection devices. Performance management tools can range from $10,000 up to $100,000, depending on the types of functions needed. In addition, if there is no expertise in using the various network tools within the organization, it may be necessary to budget for the costs of a consultant to help with the project activities.

Network Tools

Data collection and analysis tools and performance management tools are needed to facilitate the network planning cycle. These tools are used to collect and report data, generate a baseline model of a network, and model and analyze that network.

One of the key tasks in setting up an NRP project is to determine the set of tools most appropriate for the tasks to be accomplished. All tools have limits, and all tools are invested with an implicit methodology and set of data characterizations and constraints. These must be taken into account relative to the needs of the planning activities.

Data collection and analysis tools are very important for collecting live data from networks for use in performance management tools. For most NRP projects live data will be required, because it is literally impossible to know the traffic flow within a network well enough to enter it into the performance management tool. The network planner must ensure that sufficient data collection devices are available to collect whatever data is needed to meet the objectives, as was discussed earlier in the section "Define a Data Collection Strategy."

Several data collection and performance management tools are available that may play a role in an NRP project. The types of tools were discussed briefly in Chapter 2, "The Network Resource Planning Process." Appendix B, "Network Resource Planning Tools," provides an overview of many of the tools currently available for use in an NRP project.

Once you have defined your NRP objectives, marshaled the resources needed (equipment, software, budget, staff), and determined a realistic timeline, you are ready to proceed with the NRP activities. The next three chapters provide a detailed look at executing the baselining, application planning, and capacity planning activities that make up a full NRP project.

4

Baselining the Network

This chapter discusses in detail the techniques and processes of baselining an enterprise network. Baselining is the first of the three cycles that make up the complete Network Resource Planning (NRP) process (see Figure 4-1). Baselining is the fundamental step in characterizing a network and is the foundation for all other planning activity. The baselining process gives the network manager a clear picture of the performance and capacity utilization of the existing network and provides the starting point, or baseline, on which an analysis of a proposed enterprise application deployment can be based. The goal of baselining is to produce an accurate understanding of the network as it currently exists.

Baselining is the process of documenting the existing network in order to understand what is available and how it is typically being used. This includes an accurate rendering (topology map) and characterization of the network infrastructure, as well as many snapshots of network activity or traffic flow.

Figure 4-1
Baselining as a
component of the
NRP cycle.

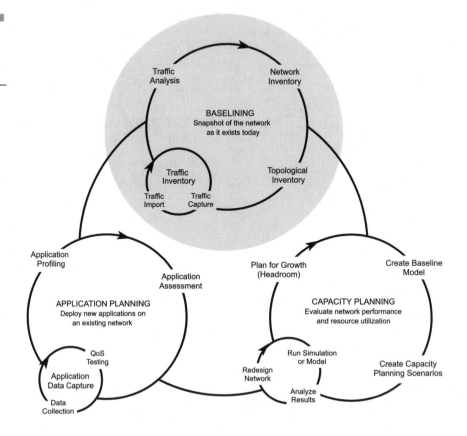

Baselining Defined

The term *baselining* is often used and rarely defined. The term is now used frequently by many companies and on many World Wide Web sites, but with many slants and variations to the meaning. In mid-1996, a search on the World Wide Web using the keywords "network" and "baselining" yielded about 100 hits. One year later the number of hits was over 9000. The term "baselining" suffers from a use-to-definition ratio problem—the word is commonly used but without agreement on a generally accepted definition.

Webster's Collegiate® Dictionary (Merriam-Webster, 1994) includes the following definitions of *baseline:* "1: a line serving as a basis; esp. one of known measure or position used (as in surveying or navigation) to calculate or locate something; ... 4: a set of critical observations or data used for comparison or a control; 5: a starting point <the baseline of this discussion>." These definitions emphasize the point that a baseline serves as a starting point or known reference point for additional analyses or discussions.

In the context of this book relative to NRP techniques, baselining is defined as the process of documenting the current network in order to understand what the network resources are, how those network resources are being utilized, and how much of those resources remain available.

Creating a Baseline versus Baselining

It is important to distinguish between *creating a baseline* as a unitary activity in support of a specific NRP task, and the ongoing process of *baselining*, which focuses on periodically validating and updating the network baseline for purposes of monitoring changes in the network's behavior.

For NRP capacity planning purposes, you need a "baseline model," which is a single snapshot of network activity that represents the network's behavior. You use this model as the basis for creating "what-if" scenarios that predict network behavior under different potential conditions.

Baselining as an ongoing activity lets you look at the changes that occur in the network over time and can help identify patterns in the network's behavior. Once understood, these patterns of behavior can be fed back into the baseline model created for NRP purposes, helping you understand more accurately what is "typical" network behavior (or worst-case behavior, depending on the types of analysis you are interested in doing). Identifying patterns of growth and change can also give you an idea of how the network is evolving over time and may give some ideas of the kinds of issues that need to be addressed in planning activities.

A network baseline should document the following aspects of a network:

- Current network topology
- Current utilization of the available network bandwidth
- Application-specific traffic data as applicable

To "baseline the network" in the context of NRP means to gather the information needed to create and document these aspects of your network. The process of creating the baseline is the initial collection of network data and documentation that is the starting point for NRP, the "stake in the ground." It is a "snapshot" of network performance and utilization in time, a reference point used as a control and for comparison. However, this does not mean that this stake in the ground is static and must remained fixed.

Over time, as the network changes, the baseline will need to change also. "Baselining the network" in this context means that multiple sets of measurements of network utilization are collected and documented, and that usage and application-based data measurements will continue to be collected at specified intervals. Baselining as an ongoing process acknowledges that the various elements within the network will change, and it recognizes that it is important to the planning process to understand how those items are changing and why.

Specifically, baselining uses data collection tools to collect network performance metrics and then uses performance management tools to analyze those metrics to determine the current behavior of the network. By analyzing performance metrics on a consistent basis (weekly, biweekly, or monthly), you can begin to identify the enterprise system behavior patterns of the network. Depending on the nature of the changes, it may be appropriate to replace the previous baseline model with a newly created baseline model to provide a more accurate basis for the NRP activities that depend on it.

Baselining requires a network sleuthing mentality and almost always reveals some surprises. Even when the network has been carefully and consistently managed, baselining may reveal application traffic that had not been suspected or that is making far different usage demands than expected. It may also point out circuits running at different speeds than expected, routers that you did not know existed, and so on.

Baselining can reveal a whole range of valuable information about an existing network. However, the results of a baselining activity must always be evaluated relative to the goals of the overall NRP project. Baselining will provide a great deal of data and may suggest many areas that should be investigated further, but unless these investigations are specifically related to the objectives for an immediate NRP project, you should not allow them to distract your focus. For example, if you are analyzing the effects of replacing existing SNA (Systems Network Architecture) traffic with traffic from a client/server application such as SAP R/3, then the data you find on the usage of various email protocols, however surprising or interesting, should probably be left for another NRP analysis project at a later time.

Why Use Baselining Techniques?

With any planning effort, and particularly with a significant application deployment such as SAP R/3, BAAN IV, or PeopleSoft, the first question most people want answered is whether their current network has the capacity to support the new application's traffic properly at the required quality-of-service levels while continuing to support existing application traffic. Baselining provides the foundation that makes it possible to answer that question. The goal of baselining is to identify the performance and behavior patterns of the network *as a total system*. All additional planning activities require that these characteristics and patterns be known for the network as a system.

The next level of understanding is to analyze the specific components that contribute to the network system. Analyzing the behavior of components such as local area network (LAN) utilization or wide area network (WAN) circuit utilization can identify how each component contributes to the total picture, which can then suggest how to make changes to specific components to improve client/server performance. It is very likely that some changes will be required within the network infrastructure in order for the network to provide an acceptable quality of service for the new and existing applications. Baselining provides the basic information needed to determine what changes may be required.

Repeated baselining is also important because of the time frames involved in a successful enterprise application deployment. The deployment schedule for an application like SAP R/3 can span one to five years. The network planning process must take this time factor into account, because changes to the network can and will occur over such an extended period. Many of these changes may be relatively minor in comparison to an enterprisewide SAP R/3, BAAN IV, or PeopleSoft deployment. However, they will still affect network utilization, and the initial baseline will not reflect those changes. A well-thought-out NRP project will provide a set of criteria for measuring, documenting, and tracking how changes will affect the network's behavior patterns over time.

How Much Baseline Data Is Enough?

In some discussions of baselining it is suggested that in order to baseline a network there must be months' or even years' worth of historical data available. That claim is not true. That myth prevents many network managers and planners from making a start at gathering simple performance metrics, in the belief that what they collect will not be useful. Even a few simple performance metrics about an enterprise network, collected over a short time (one or two days), can provide extremely valuable clues about how the network is behaving and what performance can be expected when looked at on a systemwide basis. The key is that in order to answer the types of questions needed for a successful NRP effort, it is not necessary to have a high degree of precision to your data. For example, it probably makes a significant difference whether a given WAN circuit is utilized at 10% of capacity or at 80%, but it probably does not matter whether the actual utilization is 79%, 80%, or 81% at any given time.

Baselining versus Trending

The myth that baselining takes months of data collection arises from confusion between baselining and trending. Creating a baseline is indeed the first step of trending, but establishing the initial stake in the ground doesn't take months to accomplish. Because a baseline is a representative snapshot for the purposes of a reference point, a historical trend is not needed.

In fact, creating a baseline from historical data may produce a less reliable, less representative baseline. Just as it would not make sense to determine an adult's height by averaging his or her height measurements since childhood, it does not make sense to determine a network's current performance by looking at data that is outdated. Performance characteristics of the network six months ago may not be relevant to current usage and may skew the baseline to reflect characteristics that no longer exist.

Taking multiple baseline measurements over a specified short time frame (consecutive days) is appropriate, however. Doing so makes it possible to account for short-term variations such as time of day, day of the week, or other periodic variations in network activity based on the organization's business cycle. Long-term historical data, however, is not necessary to start the baselining process.

At the same time, data sets can still be kept and archived in order to analyze trends. Even in that case, though, the required process is not as complicated as some managers have been led to believe. It is possible to tell a great deal about a network's performance from a relatively simple set of data points collected over just a few iterations of baselining.

One of the issues that network managers frequently encounter when they attempt to collect network metrics is an oversupply of data. Too much data or the wrong data can get in the way of a successful analysis. For a successful NRP effort, it is important to look carefully at the performance metrics being collected. Is the type of data worth tracking? Does it really answer questions about the network behavior? How much is involved in collecting the data relative to its worth? Are some results inconsistent with expected network behavior? Can what is being found be validated with existing network documentation?

The Data Required for Baselining

Baselining requires a combination of data collected from the actual network and data obtained from existing network documentation. At least initially, the actual collected network data may not be sufficient. The results of the baselining activity must be validated by comparing what it found with what is documented, because the baselining process can miss elements of the network. For example, the performance management tool may not have SNMP (Simple Network Management Protocol) access to all the network devices and thus may not be able to discover some devices. After any data collection problems are fixed (SNMP access enabled, for example) and several iterations of baselining have occurred, however, you can routinely use actual network data to assess changes and patterns by comparing the data collected from week to week.

You need the following types of data and documentation for a successful baseline:

■ Existing network documentation: diagrams, addressing, network devices, circuit lists, and so forth

■ Topology data collected from the network

■ Usage-based data collected from the network

■ Application-based data collected from the network

Figure 4-2 shows the hierarchical relationship between these types of network data. Building from the bottom of the pyramid, each layer depends on but also refines and provides more details about the layer below it. The bottom layer of the information pyramid is the existing network documentation, which is usually very general, rather static,

Figure 4-2
Baseline data
pyramid.

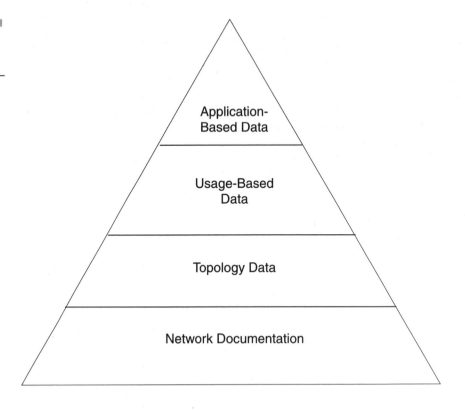

and often out of date. The second layer is the topology data. Topology data describes what components exist on the network and how they are interconnected. Topology data is often used to maintain and update the network documentation.

The third layer of data shown in Figure 4-2 is traffic volume or usage data. Data at this level is somewhat basic but is much more dynamically updated than data at the topology level. The data at this level provides general information about the traffic moving through the network. It answers questions such as how much data is moving between directly connected sites (total volume of bytes over a given time interval), in what direction the data is traveling, and at what time of day this activity occurred.

The fourth layer shown in Figure 4-2 (application-based data) also deals with traffic, but is more specific and more dynamic. The traffic data collected at this level can identify which hosts are doing the talking, what type of conversation took place (such as FTP, Telnet, or SAP R/3), the approximate start and end times of the conversation, and the number of packets and bytes in each direction.

lifferent levels of data together in a coordinated way
e to identify traffic behaviors and patterns on both a
is as well as a component (LAN, WAN, etc.) basis. The
presented at the higher levels of the pyramid provide a
etter and more specific view of network traffic when
e data shown at the bottom of the pyramid.

Network Documentation

mentation refers to the existing lists and diagrams that
n already possesses to describe its network. This informa-
iay not be current. The information could come from a
igement platform such as Hewlett Packard's OpenView,
ply consist of lists maintained in a spreadsheet. In any
ortant to validate that information found through the
ivity correlates with what is documented. Seldom does
on from these two sources actually match at the outset. A
uires some sleuthing to determine why the data collected
rom the existing documentation. In some cases it may be
umentation is erroneous (out of date or incomplete). In
ie baselining process may not have been able to access all
he network (as in the case of lack of SNMP access to key
the baselining process needs to be run again after these
issues are resolved.

In some organizations there may be little or no network documentation. An organization whose documentation is severely out of date also
fits into this category. The data collected to build the first baseline can
serve as the initial network documentation. It provides a place to start
or a stake in the ground. If the baselining effort is ongoing, "network
documentation" may simply be last week's baseline. The baseline data
still requires some sort of validation, however, even if it is just using
the network manager's own knowledge of the network, to ensure that
the baseline is reasonably complete.

Topology Data

Topology data describes the physical network components (such as
routers, circuits, and servers) and how they are connected. Topology
data includes the location and configuration description of each internetworking device on the network, how those devices are connected

(the circuit types and speeds), the type of LANs that are connected, and the location of the servers (although not all network tools can discover all types of components).

There are four ways that the performance management tool doing the baselining can acquire the needed topology data:

- *Enter the data manually.* Using existing network documentation and known information about the network, each of the network components can be built within the performance management tool. Depending on the performance management tool, this data can be entered either through the tool's data entry interface or through an ASCII import function, if available. Generally this method is the most time-consuming and is no more accurate than the network documentation on which it is based.

- *Access SNMP MIB data.* Several performance management tools use SNMP to query the Management Information Base (MIB) maintained by the SNMP agents resident in the network's routers and other internetworking devices. This process is known as an SNMP discovery. The data maintained in the MIB provides most of the information needed to build a representation of the topology data for the network in question. With this method, data can be acquired from a wide variety of internetworking devices, because most vendors support the standard SNMP MIB II definitions for routers. All that is required for this type of discovery is a starting point address (seed address) and the read-only access community string password for each of the internetworking devices that need to be discovered.

- *Import data from router configuration files.* For Cisco routers data can be imported directly from the routers' configuration files to build a representation of the topology data for the network in question. This method provides a very complete data set for each of the Cisco routers in the network, but it does not address non-Cisco routers.

- *Use topology data from a network management platform.* Some performance management tools can import data using the map file from a network management platform such as HP OpenView or IBM NetView. Using the network management platform's export function, a file can be created that can be imported by some performance management tools. This provides a limited, minimal data set that serves as a starting point. In many cases it must be manually configured with additional information in order to be useful for Network Resource Planning.

Figure 4-3

Example of a discovered network topology map. (© Optimal Networks.)

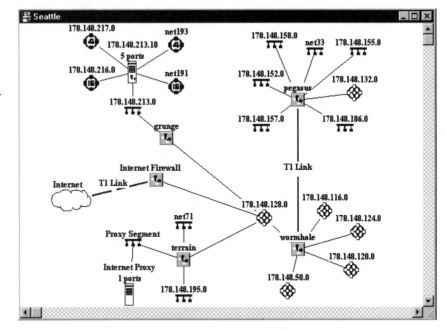

Figure 4-3 shows an example of a network map that is a representation of the topology of a network. This network was collected using the SNMP-based topology discovery capability of the Optimal Surveyor tool from Optimal Networks. The network map shows routers, circuits, servers, and the discovered connectivity.

Usage-Based Data

Usage-based data can be gathered from SNMP agents in routers or other internetworking devices that support MIB II. SNMP queries to the routers provide statistics about the exact number of bytes that have passed through each LAN interface, WAN circuit, or Frame Relay permanent virtual circuit (PVC) interface. This is the most complete way to determine the total volume of traffic; most traffic analyzers and Remote Monitoring (RMON2)-compatible probes in use today lose some traffic data information. You can use this data in turn to calculate the percentage of utilization of the available bandwidth for each WAN circuit or Frame Relay PVC. It can be important that the queries be launched in a multicast fashion (that is, that all queries be as close to simultaneous as possible). The data from each router then represents usage at approximately the same point in time, which lets you build a system view of activity and utilization by time of day for an enterprise network.

Application-Based Data

Data from traffic analyzers such as Network General Sniffers or from RMON2-compatible probes provides specifics about the application traffic on the network. Strategically placed data collection devices can gather enough data to provide clear insight into the traffic behavior and flow patterns of the network system. The information collected by traffic analyzers or RMON2-compatible types of probes should include the following:

- The type of applications (FTP, Telnet, Oracle, SAP R/3)
- The hosts that are communicating by network layer address (i.e., IP address)
- The duration of the network conversation between any two hosts (start time and end time)
- The number of bytes in both the forward and return directions for each network conversation
- The average size of the packets in the forward and return directions for each network conversation

Many performance management tools can use this data to calculate a throughput rate in packets per second (pps) or bits per second (bps) for each network conversation.

The Relationship between Usage-Based and Application-Based Data

The primary difference between usage- and application-based data is the degree of detail that the data provides and therefore the conclusions that can be made based on the data.

Collecting traffic data on an enterprise network is in many ways analogous to collecting vehicle traffic data on a highway. One way to estimate highway usage is to assign someone at each on-ramp and off-

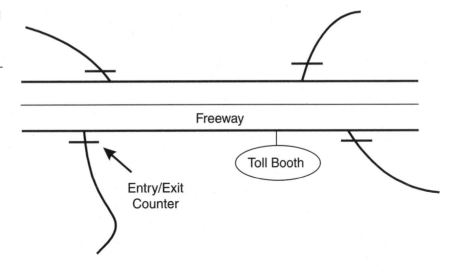

Figure 4-4
Highway data
collection analogy.

ramp to count how many vehicles enter and exit the highway. Figure 4-4
shows a highway with counters placed on all on- and off-ramps to count
the vehicles entering and exiting the highway. Calculations can be done
on the data collected to determine the volume of traffic (number of
vehicles) that moved through the highway system at any point in time
(the average flow). Those numbers can then be plotted and a behavior
graph developed. This process could be repeated for several days in a
row, and at the end of the week, traffic patterns would emerge.

If the maximum capacity of the highway (the maximum number of
vehicles that could use the highway and still travel at the speed limit,
for example) is known, a percentage utilization can then be calculated
at any given point. That computation is very similar to the methods
used to collect and analyze usage-based data from network devices.

Often, however, just knowing usage statistics and percentage of utilization may not be sufficient to understand a network's behavior. If
you know that utilization is very high at certain points in time, the
next logical set of questions involves the reasons for this pattern. Simple usage data cannot address those questions. Information is needed
about which applications or hosts are using the network and what type
of demand each one makes. In the highway analogy shown in Figure
4-4, a monitoring station similar to a toll booth could be placed at a
strategic point on the highway, and much more could be learned
about the vehicles that use the highway (to the great annoyance of the
drivers). This special monitoring booth could stop each vehicle and

record details such as the make, model, and color of each vehicle, how many passengers it carries, how many doors, where the vehicles came from, where it is going, and so on. (Weigh stations actually do this type of monitoring for trucks today.) When this information is combined with the related usage-based data, many more conclusions can be made about the traffic on the highway. This special monitoring booth is analogous to a data collection device such as a traffic analyzer or RMON2-compatible probe used on an enterprise network.

As a general rule, you need to collect both usage-based and application-based data in order to get a complete picture of network traffic patterns. There are two reasons not to depend only on data from data collection devices (traffic analyzers or RMON2-compatible probes) to determine the utilization of network components. One reason is that it would be a very expensive method to use. You would need to collect traffic from every segment in the network (or at least in the portion of network that is under study), and that would require placing a data collection device on every WAN circuit or LAN. In the highway analogy, it is much more expensive to construct and instrument a toll booth or weigh station than it is to hire temporary workers to sit at the on- and off-ramps and just count cars. Similarly, collecting usage-based data is low-cost, because it can be collected from existing SNMP agents on the internetworking devices. Traffic analyzers and RMON2-compatible probes can cost anywhere from $1000–$2000 (for software-only collectors) up to the $20,000 range for the more sophisticated hardware-based devices. Instrumenting a network sufficiently to get a complete traffic picture using traffic analyzers or RMON2 probes is likely to be prohibitively expensive.

More importantly, even if it were possible to install data collection devices at strategic locations so that statistics for all the network traffic of interest could be collected, this still would not be sufficient to get a complete traffic picture, at least with today's data collection devices. Just as weigh stations can collect information only from trucks and only when they are open, most data collection devices in use at the time of writing this book lose some of the data that passes by. Data can be lost because of router updates or broadcasts that are not archived or because the data collection device simply runs out of space to store all the data it is receiving. Such losses are especially likely on busy WAN circuits or backbone LANs. Therefore, in most cases, usage-based statistics from routers need to be collected to supplement the data captured by the data collection devices and to provide a reasonably accurate view of total system activity.

Creating a Baseline

The goal of baselining is to produce an accurate model of network behavior as it exists today. A baseline is the combination of topology data that has been through a validation cycle with usage-based data, application-based data, or some combination of both that represents current traffic flow on the network. The baseline model can be used by itself for analysis of network utilization and to document the network, or it can serve as the basis for application or capacity planning. Either way, the point of developing this baseline is as a reference point for use in future comparisons. Therefore, the processes used to create the baseline must be repeatable. You want to be able to take measurements on the network in the future and compare them meaningfully to the existing baseline to determine how things change over time.

The diagram shown in Figure 4-5 illustrates the tasks that make up a complete baselining project. The model is shown as a circle because baselining activities are cyclical. The first step is a network inventory, but baselining then goes on as a continuous process. The cycle is repeated as the network changes over time so that the baseline reflects the network's current state.

The steps to building a baseline are as follows. Each of these steps is discussed in much greater detail later in this chapter.

Figure 4-5
Baselining cycle of activities.

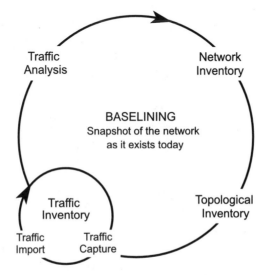

Traffic Analysis

Network Inventory

BASELINING
Snapshot of the network
as it exists today

Traffic Inventory

Topological Inventory

Traffic Import

Traffic Capture

1. *Network inventory:* Collect what is already known about the network, including a review of currently available network documentation and querying the appropriate staff.

2. *Topological inventory:* Gather topology data from the network and import into a performance management tool of choice. Validate the network representation/model of topology against the network inventory (network documentation) and fine-tune the topology model.

3. *Traffic inventory:* Gather usage-based and application-based traffic data according to the project objectives and import both types into the performance management tool of choice.

4. *Traffic analysis:* Analyze usage-based data to determine network utilization and available capacity. Analyze application-based data to generate a list of the major applications transiting the network, how they behave, and how they use network resources.

Typically, the network baseline provides a reliable representation of the network infrastructure and a snapshot of the network activity or traffic flow. These two data sets yield a tremendous amount of information about the network, how it is being used, capacity utilization of its WAN and LAN components, as well as providing the foundation for other planning activities. However, completing all of the four steps is not required to gain value from a baselining effort.

Depending on the objectives that you have identified for the NRP project, not all of the steps outlined in the diagram may be necessary. Some organizations maintain only the topological inventory of the network and gain value from keeping that information current. In that case only the first two steps (network inventory and topological inventory) will be used, and much useful information can be learned about the network over time. In other cases, depending on the NRP objectives, all the steps of the cycle may be needed. The types and amount of data and the types of analysis will depend on the baselining objectives. Setting NRP objectives was discussed in Chapter 3, "Getting Started."

Baselining Objectives

An NRP project is typically conducted in the context of a high-level set of objectives relating to the business needs that the corporate network supports on a continuous basis. This book focuses specifically on baselining objectives related to the deployment of an enterprise client/server application such as SAP R/3, BAAN IV, or PeopleSoft. Within the overall NRP objectives a wide range of goals and constraints can dictate how the enterprise application deployment will be handled. That decision in turn dictates the types of information needed in the baselining phase. The following three scenarios illustrate how baselining activities relate to different types of NRP objectives. Most organizations will follow one of these scenarios, with the second scenario being the most common.

The first scenario represents an organization where significant time or financial constraints dictate that the new enterprise application be added to the existing network on top of its current application mix. The only adjustments that can be made within the network are to change circuit capacity to provide acceptable quality of service for the new application. In addition, the time frame for decision making is very short, so the data collection and analysis needs to be completed within one to two weeks. This is a situation where the need for network planning has emerged as an afterthought in the application deployment process, arising only when the actual deployment of the application is imminent. This typically happens when the group that manages the enterprise network is not included in the planning cycles during the development of the new application.

The minimum set of baselining activities needed for this type of project are

- To collect network documentation and topology data
- To collect usage-based traffic data for at least one or two business days
- To analyze usage-based traffic for performance issues and saturated circuits

Application-based data is not used in this scenario, because the time frame of the project does not allow for the collection of the data, and because overall usage-based information is sufficient to determine circuit capacity adjustments for minimal network redesign.

The second scenario is probably the most common. In this scenario the organization does not have much information about the current network but understands that the proposed enterprise application deployment could require changes. This type of organization understands the need for network planning, and allows time to do a more complete NRP project. The ideal is to minimize the number of changes, but because the organization does not have a good understanding of what is already there, it is open to doing whatever is necessary, including a more substantial network redesign if required.

The baselining steps for this type of project are

- ▪ To collect network documentation and topology data
- ▪ To collect usage-based and application-based traffic data for at least one to two business weeks
- ▪ To analyze both usage-based and application-based traffic for application mix, performance issues, and saturated circuits

In this case, utilization data alone is not sufficient. Some information about the applications that generate the traffic is also required. The analysis can address questions such as whether some of the existing traffic can be reduced, such as Internet traffic that might not be work-related. In addition, some existing traffic may be replaced by traffic from the new application. For example, some or all SNA traffic may be replaced by an enterprise application such as SAP R/3 after deployment is complete.

The third scenario is one in which the existing network is already having problems meeting application demands. Network users have been complaining, and it is time for some major changes and restructuring, possibly involving a major network redesign. In this scenario, a redesign of the network may have already been proposed, but with little or no analysis of network usage to back it up. A major enterprise application deployment effort provides the motivation and justification for making these changes now. Redundancy (the ability of the network to continue to function when portions fail) has also been identified as a need for this network.

A redesign proposed under this type of scenario typically includes increasing the bandwidth on many existing circuits. This type of redesign will almost always dramatically increase the organization's monthly telecommunications costs, especially if the network is international. While this type of solution may be easy to conceive and may seem obvious, it may not necessarily be the most cost-effective solution. Furthermore, it may not even solve the performance problems. A network analysis is required to determine whether adding capacity is really the appropriate solution.

An NRP project will focus on validating the proposed redesign and determining whether it meets the objectives for quality-of-service goals. The project will evaluate current network behavior to determine current traffic flow (who's talking to whom), types of applications, and usage of circuits. The project goals will be to attempt to reduce the cost of the proposed redesign while maintaining performance goals.

This scenario may need more than one baseline snapshot (multiple weeks). Special-event traffic sets may need to be captured, such as network traffic reflecting end-of-month or end-of-quarter business cycles. All the baselining activities will be done at least once for this project. The following baselining activities will need to be performed:

■ To collect network documentation and topology data

■ To collect usage-based and application-based traffic data, during peak periods of network usage for one to two weeks, and during specific time periods such as the end of the month or quarter

■ To analyze both usage-based and application-based traffic for application mix, traffic flow, performance issues, and saturated circuits

The primary differences between this scenario and the previous scenario are the completeness of the data required, the time required to complete the data collection and analysis, and whether the network infrastructure will be changing. This scenario requires that the application-based data set be very complete and represent most of the traffic in the network as accurately as possible (this may be difficult to accomplish). This may mean that more traffic analyzers or RMON2-compatible probes will be required to collect the needed application-based traffic. In addition, usage-based traffic must be used to validate the application-based data to ensure that the data collection devices are placed correctly and to verify the completeness of the traffic they capture so that the application-based data accurately represents the available capacity of the network. These issues are dealt with in detail in Chapter 6, "Capacity Planning."

The following sections detail the activities in conducting a baseline analysis.

The Network Inventory

This step focuses on gathering the existing network documentation and determining the existing components of the network. This step effectively defines what the baselining effort is expected to find, but it also provides information that may be used as input into the baselining process.

The information that needs to be gathered includes

■ The number, classes, and names of network devices (router names)

■ The sites or campuses to be baselined by name and location

- A list of leased-line circuits, Frame Relay PVCs, and so forth, with end points (router names) and their speed (or capacities)
- The number and location of servers by network address
- Addressing schemes as well as exact addressing for routers
- A list of applications thought to be in use on the network, such as SAP R/3, Telnet, or HTTP
- The protocols thought to be in use on the network, such as TCP/IP or IPX
- Passwords as applicable (SNMP community strings for routers, router passwords for configuration information)

The goal is to collect all information that is currently known about the network.

The Topological Inventory

The topology inventory provides a view or "map" of the network showing the logical position and sometimes the geographical position of network components relative to each other. The topology inventory as needed for NRP purposes can be generated in one of several ways:

- By using the SNMP network discovery function in products such as Make Systems Inc.'s NetMaker XA Visualizer or Optimal Networks' Surveyor
- By using functionality provided by Cisco's NETSYS Performance Baseliner to create a topology view from Cisco router configuration files for Cisco-only environments
- By exporting the network map file from a network management platform (such as HP OpenView or IBM NetView) and using the import capability provided by CACI's ComNet Baseliner
- By manually entering the data from the network inventory to represent the topology of the network

Validation

Aside from defining the overall project objectives, validating the results of the topology inventory is the single most important step in the baselining process. The validity of all further NRP activities depends on the degree to which the topology inventory accurately represents the network under study.

You should review all specific items for correctness—make sure that they match what is known about the network according to the network documentation. Usually, discrepancies will be found. There may be unknown devices attached to the network or errors in routers' SNMP MIB data. In addition, you may discover that devices are misconfigured. When you attempt to validate your topology inventory for the first time, plan to work through the information piece by piece and also to check that the information makes sense. For example, the topology inventory may show a T1 circuit between two locations where no such circuit is documented. The time spent validating the topological data is well spent, considering that it is the foundation for accomplishing the rest of the baselining objectives and thus the overall NRP objectives as well.

The following items should be checked against the documentation gathered in the network inventory step:

- Check for general network completeness—that is, that all internetworking devices have been found or manually entered and all circuits identified.
- Check for any unconnected routers, LANs, or servers.
- Validate circuit speeds with knowledgeable network management staff and against network documentation.
- Validate router chassis types and vendor types.
- Verify router protocol configuration.
- Verify that network addressing is compete for all network protocols.

The process of creating and validating the network topology is iterative. The first pass may be tedious and slow-moving. In many cases there will be additional manual input to the model as well as manual correction to settings in the actual network. In some cases it may make sense to collect the topology data again after the network settings have been reconfigured. The decision to re-collect the topology data largely depends on the number of changes that have been made in the actual network compared to the model that has been generated.

The Traffic Inventory

Building a traffic inventory is the step within the baselining process that documents how much traffic is on the network—especially, for the purposes of this book, the wide area portion of the network. Traffic inventory activities focus on the WAN because it is typically the capacity- or performance-limiting resource within an enterprise network. The WAN is also usually responsible for the largest portion of recurring costs within the network and provides the most opportunity for cost control.

The traffic data used in building a traffic inventory is collected from two different sources that provide different types of data. Usage-based traffic data is collected from routers' SNMP agents (MIBs). Application-based traffic data is collected with data collection devices such as traffic analyzers (Network General Sniffers, for example) or RMON2-compatible probes. It is strongly recommended that you coordinate the two types of data collection efforts so that you can capture both types of traffic samples at the same time.

Coordinating the collection of these two types of data is sometimes difficult, but the benefits are many. With two coordinated sets of data, you can examine the conversations that created the traffic volume found in a specific usage sample. The usage-based samples pinpoint exactly which application traffic samples are of interest to analyze, and the application-based data provides the details on the conversations of interest. Correlating usage-based and application-based traffic samples can provide validation that a high level of usage represents meaningful, normal activity, or else that it represents traffic that requires further investigation.

In light of the overall NRP goals (to facilitate the effective deployment of the target enterprise application modules), the specific steps for developing a traffic inventory are the following:

1. To collect usage-based traffic samples, so that the utilization of the network resources can be identified and documented

2. To collect application-based traffic samples to determine which activities or applications contribute to the observed usage patterns

3. To import both types of traffic data into a performance management tool for analysis

Collecting Usage-Based Data

In order to collect the usage-based data needed to build an overall, or system, view of the network, data collection or performance management tools that support simultaneous SNMP queries are required. Usage-based data is gathered using router statistics, because today's routers are the internetworking devices that terminate WAN interconnections. In the future, other internetworking devices, such as Asynchronous Transfer Mode (ATM) edge switches or ATM backbone switches, will become the WAN connection termination points, and collection and measurement techniques will evolve to take these into account.

An enterprise network system's behavior patterns will typically emerge after analysis of as few as two or three consecutive days of usage data samples. Collecting usage-based samples for more than two or three days provides further validation of the emerging patterns but is usually not absolutely required to establish the patterns. However, gathering usage-based samples for an entire week (five 24-hour periods) provides a robust data set for determining the busy times for consecutive days.

It is important to determine whether there are specific business processing cycles that need to be captured, such as month-end processing or closing of an accounting period. The capture period should be coordinated to include this activity in order to get a usage picture that will include these peak load periods.

By collecting data from the entire network under study, you can look at overall system activity and trends. The specific performance metrics you need are taken from the SNMP MIB II variables IfInOctets and IfOutOctets as well as the in and out packet counts. These MIB values contain counts of the total number of octets and packets that have passed through a particular router's interface in the forward (out) and return (in) directions since the router has been operational, or since the counters last rolled over and reset.

Figure 4-6 shows the query points (interfaces) that a data collection or performance management tool would query to collect the data needed (in and out octets and packets). These interface values are collected at time t_0 and then again at times t_1 through t_n. Because the MIB variables provide a running total of the octet or packet count, the actual volume of data transiting the system within the time interval must be calculated by subtracting the value of the MIB variable at t_0 from the value of the same variable collected at t_1, and so on.

All routers in the enterprise network should be queried simultaneously (as nearly as possible). This allows the values obtained from the individual routers to be aggregated to calculate a volume (delta bytes) for the entire system, for any particular time period.

System Volume or Activity

Figure 4-7 shows the number of bytes aggregated on a half-hour basis for a 50-site network in Asia, starting from approximately 6:00 A.M. to

Figure 4-6
Collection of usage-
based data (in and
out octets).

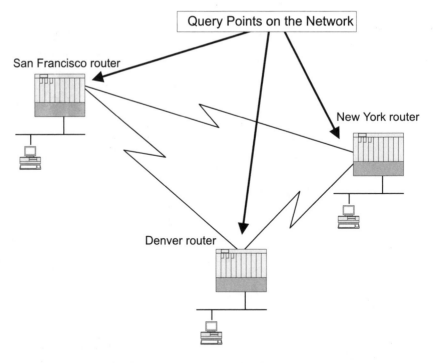

Figure 4-7
System volume chart.
(© Make Systems,
Inc.)

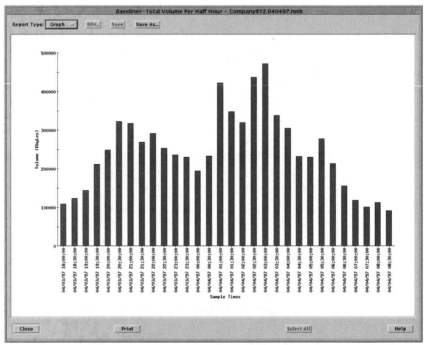

9:00 P.M. Asian time. (The actual data was collected domestically, using the Netmaker XA Baseliner tool running on a Sun workstation, and is time-stamped in the report using Eastern Daylight Time.) The x axis is the time the bytes were collected. The y axis shows the aggregated number of bytes for the entire system.

By gathering data as described above, the busy time for the enterprise WAN as a system can be determined, as well as the frequency of this behavior. The "busy hour" is the hour during the day when the maximum network activity and utilization are observed. For example, in the diagram shown in Figure 4-7 the busy hour is at 02:30 to 03:30 A.M. EDT (which is approximately 2:30 to 3:30 P.M. in Asia). Usually, at least 24 hours of data collection are required, even though the analysis may focus on a shorter period of time, such as the 15 hours of the Asian business day shown in Figure 4-7.

Individual Circuit Utilization

Individual circuit utilization starts with the same data as shown for the system volume chart, but it breaks the data down by each WAN circuit. It shows the data in terms of utilization instead of total volume. By dividing the volume (in bytes) by the number of seconds in the interval $(t_1 - t_0)$, a value in thousands of bits per second (Kbps) can be generated in both the in and the out directions for a router interface that connects to a particular circuit. When this Kbps value is compared to the WAN circuit or Frame Relay PVC capacity (also in Kbps), a percent utilization value can be calculated. For example, if the calculated usage in one direction on a circuit is 32 Kbps and the capacity is 64 Kbps, 32 Kbps/64 Kbps yields a 50% utilization of the circuit in that direction.

Figure 4-8, an individual-circuit utilization chart, shows the forward and return utilization on a 128 Kbps circuit from the time starting around 8:00 A.M. to about noon, Asia time. The x axis is the circuit name and time (EDT); the y axis shows the percent utilization in both the forward and return directions.

The Data Collection Interval and Time Periods

The collection interval for collecting usage-based data is normally set at five minutes. For usage-based data from routers, five-minute intervals

Figure 4-8
Individual circuit utili-
zation chart. (© Make
Systems, Inc.)

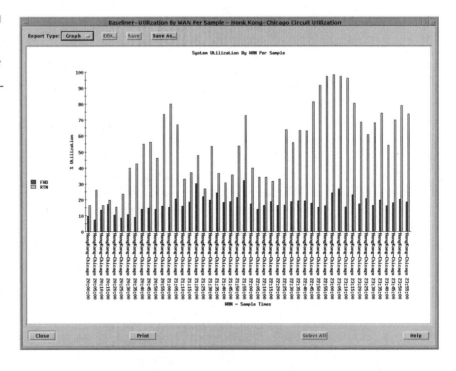

have been determined to be sufficiently discrete to show the peaks and
valleys of the network traffic load, but not so large an increment as to
lose the peaks and valleys when computing the average load in kilobits
per second (Kbps). In addition, research shows that most network conversations today are completed within a five-minute window.

If data is to be collected across divergent time zones, it is very helpful to pick one time zone as the base time and to configure all the
data collection devices to use that time. That way the resulting data
will all refer to the same times, making the job of correlating the data
much easier. For example, if the data collection tools doing the sampling are on the East Coast of the United States, a good strategy would
be to use Eastern Time as the base time for all devices collecting data.
This method simplifies the correlation of all the usage-based and
application-based traffic data from the various locations.

Collecting Application-Based Data

In order to collect application-based data for use in baselining, data collection devices that can identify key information about the applica-

tions using the network are needed; either traffic analyzers or RMON2-compatible probes can be used. When you choose your data collection devices, it is important to select devices that can export the data in a form that can be imported into the performance management tool you plan to use for the data analysis. Possible formats can be determined by consulting with the vendor of the performance management tool. Most vendors update their products regularly to add or enhance support for a variety of data collection devices.

Data Collection Placement Strategy

A placement strategy for the data collection devices is very important. In order to create a focused and cost-effective data collection strategy, you must thoroughly understand the data that is needed. This will ensure that the data collection effort is on target to realize the project objectives. For example, if the project objective is to look at traffic between remote clients and servers in centralized data centers, you will need a different collection strategy than if the objective is to look at electronic mail within one campus LAN.

In order to determine a cost-effective data collection placement strategy, the following two steps are needed:

■ To identify where the primary network resources for the application of interest are located

■ To identify the possible paths that the traffic of concern could take

In most cases, it is not necessary to place collection devices on every WAN circuit or every LAN. By determining where the key resources are located, and the possible paths from the clients to those resources, you can significantly reduce the number of data collection devices needed to collect the traffic of real interest. For example, depending on the topology of the network, it may be sufficient to put collection devices only on key backbone WAN circuits to see all critical application traffic between remote clients and centralized data center servers.

Figure 4-9 shows a network with client sites in Asia and one key server site in the United States. Because the traffic of interest is all going to the Chicago site, all traffic from the downstream Asia sites can be captured by placing WAN traffic analyzers or RMON2-compatible probes on the three circuits to Chicago.

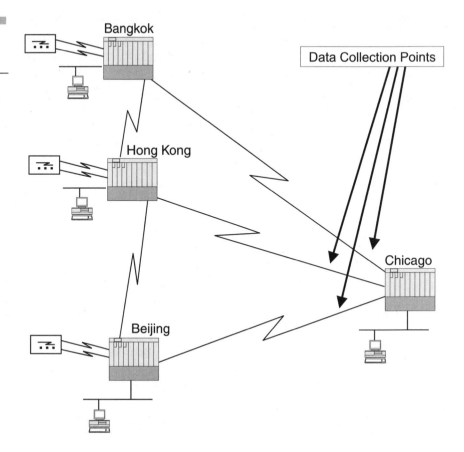

Figure 4-9
Data collection
device placement.

Configuring the Data Collection Devices

In order to be useful for analyzing traffic usage patterns, application-based data collection must cover the same time periods and use the same collection intervals as the corresponding usage-based data for the WAN circuit in question. For example, if a major backbone is at saturation (100% utilization) during certain periods of the day, you need to have application-based data collected during those same time periods (and at the same sample intervals) in order to analyze the application traffic that is causing the saturation. This can mean that data collection device placement and scheduling of data collection must be coordinated across multiple physical locations, possibly including locations that are geographically widespread.

Some data collection devices, such as Network General Distributed Sniffer Servers, can be controlled remotely through the network, so collection can be started and stopped for many DSSs from one location, as long as the appropriate network access is available. In other cases, correlated data collection will require the cooperation of multiple people at the various different locations. Each separate data collection device should be scheduled to use the same sampling interval (for example, five-minute periods) and the same synchronized start and stop times.

As with usage-based data, if data is to be collected across divergent time zones, it is helpful to pick one time zone as the base time and configure all the data collection devices to use that time. That way, the resulting data will all refer to the same times, making the job of correlating the data much easier. For example, if the data collection tools doing the sampling are on the East Coast of the United States, a good strategy would be to use Eastern Time as the base time for all devices collecting data, even if the target time period for the analysis is the Asian business day (8:00 A.M. to 6:00 P.M., 12 hours ahead of Eastern Time). All the traffic analyzers, RMON2-compatible probes, and data collection or performance management tools querying the routers would be set to Eastern Time, irrespective of the actual time at their physical location. Thus, data collected at 8:00 A.M. in Tokyo would be time-stamped 8:00 P.M. Eastern Time (the previous day). This method simplifies the correlation of all the usage-based and application-based traffic data from the various locations.

Traffic Analysis

Once the usage-based and application-based traffic samples have been collected, all the data needs to be analyzed to determine the behavior of the enterprise network. You should first analyze the usage-based data to determine both the system trend and the individual circuit utilization across multiple days. Analyzing multiple days of usage-based data should show similar behavior for both the enterprise network as a system and the WAN circuits.

Once the usage-based data has been analyzed, you can analyze the application-based data, in terms of both overall application distribution and throughput, and relative to the specific time periods of interest (usually periods that show high-volume usage) that emerged from the initial analysis of the usage-based data.

All the collected data then needs to be analyzed to determine which samples best represent the behavior of the enterprise network so that a baseline model can be generated. The selection of the samples used to create the baseline model is important because it is the representation of the network that will be used as the basis for capacity planning activities. The strategies for creating a baseline model are discussed in Chapter 6, "Capacity Planning," and in detail in Appendix A, "Baseline Model Creation Strategies."

Analyzing Usage-Based Data

The following steps are involved in analyzing the usage-based traffic samples to identify patterns of network activity:

- To create usage charts and review the traffic samples for each 24-hour period, for both system view and individual circuits, across multiple days
- To identify patterns from the system usage chart across multiple days
- To identify the "busy hour" for each 24-hour sample across multiple days
- To identify the patterns (percent utilization) for critical (backbone) circuits across multiple days
- To validate (if possible) that this information represents true behavior patterns of the system

These steps can all be accomplished using router MIB statistical collection tools as discussed in Chapter 2, "The Network Resource Planning Process."

Reviewing the usage-based data in blocks makes the task of analyzing the data more manageable. You can choose blocks that make sense in terms of the analysis, such as business mornings and business afternoons, or they can be arbitrary, such as contiguous six-hour periods.

Finding the "Busy Hour" for the System

The review and validation of the data should always include an analysis of whether the patterns make sense in terms of what is known about the organization's expected usage and business cycles. Notice that in the system volume chart, Figure 4-10, the samples taken between 22:30 and 23:30 (Eastern Time) represent the peak hour for this business day in Asia. This would be the network's "busy hour." It also shows that

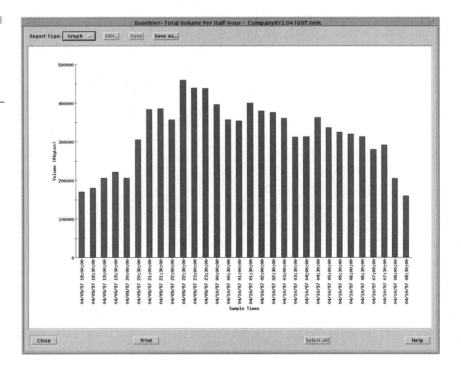

Figure 4-10
System volume chart showing more activity. (© Make Systems, Inc.)

network usage dips to a lower level during the Asian midday or lunch time. There is another spike in usage at approximately 04:30 (Eastern Time), which could represent Asian employees wrapping up activities to prepare for the work day's end.

Analyzing Backbone Circuit Behavior

Another way to determine whether a particular sample period contains significant activity is to look at the usage charts on a per-circuit basis; that is, usage charts for each leased-line circuit, Frame Relay PVC, and so on. In looking at patterns for individual circuits, it will usually become apparent that some circuits (particularly backbone circuits) mimic the system behavior—the peaks and valleys are the same as observed for the system as a whole. These backbone circuits are usually the key contributors to the overall system behavior. Other circuits may not show the same type of pattern as the system and are usually circuits that have less impact on the overall performance of the network.

Figure 4-11 provides a more detailed look at usage-based traffic data for one of the backbone circuits between Asia and the United States. It clearly shows that peak utilization is in the morning at the same time

Figure 4-11
Circuit utilization
chart. (© Make Sys-
tems, Inc.)

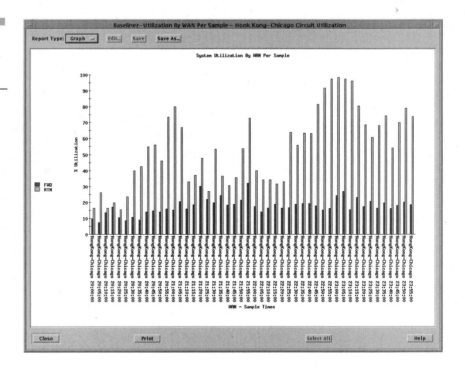

as the system busy hour (from 22:30 to 23:30 Eastern Time, as shown in Figure 4-10). Note that Figure 4-11 shows utilization in five-minute intervals rather than the half-hour intervals shown in Figure 4-10. This backbone circuit mimics the overall system behavior and is also almost saturated (100% utilized) during about half of the busy hour. Because this is one of the major backbone circuits for the Asian network, the applications using this circuit should be analyzed further to see what is causing this traffic. This level of understanding is also critical to deciding what usage-based data set to use for capacity planning purposes. You want to make sure to select a set of traffic data that represents network behavior that is relevant to your NRP goals. (The issues involved in creating a baseline model for use in capacity planning will be discussed in more detail in Chapter 6, "Capacity Planning.")

Validating the Analysis

Once the usage-based samples of interest have been identified, it is important to validate the hypothesis that those samples are truly representative of network usage. You can review the application-based data that corresponds to the time frame of interest, analyzing the specific network conversations to understand which conversations contributed to the usage for that time period. The application-based data should identify the applications that are causing the observed usage, thus helping to determine whether the activity is representative of what is considered to be valid network usage.

It is also important to determine whether the observed usage pattern is standard behavior for the network or is a one-time or anomalous occurrence. That determination can be done in several ways. Looking at usage-based data across multiple days to see whether the same behavior is repeatable is probably the best way to validate the activity patterns. You can also look at usage-based data from another source, such as a network management platform (such as HP OpenView), to see whether it shows the same types of patterns for individual circuits. Finally, you can validate your data against known uses of the network—whether the patterns match what you expect, given the normal business activities that should affect network usage.

Analyzing Application-Based Data

Analyzing application-based traffic makes it possible to characterize in some detail the behavior of individual applications and users (or hosts). This includes information about the number of conversations, the number of users, what kind of traffic volume the application represents, the host from which the traffic originated, and the host to which the traffic is going.

An application-based traffic analysis can provide the following types of information:

- The distribution of applications on the network—the top application types used (FTP, SNA, WWW-HTTP, and so forth) in order of the amount of usage
- The behavior of network conversations for any individual host or application (stated as throughput in bits per second, duration, etc.)
- The top hosts (which clients and servers are using the network the most)

Application Distribution

One outcome of the application data analysis will be an application distribution report, which is a listing of the application types that are using the network, along with metrics on how much of the network's resources each application type is using. The report is usually presented in the order of usage, from the application types with the highest usage to those with the lowest. Depending on the performance management tool you use, the report may not list all application types on the system but only some number of the top applications (10 or 20, for example).

Figure 4-12 shows an application distribution report generated by NetMaker XA from imported Network General Sniffer data for the top ten application types that correspond to one hour of the usage-based data shown in the system volume graph of Figure 4-10. The information in the column labeled "Name" shows the application type, and "# of Demands" shows the number of sessions of that application type. The column "Total (KBytes)" shows the total number of kilobytes for this circuit across the busy hour for that application type. The column "KBytes-Fwd (%)" shows the amount of the data that moved in the forward direction, relative to the hosts involved in the conversations for the application type, both as the number of kilobytes and as a percentage of the total. The "KBytes-Rtn (%)" column shows the amount of the data that moved in the return direction relative to the hosts in the conversation for the application type. For many application types, the usage is asymmetrical—most of the bytes are going in one direction.

Figure 4-12 shows the top ten application types for the busy hour of the 15 hours shown in Figure 4-10 (22:30–23:30 Eastern Time). The top application type is WWW-HTTP, which could be Internet or intranet web traffic. It is very asymmetrical, as might be expected—a request

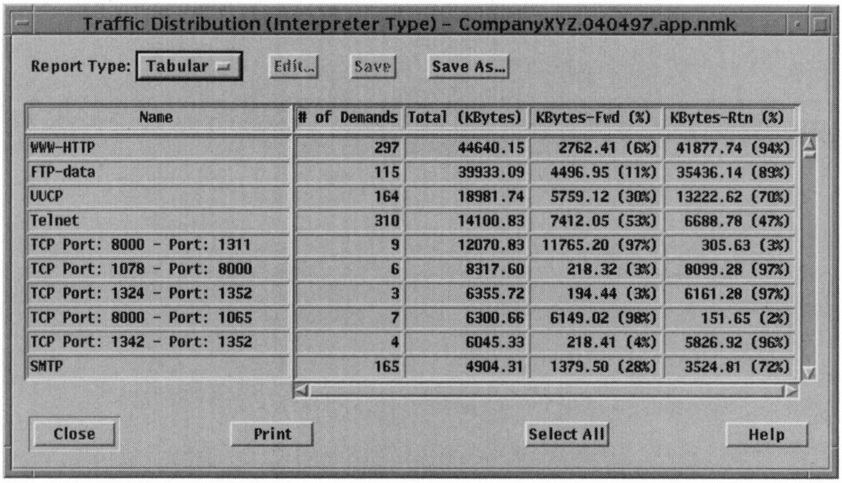

Figure 4-12
Application distribution report. (© Make Systems, Inc.)

Traffic Distribution (Interpreter Type) – CompanyXYZ.040497.app.nmk

Report Type: Tabular | Edit... Save Save As...

Name	# of Demands	Total (KBytes)	KBytes-Fwd (%)	KBytes-Rtn (%)
WWW-HTTP	297	44640.15	2762.41 (6%)	41877.74 (94%)
FTP-data	115	39933.09	4496.95 (11%)	35436.14 (89%)
UUCP	164	18981.74	5759.12 (30%)	13222.62 (70%)
Telnet	310	14100.83	7412.05 (53%)	6688.78 (47%)
TCP Port: 8000 – Port: 1311	9	12070.83	11765.20 (97%)	305.63 (3%)
TCP Port: 1078 – Port: 8000	6	8317.60	218.32 (3%)	8099.28 (97%)
TCP Port: 1324 – Port: 1352	3	6355.72	194.44 (3%)	6161.28 (97%)
TCP Port: 8000 – Port: 1065	7	6300.66	6149.02 (98%)	151.65 (2%)
TCP Port: 1342 – Port: 1352	4	6045.33	218.41 (4%)	5826.92 (96%)
SMTP	165	4904.31	1379.50 (28%)	3524.81 (72%)

Close   Print   Select All   Help for a page goes forward, and the whole page returns. This application type should probably be analyzed further to determine whether the usage is indeed all legitimate business usage.

Identifying High-Volume Applications

Applications such as WWW-HTTP, FTP, and Telnet are identifiable because they use well-known TCP ports or sockets reserved for those application types. Some traffic analyzers and RMON2-compatible probes can map these well-known ports to the names of the application types and include the names in the data they provide.

Several other applications listed in the report shown in Figure 4-12 do not use well-known ports, so the data collection device cannot identify those application types by name. If these application types cause significant traffic volume relative to other application types, it is important to determine what type of applications these are. For example, if "TCP Port: 8000" in Figure 4-12 turns out to be the port for proxy servers for Internet traffic (meaning that "WWW-HTTP" represents intranet traffic only), then the report shows that Internet, intranet, and electronic mail (UUCP and SMTP combined) represent a significant portion of the top applications using this network. These applications should then be analyzed further to show how their behavior affects network performance over time.

Analyzing Application Throughput

Tracking application throughput shows how an application behaves in a specific environment. Application throughput is a metric (in Kbps) that shows how much bandwidth a particular session is using within a particular time period. For a given application, an individual session's throughput is calculated by counting the bytes in either direction and dividing by the duration of the session. Looking at many sessions of the same type, such as multiple conversations from users running the SAP R/3 GUI, you can gain a sense of how the application is using the network overall.

For example, some applications (such as FTP or HTTP) are variable in their bandwidth usage and may behave differently from session to session or in different network environments. Other applications or protocols, such as the SAP R/3 GUI or Telnet, exhibit similar behavior from session to session and on many different networks.

A lightweight application, such as Telnet or SAP R/3, is one where the throughput is always low (less than 10 Kbps, and typically 1 to 2 Kbps when active). There is a good chance that this type of application will not be a problem, at least in terms of creating performance problems on the network. However, the number of simultaneous sessions and the paths taken by the conversations of such an application must still be considered in evaluating its overall impact.

Table 4.1 shows an example based on samples collected using three transactions from a PeopleSoft HRMS application. The transactions shown are

■ Login activity using the native PeopleSoft client

■ Hire Employee activity using the native PeopleSoft client

■ Hire Employee using a Citrix WinFrame client

PeopleSoft Version 6 HRMS is a two-tier application. The native PeopleSoft Version 6 client is a "fat" client that talks to the PeopleSoft database server. Citrix WinFrame is an alternate to the native PeopleSoft Version 6 GUI that provides a thin client and an intermediate server between the client and the PeopleSoft database; it is recommended for PeopleSoft Version 6 installations with significant numbers of small-capacity WAN circuits in the 64–128Kbps range.

The "Source" shown in Table 4.1 is the server side of the conversation in all cases—either the native PeopleSoft server (10.10.200.1) or the Citrix WinFrame server (10.10.200.2). The destination is a Pentium client (10.10.100.1) running either the native PeopleSoft client or the Citrix WinFrame client. Start and Stop times are the times recorded by the data collection device as the starting and ending times of the session. "Bytes forward" is the number of bytes from the server to the client. "Bytes return' is number of bytes from client to server. The "Average Kbps forward" and "return" are calculated as the number of bytes (forward or return) multiplied by 8 and divided by five minutes (the duration of the session). All three HRMS activities were completed within the five-minute interval.

In Table 4.1, the "Average Kbps" is the throughput for these individual HRMS transactions in each direction. Based on these single samples, it appears that these transactions are relatively lightweight in terms of application throughput, though not as lightweight as most SAP R/3 or Telnet sessions.

TABLE 4.1

Collected Application Transactions for PeopleSoft Showing Throughput

Session Type	Source	Destination	Start Time	Stop Time	Bytes Forward	Bytes Return	Average Kbps Forward	Average Kbps Return
HRMS Login	10.10.200.1	10.10.100.1	11:05:00	11:10:00	357226	36121	9.53	0.96
Citrix Hire Employee	10.10.200.2	10.10.100.1	11:10:00	11:20:00	204811	94710	5.46	2.53
Native Hire Employee	10.10.200.1	10.10.100.1	13:35:00	13:40:00	159514	100564	4.25	2.68

Determining the Applications to Analyze

In analyzing your applications, a good place to start is with the applications that appear as the top application types in the application distribution report (the report shown in Figure 4-12 is an example) or are of particular interest for the planning effort. Some application types use well-known TCP ports or sockets and will be listed by name. Others do not use well-known ports, and you need to determine which applications are using those ports by querying the server where the application is installed.

At a minimum, if an application is in production, you should analyze several hundred sessions of the application in order to get an accurate picture of throughput. Looking at the behavior of the various sessions over time lets you understand the application characteristics relative to the network. In most cases there will be some applications, such as Telnet, that are consistently low-bandwidth, whereas others (such as FTP) can use large amounts of bandwidth for extended periods of time (multiple minutes). If a large number of these bandwidth-intensive users use the network regularly, they increase the possibility of having saturated circuits during certain times of day.

Even lightweight applications can cause problems if too many sessions are run at the same time. For example, on a small-capacity circuit (64 Kbps), multiple users attempting to run the PeopleSoft Version 6 HRMS login activity at the same time (first thing in the business morning) could saturate the circuit temporarily, even though an individual login activity does not use a terribly large amount of bandwidth (less than 10 Kbps when active).

Correlating Usage and Application Data

As discussed previously, there are many benefits to collecting usage-based and application-based data simultaneously—at the same time intervals and over the same duration. Usage-based data shows you the total utilization of the network (circuit by circuit), and the application-based data shows you the applications by network conversation that are causing the utilization, as long as the two data sets cover the exact same time periods.

For example, if usage-based data shows that there is one circuit with consistently high utilization, you can use the application-based data to tell you which application types are creating the most utilization demands and who are the participants (source and destination hosts) in the conversations that make up that traffic. If there is one consistent busy hour during the day, analyzing the application mix during that hour can help you understand which activities are causing the situation, possibly letting you develop strategies for spreading the processing load across other time periods. Figure 4-10 shows the overall system volume for a network, and Figure 4-12 shows the distribution of application types for the busy hour identified in the system volume chart.

In addition, coordinated usage-based and application-based data sets let you use one set of data to validate the other set. For example, because traffic analyzers do not always pick up 100% of the traffic that passes by them, the related usage-based data helps to determine whether the application-based data is sufficiently complete for a given time period. Conversely, you can use application-based data to validate that the usage-based data you are observing is actually what you think it is, or to validate that the traffic routing is happening as you expect (that is, that network conversations of a particular application type are traversing the correct circuits).

By using a well-coordinated set of both usage-based and application-based data, you generally will have sufficient information to create a robust baseline model for the purposes of capacity planning.

Using Baseline Data to Create a Capacity Planning Baseline Model

If you intend to do capacity planning activities as part of your NRP project, one of the important uses of baseline data is the creation of a baseline model for capacity planning purposes. Baseline model creation starts from the topology model (or map) created from the topology inventory and adds to that model the traffic (usually usage-based traffic) that represents "typical" network usage.

You create the baseline model by loading the traffic data that you have selected as representative of the baseline traffic for the purposes of application and capacity planning. The goal of creating a baseline model is to ensure that you define and build a sufficiently robust network traffic model in keeping with the project objectives. If the baseline model does not accurately represent the usage and characteristics of the network activity as it actually exists, then all analyses, planning, and decisions based on the model are of limited validity and usefulness.

The traffic data you use for the model must be scrutinized to ensure that the following conditions are met:

- All important traffic elements have been included (the topology is complete as far as is relevant).

- Sufficient usage-based samples were collected to ensure that the traffic represents "typical" usage and is not an anomaly.

- The usage-based samples were collected on days and at times of day that are representative of the traffic flows that are relevant for planning.

- Variations in the network usage over the week and over the month have been fully considered and accounted for.

There are several approaches or strategies to selecting the samples to be used to represent the network load for capacity planning purposes, depending on the goals of the planning effort. Some of the factors to consider include whether the baseline model should be based on average utilization, peak (worst-case) utilization, or somewhere in between. These strategies are discussed in Chapter 6, "Capacity Planning," and in detail in Appendix A, "Baseline Model Creation Strategies."

Tracking Changes in Network Activity

The initial baselining process creates the starting point or foundation for all other network planning. Once you have established the baseline, you will then want to continue to collect traffic data and analyze it on a periodic basis to track changes in the network over time. Watching for changes in the baseline data lets you recognize when unexpected events occur and also lets you validate that planned changes are having the expected effects. Monitoring change and usage trends also helps you predict when network enhancements, such as adding capacity, may be needed. You should track changes in the topology inventory and traffic inventory to monitor the utilization of the system and its components.

It is not necessary to capture and analyze data on a day-to-day basis. Once a week, once every two weeks, or once a month should be sufficient, depending on the usage characteristics of the network. In a rapidly changing network environment, it may be necessary to capture data weekly (the busiest one or two days of the week) and do an analysis twice a month. Network usage can change quickly, especially in an environment with emerging Internet and intranet usage. In this type of environment, noticeable changes in activity may be observed even over a two-week period. In a more stable environment, analysis may be done less frequently. However, it is a good idea to capture data frequently (at least weekly), even if you do not analyze it weekly. Then if, for example, you have been analyzing data once a month and a sudden unexpected change appears, you have the additional data that can help you identify when in the month the change actually began to take place.

Relatively frequent data collection can also help you determine whether a change is an anomaly or an actual shift in network activity patterns. For example, you might see a short-term spike in FTP activity because a specific user is sending or retrieving very large files for a one-time project. On the other hand, you might see FTP spikes related to downloading information from the Internet on behalf of multiple users; that activity may not be a regular occurrence for any one user, but the overall pattern of users accessing the Internet and transferring files may be a repeatable trend that must be investigated further.

Changes in the Topology Inventory

Once the topology inventory has been collected and the validated network model has been built, it is important to watch for changes over time. Because an NRP project may span a significant time frame (months or years), network changes will undoubtedly occur that affect the validity of the network model. It is a good practice to update the network model at least once a month, using the performance management tool.

Changes that generally affect the topology are addition of routers, changes in circuit speeds, addition of circuits, or addition or moving of entire sites. These items can significantly affect how the network will support mission-critical applications.

An accurate network topology model, as shown in Figure 4-3, is the foundation for meaningful data collection and baselining activities. However, the network's topology tends to be a less dynamic aspect of the network as a whole, with changes occurring relatively slowly and generally more deliberately, as compared to network traffic utilization changes, for example.

If the staff responsible for network planning are not directly involved with daily maintenance of network operations, it may be appropriate and valuable to set up a process that alerts the network planners whenever certain types of network changes occur. This way, whenever the topology inventory is updated, the planners will know what types of changes to expect and can quickly validate that those changes have occurred as expected. Any capacity planning baseline models based on an outdated topology model should also be updated to reflect these changes. Maintaining the network baseline ideally should become an automatic part of the network change process.

Changes in Network Utilization

If you suspect that network usage changes have occurred in the enterprise network system, there are several ways to evaluate the nature of these changes. First, you can look at the change in the overall volume of bytes moving across the wide area network (overall system activity data). Second, you can look at how the utilization on individual WAN backbone circuits has changed, helping localize the causes of the system utilization change. Third, comparing the new usage-based data with new application-based data showing the application distribution and throughput can help determine why the changes are occurring. Understanding why a change has occurred can be extremely important.

Changes in System Activity

Figures 4-13 and 4-14 are two system usage charts that, when compared to each other, show a change in overall system activity. The two charts were collected on different days at the same time of day, both spanning the business day in Asia (the time stamps are shown in Eastern Daylight Time). The chart in Figure 4-13 represents the baseline system activity, showing the usage believed to be typical for the network. The chart in Figure 4-14 shows a fairly dramatic change in system activity during the morning hours. Further measurements showed that this change continued over time and was not a short-term anomaly.

This type of change warrants further investigation. Because this was a sudden change, it is probably due to a change in a specific area of the network rather than to a systemwide increase in activity. At this point,

Figure 4-13
System usage chart showing current system activity baseline. (© Make Systems, Inc.)

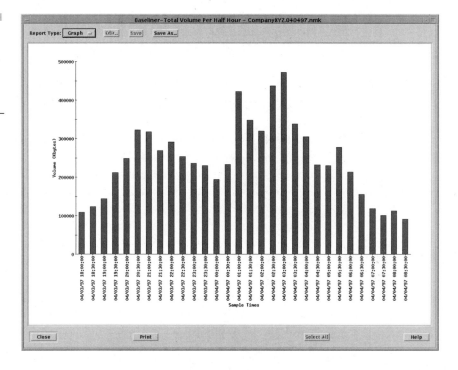

Figure 4-14
System usage chart showing changes in system activity. (© Make Systems, Inc.)

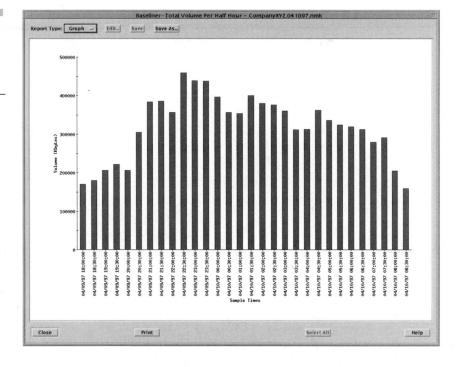

the area of the network that is causing the change must be pinpointed. Therefore, the next step is to look at individual backbone circuits to identify where the change is occurring.

Changes in Circuit Utilization

Figures 4-15 and 4-16 show changes in the utilization of one backbone circuit. Because this is a major backbone circuit, it is of definite concern. Figure 4-15 shows the existing usage baseline for this circuit. Figure 4-16 shows what has turned out to be a repeating pattern of circuit saturation (100% utilization). This circuit may be the reason for the changes in system activity shown in Figure 4-14.

Because there are many possible causes for this type of change, additional investigation is needed. One possible cause for this type of behavior could be the deployment of a new business application in one business unit without the use of NRP processes to anticipate the effects on the rest of the organization. Another possible cause could be new Internet users, if Internet access was not previously allowed.

Figure 4-15
Circuit utilization chart showing current circuit utilization. (© Make Systems, Inc.)

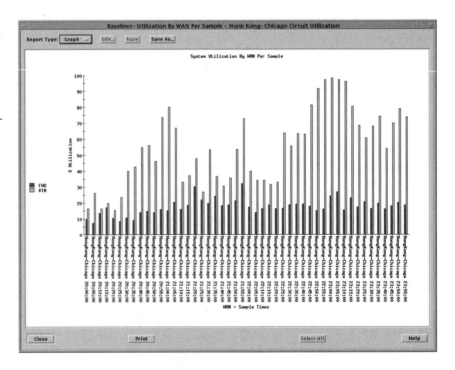

Figure 4-16
Circuit utilization chart showing changes in circuit utilization. (© Make Systems, Inc.)

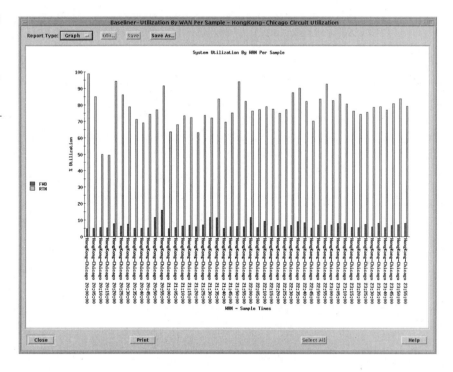

Correlating Application-Based Data with System Activity

If application-based data is available and is synchronized with the collection of usage-based data, a change can be investigated by reviewing the application-based traffic samples of interest during the time period of concern. If application-based data is not available, traffic analyzers or RMON2-compatible probes will have to be deployed to collect the required application-based data.

Key events to look for are network conversations of a particular application that are using the bulk of the circuit's bandwidth, a new application type that suddenly moves into the top five in an application distribution report for that circuit, or an application type that has never been present before.

Changes in Application Distribution

Reviewing the application distribution for the enterprise network (or a portion of it) on a regular basis provides an opportunity to identify shifts and changes in application use from a system perspective. Some things to watch for are

■ An application type that has not usually been one of the top 10 applications (in terms of total number of bytes) but has now moved into the top 10 and stays there

■ An application type that has been in the top 10 but has suddenly changed location (moved up) or whose total number of bytes has increased dramatically

■ An application that has previously been confined primarily to a campus LAN but whose sessions are now occurring over the WAN

Figures 4-17 and 4-18 show changes in application distribution for the backbone circuit shown in Figures 4-15 and 4-16. The changes specifically involve the application type SMTP (Simple Mail Transport Protocol, a mail transport protocol used for Internet email and within corporations). In this example, SMTP has typically been at the lower end of the top 10 applications. As shown in Figure 4-17, SMTP is number ten, with 165 sessions ("# of Demands") and 4904 total Kbytes. Figure 4-18 shows that SMTP is now the number one application type, with 1932 sessions ("# of Demands") and almost 90,000 total Kbytes—an order-of-magnitude increase. The additional SMTP traffic may be responsible for the observed changes in system activity and for the saturation of a major backbone circuit for this network.

It is most important to determine why a change such as this has occurred. Are there faulty mail servers, causing lots of errors and

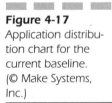

Figure 4-17
Application distribution chart for the current baseline. (© Make Systems, Inc.)

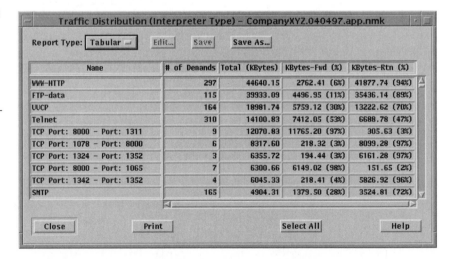

Traffic Distribution (Interpreter Type) – CompanyXYZ.040497.app.nmk

Report Type: Tabular   Edit...   Save   Save As...

Name	# of Demands	Total (KBytes)	KBytes-Fwd (%)	KBytes-Rtn (%)
WWW-HTTP	297	44640.15	2762.41 (6%)	41877.74 (94%)
FTP-data	115	39933.09	4496.95 (11%)	35436.14 (89%)
UUCP	164	18981.74	5759.12 (30%)	13222.62 (70%)
Telnet	310	14100.83	7412.05 (53%)	6688.78 (47%)
TCP Port: 8000 - Port: 1311	9	12070.83	11765.20 (97%)	305.63 (3%)
TCP Port: 1078 - Port: 8000	6	8317.60	218.32 (3%)	8099.28 (97%)
TCP Port: 1324 - Port: 1352	3	6355.72	194.44 (3%)	6161.28 (97%)
TCP Port: 8000 - Port: 1065	7	6300.66	6149.02 (98%)	151.65 (2%)
TCP Port: 1342 - Port: 1352	4	6045.33	218.41 (4%)	5826.92 (96%)
SMTP	165	4904.31	1379.50 (28%)	3524.81 (72%)

Close   Print   Select All   Help

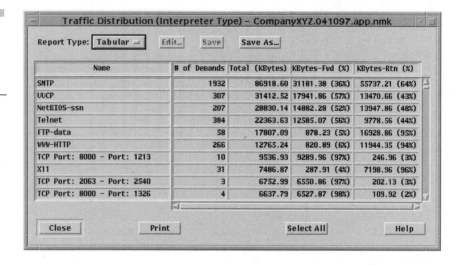

Figure 4-18
Application distribution after change.
(© Make Systems, Inc.)

retransmissions? Or do the changes make sense and correlate with known changes in the business? For example, has there been a major increase in user population, such as the availability of wide area network access to groups of users that previously had only local access?

The Baselining Life Cycle

Repeated baselining provides the data sets needed to identify changes in network usage as well as to create current and accurate baseline models for application and capacity planning activities. The frequency with which an organization updates its baseline data sets depends on the resources the organization believes it can devote to this activity in relation to the benefits that will be gained. However, measuring and documenting the network on a weekly basis (if possible) provides data with sufficient resolution to identify changes in network behavior and to separate anomalies from long-term network changes.

The baselining process (Figure 4-19) is cyclical in nature because the validity of each step depends on accurate information from the previous step; as the network changes over time, so must the baseline.

The following are guidelines for how often you should update your network information:

■ *Topology inventory:* At least once a month. This is usually the slowest-changing aspect of the network and the least likely to change unexpectedly.

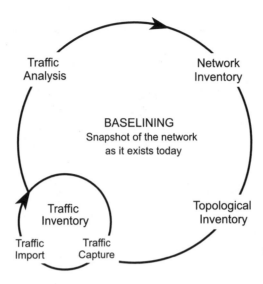

Figure 4-19
The baselining cycle of activities.

- *Traffic inventory:* At least once a week. You may not choose to analyze the data you collect every week, but having it available can be extremely valuable if and when users complain or unexpected changes arise.

- *Traffic analysis:* Once every two weeks or once a month, depending on the stability of your network environment. If you collect data more frequently, you can always go back and analyze the additional data if the need arises.

The following information should be tracked on a recurring basis, using the information collected as a result of the baselining tasks:

- Topology changes
- System activity usage changes
- Circuit utilization changes
- Application distribution and throughput changes

As a result of monitoring this information, significant network changes will become more visible and quantifiable at an earlier point in time. It will become possible to investigate what the changes may mean to other areas of the network before problems arise. Reviewing each new baseline against the previous baseline enables you to understand how the enterprise network is behaving as a system and how that behavior affects application performance.

Application Planning as the Next Step

The results you accomplish through your baselining activities are of great value in their own right. You can also use your baseline data as the basis for capacity planning activities. If the network already has utilization problems, and you want to test a capacity redesign in light of the current application mix, you can go straight to the capacity planning phase, using the baseline data you have collected to create baseline models for "what-if" analyses on various capacity redesign scenarios.

However, the focus of this book is on NRP for new application deployment. In order to do capacity planning for that purpose, you will need information on the behavior of the new application in addition to baseline information on the behavior of your existing network. The next chapter, "Application Planning," covers how to characterize a new application to determine the types of demands it will make on the enterprise network when it is deployed.

References

Merriam-Webster, Inc. (1994) *Webster's Collegiate Dictionary, Tenth Edition.* Springfield, Massachusetts.

CHAPTER 5

Application Planning

This chapter discusses in detail the techniques and processes of application planning. Application planning methodologies involve creating a "profile," or workload characterization, of the behavior of an enterprise application (or of representative application transactions) and then augmenting the baseline model of the network using the profile. The resulting model makes it possible to predict the effect of the application on network behavior as well as how the network's behavior will affect the quality of service delivered by the application. Application planning builds on the successful baselining activities covered in the previous chapter. In this chapter you will learn the steps needed to accomplish application planning and how to apply the methodology to new or existing applications in your own network environment.

The Objectives of Application Planning

Application planning is the second of the three cycles that make up the complete Network Resource Planning (NRP) process (see Figure 5-1).

Application planning activities discussed in this chapter focus on characterizing the behavior of an enterprise application, such as SAP R/3, PeopleSoft, or BAAN IV, in terms of how it uses or is expected to use the network. The network planner can use this information to determine the effects of adding the application to the network (if it is a new enterprise application) or of making changes to an existing application, such as adding users, adding client locations, or moving servers. Application planning activities also allow the network planner to determine what quality-of-service levels the application can be expected to deliver to its users, based on the behavior of the network over which it is running.

Figure 5-1

Application planning as a component of the NRP cycle.

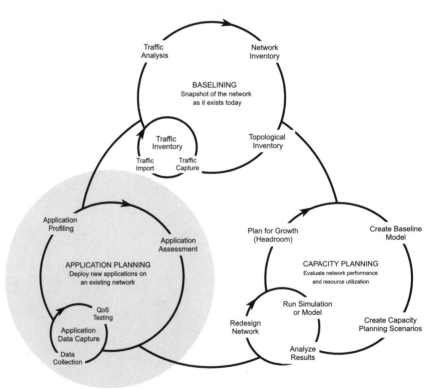

The types of enterprise applications that will benefit from application planning are those whose functionality is divided into multiple components that communicate over an enterprise wide area network (WAN)—that is, distributed applications. Application components include a *client* module that a user runs locally and that communicates across the WAN to access a *resource* (data or a service) located elsewhere on the network. In this chapter the focus is on enterprisewide, multitier client/server applications such as SAP R/3, BAAN IV, and People-Soft, but many other client/server applications, such as electronic mail (Microsoft Exchange), Lotus Notes, or Microsoft SMS, will also benefit from application planning techniques.

As with baselining activities, a commitment to planning by the organization is very important and remains a major factor in getting many of these tasks accomplished. This is particularly true for application planning, because successful application planning activities require a high level of coordination between network management personnel (the group usually charged with determining how to make the enterprise network support a new application) and the application developers. This in turn requires a belief in the value of these planning activities and a high level of commitment on the part of corporate information technology (IT) management.

In many organizations, network management personnel and application developers report to different branches of the organizational tree; these groups traditionally do not work together. In addition, application developers are often not responsible for the impact the applications they develop have on the performance of the network, and they may not be familiar with the issues involved.

If the application planning activities are proactive (meaning that their intent is to project how the application will affect the network *before* it has actually been rolled out into a production environment), then the cooperation of the application developers with the network management staff is critical. In order to measure application traffic, the network planner will need access to the application (the "test bed"), which may exist only in the development environment. A knowledgeable "user" of the application will be needed to create a benchmark (the script of application tasks that will create traffic to be measured) and to execute the application benchmark while you monitor and capture the traffic it generates. These activities may be viewed as disruptive by application developers, whose own goals and objectives do not include NRP. Thus, commitment from a higher level of management may be required to ensure that the level of resources and cooperation needed can be obtained from the application development group.

Application planning activities are often very strategic, because of the strategic or mission-critical nature of the enterprise application involved. An organization will make a commitment to NRP, and specifically to the application planning portion of NRP, for a number of reasons:

■ The enterprise application of concern is strategic and is critical to achieving the organization's business objectives.

■ The application will be used by people who are geographically dispersed, and thus depends on the wide area network infrastructure.

■ The application deployment effort is highly visible within the company, and the success or lack of success will be visible to high levels of management.

■ Concerns exist (possibly due to existing user complaints or known performance issues) that the existing WAN infrastructure may not be adequate to support the new enterprise application at the desired level of service.

As an example, a scenario used in Chapter 3 described a manufacturing company with a large international network. One of its overall corporate objectives was to implement and deploy the PeopleSoft HRMS application worldwide to handle corporate human-resources activities. Centralization of these processes would allow standardization of recordkeeping across the organization and would greatly simplify the handling of the many employees who move around between international locations. In this organization, a major redesign of the network had been proposed, in part to support this application. However, based on their own understanding of the existing network problems, the network management staff suspected that the redesign might not be entirely effective. Their baselining and application planning activities enabled them to provide quantitative, factual evidence to support their concerns and to identify the types of changes in the network that would be effective to support the new PeopleSoft HRMS application.

Requirements for Application Planning

Like baselining, application planning is largely a data collection exercise, although it is done in a very specific, targeted way. However, when compared to baselining, application planning activities place much more emphasis on process—on understanding the project objectives and defining how to collect the data that will make it possible to meet those objectives. Data collection tools play an important role in the later stages of the application planning cycle, but much work is required beforehand to understand what needs to be done and to set up an environment in which the data collection can occur.

In baselining, you can collect data without necessarily knowing what to expect in advance. The data you collect will generally give you interesting or useful information about the network, even if it is not what you anticipated. In application planning, your data collection efforts have to be very carefully targeted and controlled to monitor specific application transactions. If you do not monitor the right transactions or the right locations, the data you collect may be completely useless. Thus, much preparation is needed to execute a successful application planning project.

In order to complete the application planning phase of an NRP project successfully with valid, useful results, you must

- Understand how the application will be used on the network
- Understand the network environment in which the application is or will be deployed
- Understand the network test environment in which the application planning activities will be conducted
- Have access to application-based data from the baselining phase for the relevant parts of the network where the application will be deployed

Understanding How the Application Will Be Used

The first requirement for application planning, on which all other application planning activities depend, is to gain a thorough understanding of how the business will use the application under study. How often will various tasks of the application be performed? How long does each application transaction take? How many users might be doing a transaction simultaneously? In order to collect valid traffic data to profile the application behavior, you need to have users execute application transactions that you believe to be typical of the way the application will be used on your network. The transactions must also enable you to accomplish your NRP objectives most effectively—that is, they must be expected to use wide area network resources to a non-trivial degree. In order to select the right transactions, a thorough understanding of how the application will be used is necessary. These application transactions will form the basis of the benchmark (or script) you will use to create the specific application traffic that corresponds to those transactions.

Understanding the Application Deployment Environment

A second requirement is to understand both the logical and physical implementations of the application: how and where it will be deployed. This is critical to collecting meaningful data on the application's behavior. There are two aspects to understanding where and how to collect application data: understanding where the components of the application will be located and understanding how components will communicate over the wide area network.

First, you must know how the application components are going to be placed among the actual sites on the network. In a multitier architecture, you need to know whether the tiers will be distributed over the enterprise or whether some tiers may be collapsed or colocated. This is necessary to determine which application data traffic flows will be important to profile.

For example, in a three-tier environment, if the presentation portion of the product (the graphical user interface) is separated from the application server and communicates over a wide area network, you would almost certainly want to look at the data that the application generates between the presentation module (the client) and the application server. Conversely, if the application server and the database server both reside on the same local area network, the interactions between those servers might not be of concern. On the other hand, in a two-tier implementation such as the PeopleSoft version 6 applications, you would be interested in the interactions between the client application logic and the database server. The data flows you capture may be meaningless if you do not collect them at the right points.

Note that at the time of writing this book, a three-tier implementation of the PeopleSoft applications (version 7) had been released but was not yet widely implemented. The NRP projects the authors conducted concerning PeopleSoft implementations were all done with version 6, so only that version is discussed in this book.

The second step in understanding the network environment is to understand the types of WAN connections over which the application components will communicate. Different types and sizes of circuits have different delay characteristics. For example, the per-packet delay on a 64Kbps Frame Relay circuit could be three times that on a T1 circuit. These characteristics need to be factored into any quality-of-service metrics that you develop.

Understanding the Testing Environment

A third requirement for successful application planning is to understand how the application is deployed in the environment that you intend to use as the test bed for your application planning activities. This helps to determine where to place data collection instrumentation to capture the traffic flows of interest. If possible, application data should be collected in an isolated test environment rather than in the actual production environment, because it is easier to isolate the effects of the application under study. However, if you use an isolated test environment, you need to understand how that environment is similar to or different from the actual deployment environment. For example, it is quite common that the application data capture could occur between a client and server on the same LAN in a test bed environment, whereas in the actual application deployment the clients and servers will communicate across a WAN.

The test bed is an actual physical location where you can run the application client GUI, execute specific predefined tasks (the benchmark or script), and collect and measure the traffic associated with those activities. Carrying out these activities in a relatively isolated environment, such as a development or pilot environment, will greatly simplify this aspect of the project. In addition, it allows much more flexibility in the types of test scenarios you can create, especially if you have access to a network delay simulator that will allow you to simulate a variety of WAN environments.

If you must run your data capture activities in an actual production environment (for an application that is already deployed, for example) you need to understand and take into account other factors such as competing users and network bottlenecks unrelated to the application under study. In general, carrying out application planning activities in a production environment is more difficult and is not recommended. However, with careful planning it can be done and will still prove very useful.

Baselining as a Requirement

In most cases, the application planning cycle depends on the successful execution of at least one cycle of baselining activities. Analysis of the application-based data collected during the baselining phase can be valuable in determining what specific data should be collected for application planning—for example, to identify the amount of network usage due to existing applications that may be replaced by a new application. Or, if the NRP project's goal is to project the effects of growth on the network, you might want to do application planning analyses on the applications that baselining has shown to be the most heavily used.

In addition, if your application planning activities are in preparation for subsequent capacity planning activities, a baseline model built with usage-based traffic is needed to create a complete model of the existing network. Such a model is the basis on which the capacity planning activities discussed in Chapter 6 are built, and capacity planning cannot be done without it.

Developing Your Application Planning Strategy

This chapter will help you develop your own strategy for applying application planning techniques. How you do this will depend on the NRP objectives, the implementation of the application under study, and the way you anticipate that the application will be used. Given these factors, you need to come up with a strategy for collecting data on the application's behavior, including

■ Determining how the new enterprise application will be deployed (locations) and how often it will be used (number of users and frequency of use)

■ Creating a script or benchmark for the application tasks to be measured

■ Identifying an application test bed for doing the data collection

■ Strategically placing and configuring data collection devices

■ Determining the quality-of-service requirements for the new application

■ Running the benchmark tasks, collecting data, and documenting the data collection relative to those tasks

■ Using the collected data to create a usable statistical application profile for each transaction of interest

The Application Planning Cycle

The goal of application planning is to characterize the traffic, or workload, that an enterprise application will create. You can also project and quantify the level of performance or service that users of the new application will find acceptable and use these metrics to evaluate the results of the capacity planning activities as discussed in Chapter 6.

Application planning methodologies require that a representative set of application transactions be measured in order to determine what demands the application is likely to make on the network. These measurements are analyzed to create a workload characterization, or "profile," of the application, which can then be superimposed on the baseline model to simulate how the application load will affect the network. The three tasks that constitute an application planning activity, as shown in Figure 5-2, are application assessment, application data capture, and application profiling. As with baselining, application planning activities are also cyclical in nature and may need to be repeated to

Figure 5-2
The application
planning cycle.

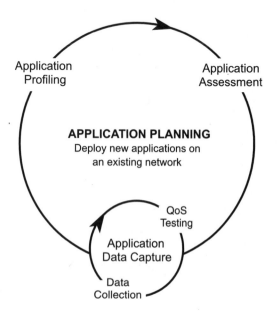

refine the information or to take changes in the application or the network environment into account.

The steps to the application planning cycle are

■ Application assessment:
- Determine an application usage scenario: projections for how the application will be deployed in terms of numbers of users and servers, locations of users and servers, and transaction rates (number of transactions in a given time period)
- Identify the specific application transactions that a typical user would perform
- Create a benchmark (a repeatable set of application activities) to be used to generate identifiable application traffic
- Identify the network environment in which the application will be deployed, including the current application mix in that environment

■ Application data capture:
- Identify a test environment in which the application can be run for purposes of data capture
- Test the application to determine and quantify the quality-of-service goals for application response time and throughput
- Capture the traffic data that corresponds to the target transactions that make up the application benchmark using a traffic analyzer such as a Network General Sniffer

■ Application profiling:
- Create representative models or profiles of the application's traffic characteristics based on the data captured

Like the other areas of NRP, application planning is most valuable when it is looked at as an ongoing, iterative process (see the discussion of life cycle management in Chapter 2, "The Network Resource Planning Process"). Ideally, it should become one of the standard processes that are a part of all enterprise application deployment projects on the network. For any given enterprise application deployment project, several cycles of application planning could be undertaken as follows:

■ During the development/pilot phase of a project, the first application planning cycle would be done to determine how the application is likely to affect the network. The feedback from this cycle enables network managers to adjust the network infrastructure as needed before the application is deployed and causes problems, and it also allows the application developers to modify the application prior to deployment so as to use network resources more efficiently. This application planning cycle should be done for each new module of the application as it goes through the development/pilot/ deployment phases.

- When a significant change is made to the application or to the enterprise network during the development or pilot phase, another application planning cycle will be needed to take these changes into account.

- When the first production deployment phase is undertaken, another cycle would be executed to validate the actual behavior of the application—especially if the actual application performance does not appear to be what was predicted.

- If significant changes are made to the enterprise network after the application has been fully deployed, such as upgrading to an ATM backbone, the application planning cycle should be redone.

- When significant changes are made to the application itself, such as updating to a new revision, the application planning cycle should be redone.

Whenever there are significant changes to the network infrastructure, or if the overall behavior of the network changes, you should do a new round of application assessment activities to validate or revise your estimates of the number of application users, their locations, and the location of the application servers. Even if the application itself does not change, you should configure the application profiles onto a new network baseline model, using a new capacity planning scenario, to determine how the application and the network will interact under these new conditions. The actual creation of capacity planning scenarios and the analysis of the changes are discussed in Chapter 6, "Capacity Planning."

NRP's Focus on an Application's Network Behavior

There is one important caveat regarding application planning. The application planning methodology discussed in this book will help you determine how your application will behave *in terms of its usage of the network*. There are obviously many other factors besides the network that determine the level of performance (quality of service) a user may see. Server capacity, competing demands on the database server, client capacity, and the design of the application itself are some examples of factors that may be very significant. In the broader sense of application planning, these are clearly areas that merit investigation and analysis. However, application planning as discussed in this book focuses only on the behavior of the network and how the network's behavior affects an application's quality of service.

Quality of service, as discussed in this book, is the user perception of an enterprise application's performance. Acceptable quality of service means that the user can use the application to accomplish a set of tasks without undue problems or "unacceptable" delays. For any networked client/server application, quality of service is affected by three components: the behavior of the client, the behavior of the network, and the behavior of the server (see Figure 5-3).

It is possible that, as a result of the application planning activities discussed in this book, you may determine that the network has sufficient capacity to handle the application—that is, the network component is not creating a problem in terms of quality of service. However, the application performance as perceived by its users may still be a problem because of other factors, such as server or client performance. In this case, the results of application planning activities may still help you diagnose the actual source of the problem, by ruling out the network as the culprit.

For example, users at a Midwestern company were experiencing very slow response times with a new client/server application. Upgrading their circuits to T1 speeds did not improve the situation. The results of baselining and application planning activities determined that the actual circuit utilization was very low (the circuits were not at all congested), and the application throughput was also low. Some of the metrics gained through the application planning activities, such as error rates and average packet size, were critical to pinpointing the source of the problems. In this case, it turned out to be the server component, not the network component, that was the cause of poor quality of service. The problem was determined to be a combination of inadequate server capacity (as indicated by high numbers of dropped transmissions,

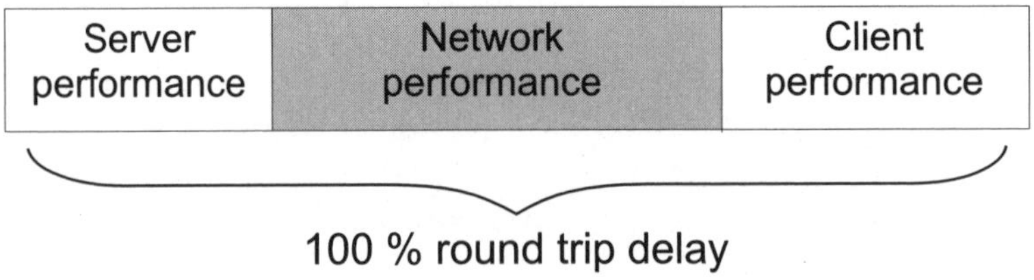

Figure 5-3
Components of
quality of service.

Server performance	Network performance	Client performance

100 % round trip delay

which got *worse* when the circuit speed increased) and poor application design relative to network usage (sending large numbers of very small packets).

Application Assessment

The application assessment process has several stages. The first is to determine the application usage scenario: how the application will be deployed on the network in terms of where users and servers will be located, how many users will be at each location, and how frequently these users are expected to do various application tasks. This information is critical in the capacity planning stage of the NRP project, but it can be time-consuming to obtain, so the effort to collect it should be started in this phase. Also, this information can help you determine which critical transaction activities to include in your benchmark.

Next, you need to determine which transactions are representative of what users (clients) on the network will do with the application. These transactions (or a subset of them) will form the script, or benchmark, used to generate the traffic data that will become the basis for the application profiles. The application profiles in turn will be used to load the network model to simulate the network as it will function when the application is deployed.

The final stage of application assessment is to define the network environment in which your application will run when it is deployed. You need to understand the existing application distribution and how the introduction of your new application may affect that distribution. Application assessment may also point out other areas of concern you will need to address when you introduce the new application, such as a high volume of existing Internet traffic.

Defining the Application Usage Scenario

In order to use the results of your application planning activities for capacity planning, you need to know the strategy for the deployment of the application: the locations of the servers and clients on the network, how many users there will be at each site, what transactions they are likely to do, and how often they will do those transactions. Specifically, you need to collect the following data:

▪ The location of the application server(s) and clients by country, city, LAN segment, and closest router name—whatever is sufficient to identify the locations of each server and client relative to the elements on your network map (topology inventory). This information will be required in the capacity planning phase so that you can allocate the additional workload due to the new application on the correct circuits and LANs in your network.

▪ The number of users at each location that will be running application transactions. In the capacity planning scenario this information will be used to compute the workload volume attributable to the new application on any given circuit or LAN (between a given location and the application server or application database).

▪ The frequency of use for each application transaction, in terms of one transaction every *x* seconds or minutes. This metric, also called the transaction rate, will be used in the capacity planning scenario to compute the workload volume attributable to the new application.

These projections will not actually be used until the capacity planning phase, but you need to start collecting the data much earlier, because it is often more difficult than you might expect to come up with these estimates. In addition, this information can help you choose the transactions to use as your benchmark, or at least to confirm your choices. Assuming you plan to do some capacity planning analyses, you want to make sure that the application profiles you create represent significant application transactions performed over the network in your capacity planning models. Your assumptions about number of users and frequency of use are also critical to the validity of your capacity planning scenarios, so it is important that these estimates be as realistic as possible, not based on vague, "off the top of the head" guesses.

Defining the Number of Users

Typically, as you begin to collect application deployment projections, you will find that the locations (client sites and server sites) proposed for the application deployment are well known. However, very often the projected numbers of users at those locations and the transaction rates for specific application transactions have not really been considered. That type of projection is typically not within the scope of the application development process.

TABLE 5.1

PeopleSoft General
Ledger
Deployment
Strategy

Location	Projected Number of Users at the Site
New Ulm	5 (2 Create Req+3 Journal Query)
Greenville	3 (1 Create Req+2 Journal Query)
Austin	42 (14 Create Req+28 Journal Query)
Bedford	4 (1 Create Req+3 Journal Query)
Irvine	2 (1 Create Req+1 Journal Query)
Canada	37 (12 Create Req+25 Journal Query)

One way to come up with projections for number of users for a new application is to make estimates based on the number of employees with certain job classifications at each client site. Typically, this information is not known within the network management organization; it requires research, which means talking to knowledgeable people about each potential client site.

You may choose to focus on only a subset of sites instead of the full deployment in order to create more manageable scenarios for capacity planning. This restriction simplifies the process of collecting information about projected users. For example, if the application is being rolled out in phases, you might choose to use only those sites that will be in the first phase. You may also choose to select a subset of possible client sites whose user characteristics (number of users, transaction rates) are considered "typical" of how you expect the application to be used. Yet another alternative is to select a subset of sites with a representative range of network connection types and speeds found in your network—one or two each of various leased-line or Frame Relay circuits, for example.

Table 5.1 shows one deployment strategy for a PeopleSoft General Ledger application. This type of information will tell you how to load the associated application profiles onto the baseline model in the capacity planning phase of your NRP project.

Defining the Frequency of the Transactions

Finally, you need to identify the probability of each transaction occurring (that is, how often one individual user will repeat this activity in an hour, or a day) for each site you plan to include in the capacity planning scenarios. This information will be used in the capacity planning phase of your project, but it also helps you determine which transactions to include in your benchmark and thus in the application profiles. Typically, depending on the goals of the "what-if" analyses you intend to do in the capacity planning phase, you want to choose transactions that have relatively high transaction rates (that is, those that are used the most often). This is especially true if you are interested in developing worst-case scenarios, which project the highest levels of usage for the new application under study.

Projections for transaction rates typically depend on factors such as the volume of business done at a particular site or, for a human-resources application, the number of employees at that location. Again, this information must often be obtained by talking to people who can help you develop realistic estimates of the volume of transactions that are likely to occur at that location.

Table 5.2 shows frequency projections for a set of typical application transactions that could be done with an Enterprise Resource Planning (ERP) application such as SAP R/3, PeopleSoft, or BAAN IV. In this table, each transaction corresponds to an application profile. Such frequency projections will help you determine how to load the profiles onto the baseline model in the capacity planning portion of the NRP project. Frequency projections may also help determine which transactions must have application profiles created for them. In this example, the Procurement and General Ledger transactions are done more frequently and are likely to be significant sources of application traffic. The Logon transaction is performed only once per day per user and thus is not likely to create significant traffic on the network over the entire business day. However, if large numbers of users log on at approximately the same time of day (first thing in the morning, for example), you might find it interesting to include that spike of activity in a capacity planning scenario.

	Transaction	Frequency (Per User)
TABLE 5.2	Logon	Once per day
Benchmark for Selected ERP Application Transactions	Procurement—Create Requisition	Every five minutes (12 per hour)
	Procurement—Approve Requisition	Every five minutes (12 per hour)
	General Ledger—Journal Query	Every five minutes (12 per hour)
	General Ledger—Journal Edit	Every ten minutes (6 per hour)

Selecting the Application Transactions

Understanding both which functions (transactions) are likely to be used within the application and the frequency with which these activities will be done across the enterprise network will help you identify the specific application transactions that can be considered "typical" for your application planning purposes.

If the application being deployed is something like a financial module of SAP R/3 or an email application like Microsoft Exchange, a given type of user transaction may occur multiple times a day or multiple times an hour. On the other hand, if the application being deployed is a human-resources application such as PeopleSoft HRMS, many important activities may be done only a few times a week or month. Understanding these activities will let you begin to select which activities you want to include in your benchmark to create a profile that will meet your application planning objectives.

Ideally, you want to focus on transactions that have a high probability of occurring (are likely to be done frequently by a large number of users) and use a relatively large amount of bandwidth (Kbps), compared to the other transactions for this application. For example, if your network is already heavily loaded, you may only need to test a few transactions that have high transaction rates (are likely to be done frequently by many users) to show that the application is likely to saturate the network. If a subset of application activities is enough to cause serious network problems, you really don't need to take the time to model the additional, less common transactions. On the other hand, however, there may be a few application functions (batch reports, for example) that, although they are not done frequently, make such high bandwidth demands that it is of interest to see how they affect the network when they are active.

Developing the Benchmark

To be useful for application planning, an application profile must accurately represent the actual way the application will be used across the network. You need to identify the specific transactions within the application that a typical user will do over the enterprise network. When you have identified these transactions (and how frequently they are likely to be performed), you can then create a benchmark to use for generating the traffic you will capture for your application profiles.

A benchmark is defined as a script of transactions with their component activities, which a knowledgeable user can perform using the application under study. To collect meaningful data for an application profile, you need to be able to correlate specific transactions in the application with the specific traffic flows on the network that result from those transactions. The benchmark provides the guide by which a user, as part of the application profiling exercise, can execute a known, bounded task (the transaction) that will create traffic that can be captured and correlated with that specific task. The set of transaction activities must be repeatable, because the application profiling activities may be done multiple times, such as to create profiles in multiple client/server configurations, and to recreate the transaction profiles at later repetitions of the application planning cycle.

In the discussions that follow, it is assumed that the benchmark transactions will be performed by an actual user. However, depending on the application and the type of transactions being studied, it may be possible to use a scripting tool or language to create benchmarks that can run without user intervention. This will require that issues such as the variable delays inherent in network response times can be handled appropriately by such a script.

The Characteristics of a Good Benchmark

Assuming that the application you are studying is not yet deployed on your network, creating the benchmark is one of the steps that will almost certainly require the involvement and cooperation of the application developers. It will require the attention of someone who not only understands the way the application will be used in the organization but also understands in detail the specific user activities that are required to execute the application functions. This "knowledgeable user" may be someone from the application development team, or a consultant or representative of the application vendor if the application is an off-the-shelf ERP application such as SAP, BAAN IV, or PeopleSoft.

A good benchmark has the following characteristics:

■ It consists of transactions that are representative of the normal transactions expected to be done with the application and that will be performed relatively frequently.

■ The transactions create activity across the enterprise network (across the WAN). If the application has functions that are executed locally (within the campus environment), these would not be relevant to looking at how the application uses the enterprise network, which is the point of application planning as discussed in this book.

■ The transactions are repeatable so that the data capture process can be done multiple times (possibly by different users) and yield sets of data that are comparable to previous data sets collected using the same benchmark.

■ The transactions can be executed within a 5–10-minute time frame, preferably within 5 minutes. This requirement forces the transactions in the benchmark to be broken down into activities that are sufficiently detailed that they are repeatable and consistent. It also simplifies the process of creating profiles that correlate well with the intervals used for collecting the baseline usage-based traffic. (The usage-based traffic will form the basis for the capacity planning baseline models.)

DEFINE ACTIVITIES WITH ENOUGH DETAIL TO BE REPEATABLE The transactions specified in the benchmark should be sufficiently detailed at a level that a knowledgeable user can run the transactions repeatedly and ensure that they generate a comparable traffic flow each time. In some cases, where the transaction involves filling in one or more screen forms and submitting them, simply specifying the name of the transaction (for example, the item to select from a menu) may be sufficient. In other cases, it may be necessary to script a transaction to the level of specifying the actual data entry items, to ensure that the traffic created by each repeat of the transaction is reasonably comparable.

For example, in an order entry transaction, entering a new customer name might invoke a secondary screen to define customer information, while entering an existing customer name would not. The benchmark needs to be scripted to the level of detail that ensures that the path taken through the transaction, and the data entered, is always the same. This detail is important because the benchmark needs to be repeatable, not just over the duration of the immediate data capture sessions but also over the entire deployment time frame. With a sufficiently detailed benchmark, you can create comparable application profiles when you introduce a revision or upgrade to the application in the future, even though different users may be executing the benchmark at that time.

CHOOSE TRANSACTIONS THAT CAN BE COMPLETED WITHIN FIVE MINUTES The individual transactions should be chosen, if possible, so that a knowledgeable user can complete one transaction within five minutes. Creating short transactions will help you break down application functions into component activities that can be specified with enough detail to be repeatable and to ensure that users can complete the activity without making errors.

Creating short transactions means that an average data rate for the transaction can be calculated within a five-minute interval. If one full application transaction can be completed within the five-minute interval, then that interval's worth of data will represent that complete transaction. This will simplify the process of creating profiles that can be mapped onto the baseline model. Just as with baselining, five-minute intervals have proven to be a useful interval because they are not so large that the actual characteristics of the data are lost when averaging the load across the interval. In addition, if your baseline was collected using five-minute intervals as recommended, then capturing activities in five-minute intervals means that the new application profiles can be used more easily with the baseline model during the capacity planning phase.

However high-level or detailed your script actually is, it must be very clear what constitutes each "complete transaction." The user running the benchmark must be able to indicate when he or she is starting the new application transaction and when the transaction is complete, because the user's start and stop times are critical to correlating the captured data with the transaction that was occurring at that time. For example, if you are profiling an electronic mail application such as Microsoft Exchange, one transaction might include the following activities:

1. Log on to mail system (may only need to be done once).

2. Read new mail messages.

3. Print mail message.

4. Create mail message (reply).

5. Send mail message.

6. Close mail.

7. Log off mail system.

The benchmark script would call out all of these activities (ideally in greater detail than shown here), but the overall transaction would be considered to start with logon and be complete with logoff of the mail system.

It is very important to test the benchmark to ensure that all the transactions work as expected. You need to make sure that the benchmark can be run repeatedly without causing errors. In addition, you need to ensure that the user who will be executing the benchmark during the data capture process knows how to execute a path that will not generate errors through each transaction. In an application still under development, you need to ensure that the user can avoid problems that may arise from existing software bugs or incomplete functionality.

A SAMPLE PEOPLESOFT BENCHMARK   Table 5.3 shows a high-level definition for transactions included in a benchmark for a People-Soft HRMS application. Note that it breaks the transactions down into smaller activities; for example, the Update Personal Information transaction is broken into separate activities for updating the name, address, and so on. It also includes the relative frequency of the occurrence of these transactions. In the actual NRP project in which this benchmark

TABLE 5.3

PeopleSoft HRMS
Benchmark

Transaction	Frequency
Administer Personnel	
Hire Employee	15% of workforce per year
Update Personal Information	2 per employee per year
—Address	
—Name	
—Phone	
—Family Status	
Update Job Information	8 per employee per year
—Promotion	
—Transfer	
—Leave of Absence	
—Terminate	
—Retire	
—Rehire	
—Change Employee Class/Type	
—Salary Change	
Logon/Logoff	3 per user per day

was used, data was captured for all the transactions in the benchmark. The frequency rates were then used, along with other factors, to decide which of these transactions should have application profiles created for them. The application profiles were then used in the capacity planning phase of the project.

In the PeopleSoft HRMS benchmark, transaction frequency was specified as transactions per year. For an application such as Microsoft Exchange or an ERP application, the unit selected would be dramatically different because in those applications users do multiple transactions every day and often multiple transactions every hour.

Assessing the Application Distribution on the Network

The final stage of application assessment is to look at the applications that are currently using your network in terms of how they are related to the specific application you are studying. This analysis is based on the application-based data you collected during your baselining cycle; it is actually just a reanalysis of that data from a different viewpoint.

An application distribution report will show you which applications are using the network and how much network resources each application type is using. The purposes of this assessment for application planning purposes are to identify the existing distribution of applications on your network and to project how the introduction of your new application might affect that distribution. The report may also point out other areas of concern you will need to address when you introduce the new application.

For example, your new application may replace one or more existing applications on the network. If so, you will need to take this fact into account in any capacity planing activities that build upon your application planning results. For example, if Microsoft Exchange mail will be deployed to replace existing SMTP and UUCP mail, you would look at the existing traffic load due to the SMTP and UUCP applications to get an idea of usage from them that might decrease or disappear. Of course, it is most likely that the new and old applications will coexist on the network for some transition period, and that must also be taken into account.

An application distribution study will also give you an idea of the characteristics of the other applications on the network that will be competing for resources with the new application. The application distribution study may provide guidance in terms of areas of change that might be appropriate in order to provide the required levels of service for the new application in the most cost-effective manner. For example, an application analysis may show that Internet and intranet traffic is responsible for the largest portion of enterprise network usage. This may point to a need to move proxy server locations or Internet access points so as to balance or redistribute the Internet traffic load and avoid congestion on the circuits most critical to the new application. It may also point to a need for new network policy on Internet traffic, such as restricting certain types of Internet usage.

Assessing the application distribution depends on application-based data from the baselining phase. If you do not have sufficient application-based data with good coverage of the enterprise network, it may not be possible to do much in this area until that data is collected.

Application Data Collection

In the application data collection step of the application planning cycle, you capture the traffic data that corresponds to the transactions that make up the application benchmark. This step consists of the following tasks:

- To make sure that you have data collection devices that can capture all the information required to create profiles of your application transactions

- To identify or create a test environment in which you can place your data collection device and work with your knowledgeable user to generate the traffic for each application transaction

- To diagram and document your test environment to make sure you understand how closely it parallels the actual deployment environment; this task also helps you determine the client and server addresses

- To place and configure your data collection devices physically

- To determine the amount of delay across the network that will be acceptable from the application user's perspective, and use that amount to set quality-of-service goals for the application

- To capture the application traffic generated by each activity in the benchmark

Selecting a Data Collection Device

To capture data for application planning, you need to use a data collection device such as a traffic analyzer attached to the network at the appropriate point (most often between the client and the application server or database server). The data collection device captures the traffic data that corresponds to the benchmark activities as they are executed one by one by a knowledgeable user as part of the data capture activity.

The data collection device must be able to capture network layer conversation data (between the source and the destination), and it must be able to timestamp the conversations with the start and end times, to the second. It must also be able to capture data bidirectionally—that is, it must be able to distinguish between data in the forward and return directions, between the data from A to B and data from B to A.

Note that the data collection process discussed here will provide data that is appropriate for use with analytical modeling techniques. If you will be doing discrete event simulation, you might need to collect packet data. The discussions in this chapter mostly assume that you will be using analytical modeling techniques to do your capacity planning analyses, because those techniques are most appropriate for obtaining the type of results that meet the needs of most NRP project objectives. The differences and appropriate uses of discrete event analysis and analytical modeling techniques are discussed briefly in Chapter 2, "The Network Resource Planning Process," and in more detail in Chapter 6, "Capacity Planning."

Figure 5-4 shows the data from an Expert Analyzer output file captured using a Network General Sniffer.

The critical pieces of data the traffic analyzer must record are

▪ The start and stop time for each conversation, to the second (shown in the columns "1stFrm" and "LastFrm," giving hour:minute:second)

▪ The network protocol being used

▪ The port numbers used by the application for the source and destination (shown under "ApplD1" and "ApplD2")

Figure 5-4
Sample application
traffic data.

1stFrm	LastFrm	Protocol	ApplID1	ApplID2	Addr1	Addr2	Frms1	Frms2	Bytes1	Bytes2
13:15:05	13:16:23	TCP	Port: 1219	Port: 3700	[10.10.201.2]	[10.10.3.56]	76	78	19936	34093
13:15:33	13:17:08	NetBIOS-ssn	Port: 1202	Port: 139	[10.10.201.2]	[10.10.237.23]	229	208	17591	18508
13:15:51	13:15:53	TCP	Port: 1222	Port: 3700	[10.10.201.2]	[10.10.3.56]	12	11	1812	1335
13:15:51	13:20:00	TCP	Port: 1223	Port: 3700	[10.10.201.2]	[10.10.3.56]	70	77	15166	32226
13:15:55	13:17:07	TCP	Port: 1224	Port: 3700	[10.10.201.2]	[10.10.3.56]	228	234	67778	73602

- The network layer addresses of the source and destination ("Addr1" and "Addr2")

- The number of frames and number of bytes in the forward and return directions ("Frms1" and "Bytes1" for the forward direction, "Frms2" and "Bytes2" for the return direction)

A Network General Sniffer in Expert mode can capture all the required data if the data is output in Expert Analyzer Output File Format. Other vendors' traffic analyzers may also be able to do so as well. RMON2 probes today typically do not provide sufficiently accurate start and stop times for each conversation and thus should not be used for capturing data for application planning.

Creating or Identifying Your Test Environment

Before you can capture application traffic data, you must identify a testing environment, or test bed. This is a location at which you have access to the application client system and where you can place your data collection device. The client system and the data collection device (traffic analyzer) should be physically close (in the same room, if at all possible), because the user who is running the benchmark needs to be able to communicate with the person controlling the data collection device. The user must be able to indicate when individual benchmark transactions are started and completed so that the data collection device can be started and stopped at the appropriate points.

SELECTING AN ISOLATED ENVIRONMENT   The ideal location is isolated from the overall production network, such as a development or pilot installation of the application, where you can capture application data without having to contend with lots of competing traffic. You must be able to isolate the traffic created by the application activities so that you can create "pure" traffic profiles, which represent the data generated by the transactions, independent of the effects of other network traffic, network bottlenecks, propagation delays, and so forth.

However, eventually the application will be deployed across an enterprise network, where delays *will* be a factor. Therefore, although you want to isolate your test environment from the uncontrolled effects of other network usage, you do want to be able to simulate the delays you anticipate encountering when the application is deployed. You can simulate these by using a WAN delay simulator (such as the

Adtech Data Channel Simulator) in your controlled environment. Network delays can affect the characteristics of your traffic, such as changing the application protocol behavior (windowing, retransmissions), so it is important to look at the traffic under these conditions. Using a WAN delay simulator in a controlled network environment lets you manipulate the amount of network delay experienced during a packet's round trip transmission. This lets you simulate the performance across circuits within your network, and is also critical to establishing acceptable quality-of-service goals.

Executing your application planning activities in an isolated environment also makes it easier to set up and test multiple different scenarios. For example, you may want to test the behavior of the application with or without a proxy server, or with and without a simulated WAN delay. For example, if you are testing a PeopleSoft version 6 application such as HRMS, you may want to do the benchmark once with the native PeopleSoft version 6 client without caches loaded (meaning the user screens are downloaded when needed), once with caches loaded (the screens are already resident in the client), and a third time using the Citrix WinFrame client and server. This will be most convenient and the least time-consuming if you can use the same knowledgeable user to execute the same benchmark repeatedly, using the same physical client system and data capture setup.

SIMULATING A WAN ENVIRONMENT   You can use a WAN delay simulator to simulate the bandwidth and delay characteristics of the various wide area circuits within your enterprise network. In most real networks, circuits between different remote locations experience different degrees of delay, and an application may meet quality-of-service goals on some circuits but not on others. Using a delay simulator lets you simulate the actual circuit speeds to your remote locations so as to see how the application will perform over those circuit types.

Using a WAN delay simulator also lets you manipulate network delay to help you establish your quality-of-service goals. Although the behavior of the network is only one of the three components of a quality-of-service metric (the other two are the behavior of the client and the behavior of the server; see Figure 5-3), this is the component of interest for NRP purposes. By testing network delays of various lengths, you can determine how much delay the user (or the application) can tolerate before the application becomes difficult or impossible to work with effectively. Once you know the range of delays that provide acceptable quality of service for the different transactions of the application, you can use them as metrics to evaluate the projected performance of your network in the capacity planning phase of your NRP project.

TESTING USING AN ACTUAL ENTERPRISE NETWORK If you cannot test your application in a simulated WAN environment, it is possible to do application planning activities using the real enterprise network. However, capturing data across the actual enterprise network makes it difficult to control other variables that affect the traffic behavior. In a real network environment, it will probably not be possible to manipulate delays to determine how much delay can be tolerated and still meet quality-of-service goals. If you are testing your application across the real enterprise network, depending on your objectives, you may want to test across a circuit that will provide worst-case response—for example, the smallest-capacity circuit with the highest network delay. This will let you model worst-case conditions for your projected application deployment and will give you an idea of the quality of service you can expect under these worst-case conditions.

Testing the application on the systems on which it is in development is usually preferable. For one thing, you will need to have most or all of the application components available (client, application server, database, proxy server), depending on the architecture of the application. In addition, the application developers may need to be involved in the profiling activities, because they are the ones with the expertise to create the benchmark and may also serve as the "knowledgeable user" for the data collection activities. Application profiling is the one activity out of all the NRP activities in which the cooperation of the application developers is the most critical.

AN EXAMPLE OF A TEST BED ENVIRONMENT Figure 5-5 shows an actual test bed setup that supports testing a two-tier PeopleSoft application in which the client communicates with a database on another LAN. Testing was done using both native PeopleSoft version 6 and Citrix WinFrame clients, so the test bed included a Citrix WinFrame server. An Adtech Data Channel Simulator, located on the same LAN with the client and the Network General Sniffer, was used to adjust bandwidth and insert delays to simulate communication across the enterprise WAN. The delay simulator was also used to quantify quality-of-service goals. By testing different values of delay, it was possible to determine at what point application response became unacceptable from the user's perspective.

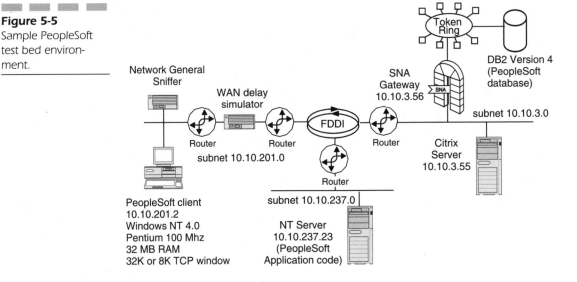

**DIAGRAMMING AND DOCUMENTING THE TEST ENVIRON-
MENT** Once you have identified or created the test bed on which
you will perform your data collection activities, you need to identify
by network address the individual components that make up the application environment—specifically, the addresses of the application
server (or database server in a two-tier client/server application) and the
client system you will be using. You also need to identify by address
the other components, such as the database server or a proxy server
(such as a Citrix server in a PeopleSoft version 6 installation). Even if
you decide not to measure traffic between the application server and
the database server at this time, you should still know where they are
located and how they are addressed (IP address, for example). In a three-
tier client/server application, you may decide later to measure database
traffic, depending on the evolution of your project (for example, if
there is a possibility of relocating the database or application servers).

It is important to draw a diagram or map of the system components
that shows the topology and traffic flows within your test bed environment, such as is shown in Figure 5-5. You must identify and document each of the components you will be studying, by name and/or
network layer address. You need to know the network layer addresses
in order to determine which conversations to collect and how to
"understand" the data that is collected.

You also need to document the components in terms of how closely
they represent the components that will be used in the production

environment. Is the client configured in a way that is similar to the way actual clients will be configured? Are they using the same transport protocols? Is the application server the same type of system, with similar capacity to the ones that will be used in the production environment? It is important to understand how the components in your test environment are similar to or different from the components that will be used when the application is deployed. For example, if a client or server has substantially higher or lower capacity than those in the production environment, or if you test using the TCP/IP network protocol when actual clients will be using IPX/SPX, the results of your application planning efforts will not provide a realistic projection of performance in the production environment.

The following diagrams (Figures 5-6 through 5-8) show application test bed topologies for PeopleSoft version 6 (with native and Citrix

Figure 5-6

Test bed for People-Soft version 6 application with native client.

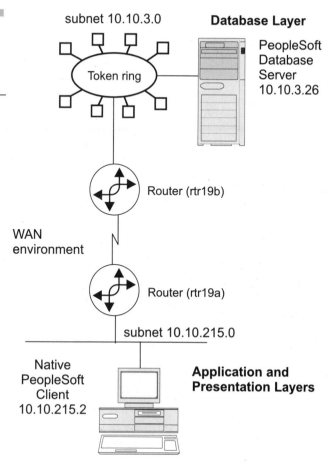

subnet 10.10.3.0

Database Layer

Token ring

PeopleSoft
Database
Server
10.10.3.26

Router (rtr19b)

WAN
environment

Router (rtr19a)

subnet 10.10.215.0

Native
PeopleSoft
Client
10.10.215.2

**Application and
Presentation Layers**

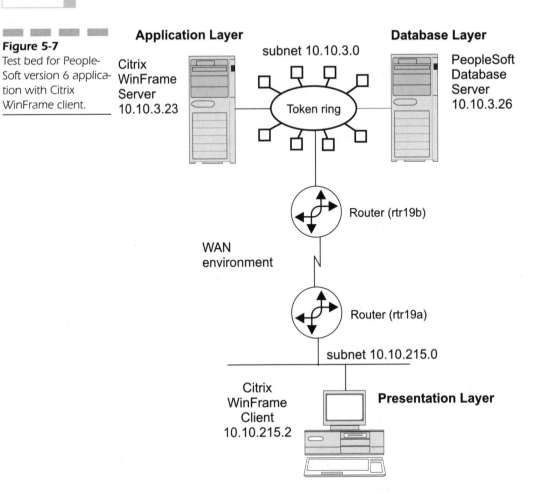

Figure 5-7
Test bed for People-
Soft version 6 applica-
tion with Citrix
WinFrame client.

WinFrame clients) and SAP R/3 or BAAN IV, annotated with names, IP addresses, or both. You should create diagrams similar to these that show the locations of your application components. In addition to helping you determine how realistic your environment is, this diagram can be the basis for determining where to place your data collection devices and your WAN delay simulator, if you will be using one.

Placing and Configuring Data Collection Devices

The next task is to determine where to place your data collection devices for the application data capture. This will depend on the objec-

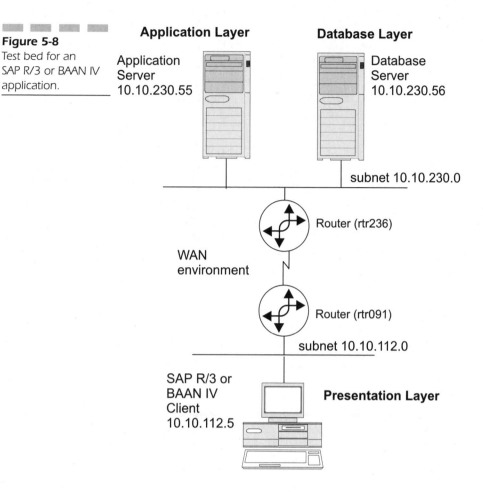

Figure 5-8

Test bed for an
SAP R/3 or BAAN IV
application.

Application Layer

Application
Server
10.10.230.55

Database Layer

Database
Server
10.10.230.56

subnet 10.10.230.0

Router (rtr236)

WAN
environment

Router (rtr091)

subnet 10.10.112.0

SAP R/3 or
BAAN IV
Client
10.10.112.5

Presentation Layer

tives of your application planning project. You also need to

■ Set up the filters on the traffic analyzer so that you collect the data
you want

■ Program a capture interval on the traffic analyzer if you plan to
capture data over fixed-length intervals

■ Test everything to ensure that it all works as you expect

DETERMINE THE TRAFFIC FLOWS TO CAPTURE First, you
need to determine which traffic flows need to be captured, based on
the objectives of your application planning activities and the architecture of the application. In a generic three-tier client/server application,
there are application-related traffic flows between the client and the
application server and between the application server and the database

server, as shown in Figure 5-9. In many cases, the primary traffic flow of interest for an NRP study is the traffic between the client and the application server. This is typically the traffic that will be traversing the WAN between remote clients and an application server located in a centralized data center. In a two-tier application such as PeopleSoft version 6, traffic between clients and the database server is the only traffic that would be relevant.

In a three-tier environment (such as with SAP R/3, BAAN IV, or PeopleSoft using the Citrix WinFrame product), you have an additional traffic flow, which you might want to study, between the application server (or the Citrix server) and the database. If these servers are on the same LAN (as is typically recommended by application vendors such as SAP and PeopleSoft), this traffic is not usually considered to be an area of concern. However, it still may be useful to look at this traffic. For

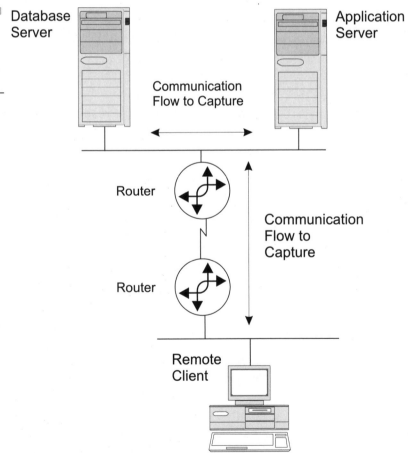

Figure 5-9
Communication flows that can be captured for a three-tier application.

example, you may find it interesting to get an idea of the volume of traffic between the application server and the database server. If there is a future possibility of separating the application and database servers, this might prove to be useful. However, in this case it is important to understand what data you are capturing, especially if you cannot guarantee that the client you are testing is the only client using the application during the time you are testing.

If the database server and application server are separated over a wide area circuit, or if the relative placement of these components is one of the issues under study, then the data flow between these two components should also be profiled. In some applications there may be a data replication function that happens between a local database server and a remote database server. In this case, the traffic flow between the two servers would need to be captured.

PLACING A TRAFFIC ANALYZER IN THE TEST BED   To capture application traffic, you need to place a traffic analyzer at some point in the route between the two end points of the conversations you want to capture. Assuming that you plan to capture the conversations between a client and the application server, you could place the traffic analyzer near either the client or the application server. However, as discussed earlier, it would generally be preferable to place the analyzer close to the client, both topologically (on the same LAN) and physically (in the same room, if possible). Physical placement of the device is important to facilitate coordination between the person monitoring the data collection device and the knowledgeable user executing the benchmark script on the client.

The diagram shown in Figure 5-10 illustrates where you would place a traffic analyzer to capture application data between the client and application server in a three-tier environment such as SAP R/3 or BAAN IV. In terms of access to the needed data, the traffic analyzer could be placed on either subnet 10.10.230.0 or subnet 10.10.112.0, but colocating it with the client is generally preferable for coordinating the data capture efforts. You would set up the traffic analyzer to filter on the client's IP address, 10.10.112.5, so that it would look only at traffic going to and from that client.

The PeopleSoft version 6 HRMS application in its native configuration uses a two-tier architecture, combining presentation and application server functionality together in a "thick" client. The only application data flow in this implementation is between the PeopleSoft native client and PeopleSoft server (that is, the database server). In this case, as shown in Figure 5-11, you would put a traffic analyzer next to

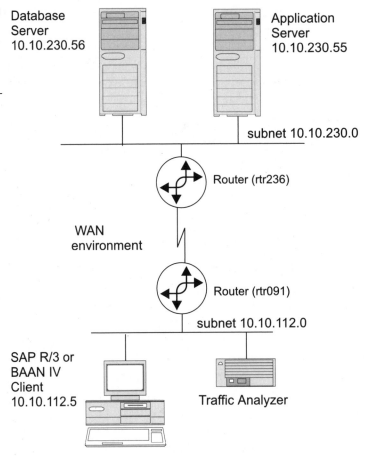

Figure 5-10

Traffic analyzer place-
ment for SAP R/3 or
BAAN IV client data
capture.

Database
Server
10.10.230.56

Application
Server
10.10.230.55

subnet 10.10.230.0

Router (rtr236)

WAN
environment

Router (rtr091)

subnet 10.10.112.0

SAP R/3 or
BAAN IV
Client
10.10.112.5

Traffic Analyzer

(that is, on the same LAN as) the client. You would set up the traffic
analyzer to filter on the IP address of the PeopleSoft client and would
look only at traffic going to and from that client.

   If you are using Citrix WinFrame software, and if the Citrix Win-
Frame server is colocated with the database server, then you could use a
similar setup to capture traffic between the client and the Citrix Win-
Frame server (see Figure 5-12). Assuming that the same client can be
used to run either the native PeopleSoft version 6 client or the Citrix
WinFrame client, you could place the traffic analyzer next to the client and filter on the IP address of the client, just as you did in the previous example.

PLACING A WAN DELAY SIMULATOR   Figure 5-12 also illustrates
the use of a WAN delay simulator, which allows you to capture appli-

Figure 5-11
Traffic analyzer placement for native PeopleSoft version 6 client data capture.

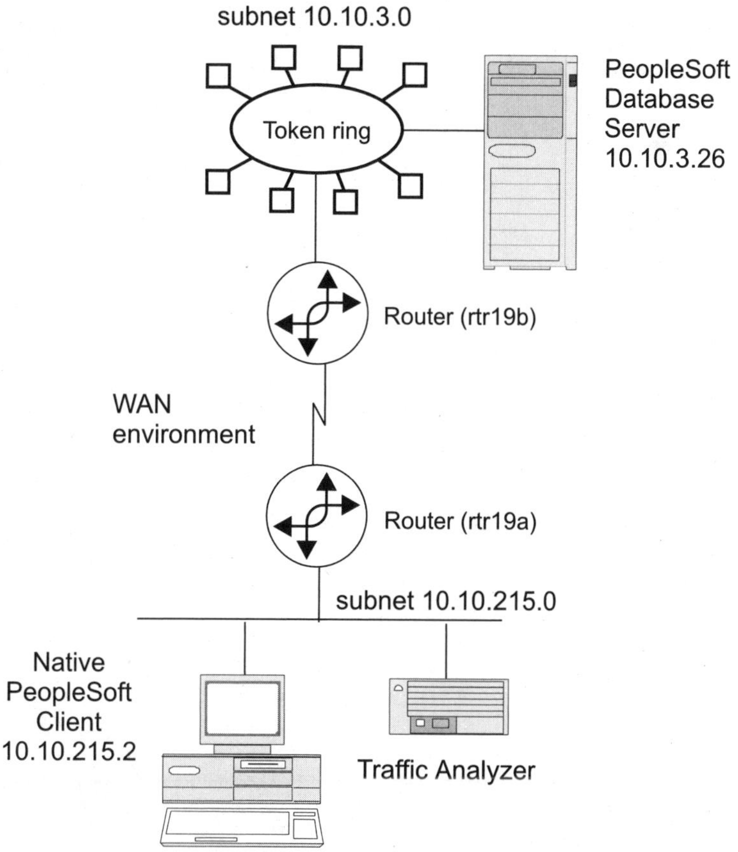

subnet 10.10.3.0

Token ring

PeopleSoft
Database
Server
10.10.3.26

Router (rtr19b)

WAN
environment

Router (rtr19a)

subnet 10.10.215.0

Native
PeopleSoft
Client
10.10.215.2

Traffic Analyzer

cation data in a LAN environment and simulate running across an actual WAN, with whatever delay characteristics the WAN may have. If your application will be deployed to remote sites with different circuit types or circuit speeds, you may decide to create multiple simulations of bandwidth and delay to model the different WAN links more accurately. Using a delay simulator also allows you to test the application under varying delay conditions to determine at what point quality-of-service goals can no longer be met. This information is very important for the capacity planning phase, because it provides the metrics you will use to evaluate the results of your network models.

The WAN delay simulator must be set up between two routers that provide serial connections, as shown in Figure 5-12. One router interfaces to the rest of the network, and the other isolates the client you are using for testing. When you set a delay using the WAN delay simulator, all components on the client side of the second router (rtr19a in

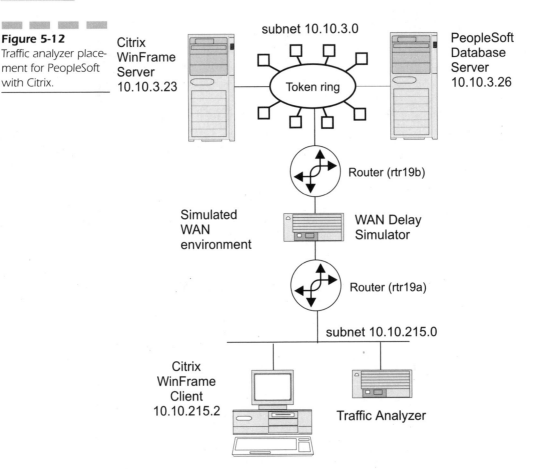

Figure 5-12
Traffic analyzer place-
ment for PeopleSoft
with Citrix.

Figure 5-12) will experience that delay for every packet they send or
receive. Thus, it is not advisable to place the WAN delay simulator
between routers that are currently being used in your production network, because then all components communicating across that subnet,
whether involved in the test or not, will be affected by any delays you
set. Ideally, you should add additional routers to your network so that
you can isolate the subnet on which you will be doing your delay testing. It is helpful if the routers and delay simulator can be set up in the
same physical location as the application client and traffic analyzer.
This makes it easier to vary the delays as needed to determine your
quality-of-service goals.

SETTING UP FILTERING   In general, if you just have one traffic analyzer to work with, you would install it on the same LAN as the client and set it up to filter on the IP address of the specific client. For example, in Figure 5-11, the traffic analyzer is placed on same LAN as the PeopleSoft client and is set to filter on the IP address (10.10.215.2) or the MAC (Media Access Control) address of that client.

If you are looking at traffic between the application server and the database server (probably a less typical situation), you could install a second traffic analyzer to filter on the address of either the application server or the database server. You would decide which server is preferable depending on how the servers are used and which is most likely to let you isolate the traffic for your application transactions. For example, if the database is used by other applications (not of interest to your project), but the application server is part of your development environment and will be accessed only by your test client during the data capture cycle, then you would want to filter on the application server address. Doing so would effectively isolate the traffic to the database generated by your application benchmark activities.

DETERMINING YOUR DATA CAPTURE METHOD   Deciding on and setting up your data capture method is an important aspect of the data collection effort. Basically, you want to use a traffic analyzer to capture data into a separate file for each separate transaction or activity in the benchmark script. The resulting data file is used to create a profile of the traffic generated by that individual transaction. In turn, that profile can be added onto the baseline model to simulate the traffic over the enterprise network caused by that transaction.

There are two ways to use a traffic analyzer to capture the data into files. One way is to control the data capture manually: start the capture when the user begins the transaction, then stop the capture and save the data when the user finishes. An alternative method, if you are using a data collection device that can be programmed to capture data for a specific interval, is to program constant capture intervals and have the user start and complete a transaction within one interval. Using a programmed interval is somewhat easier, because you do not have to keep stopping and starting the traffic analyzer.

MANUALLY CONTROLLING THE DATA CAPTURE   In   some ways the easiest way to capture data is just to start the capture with the traffic analyzer when the user starts the transaction and to stop the capture and save the data when the user finishes. Depending on the purpose for which you are capturing this data, this may be the best strategy. For example, if you are capturing a set of transactions of widely varying duration that cannot be easily fit into a fixed interval, it may be simpler to start and stop the capture around each transaction, especially if there are only a few transactions to capture. However, if you are going to be capturing large numbers of transactions or repeating your benchmark multiple times, it may be easier to use programmed capture intervals and work with those results.

USING A PROGRAMMED CAPTURE INTERVAL   With a programmed capture interval, a traffic analyzer such as a Network General Sniffer will automatically save data to a file at the end of each interval. For purposes of loading your application traffic profiles onto your baseline model for future capacity planning activities, it is simpler if your capture intervals match the sampling intervals that you used to create your baseline model. As discussed in Chapter 4, "Baselining the Network," five-minute capture intervals seem to be the optimal duration.

The data you generate for your traffic profiles will be calculated in terms of an average loading (Kbps) over the duration of the data. If the network activity associated with the transaction data lasts less than the full capture interval, the average will be computed over the actual duration of the data (down to one-second increments). If the transaction activity lasts the full capture interval or exceeds it, the average will be computed for the full capture interval. You want the sample period to be short enough that the average flow of traffic created by your transaction will not be masked by averaging, but not so short that you end up with an unmanageable number of samples. For example, if you chose a 15-minute capture interval but the transaction actually transmitted data only in short spikes at the beginning and the end of the interval, those spikes would be lost by being averaged over the full 15-minute interval.

Ideally, you want to use a capture interval that is just slightly longer than the time it takes the user to do any one transaction specified in your benchmark. If almost all activities take closer to ten minutes, then you might want to use a ten-minute interval. If most transactions take less than one minute to execute, then you might want to use a one-minute interval. If you plan to use five-minute capture intervals as recommended, you should plan each transaction specified in your benchmark to be able to be completed within a five-minute interval. Transactions that are significantly longer than five minutes should be broken down into component activities that fall within the five-minute range, unless that is not possible.

However, both the duration of the benchmark transactions and the capture interval can and should be adjusted based on the objectives of the NRP project and the characteristics of the application being studied. These characteristics include both the actual duration of individual transactions and the expected frequency of those transactions. For example, a transaction rate of one every five minutes is 12 per hour. However, some types of very short transactions (such as entering monthly customer payments) may occur at higher rates; for example, for a simple transaction one data entry person may do 30 an hour. In such a case, you need to decide whether to shorten the capture interval to two minutes, for example, or to use a five-minute interval but complete two transactions within that period and to adjust the transaction rate predictions accordingly when creating your capacity planning scenarios.

There also may be transactions that take longer than five minutes, such as generating large reports. Again, you would need to determine that capture interval based on the actual characteristics of the transactions. Assuming that the activity cannot be broken down into component activities, you still may find it beneficial to capture data in shorter (five-minute) intervals. If there is a fairly steady data stream over the length of the transaction, then you can use the appropriate set of multiple five-minute averages to represent the transaction.

TESTING YOUR DATA COLLECTION SETUP Before you begin your actual data capture, you should allow time to test the data capture setup. This means executing some transactions from the benchmark to verify that you are indeed capturing the right set of traffic data, that you can identify the actual application traffic, that the programmed capture interval (if you are using one) is appropriate and working correctly, and so on. Testing your setup will help you determine whether to use a programmed capture interval or not, and what is the best capture interval to use.

You need to identify your actual application, usually by TCP port number, so that you can tell which conversations can be attributed to that application. Some applications, such as FTP, Telnet, SMTP, or UUCP, use well-known ports, so a data collection device such as the Network General Sniffer can identify them by their application name. In most cases, however, you will need to figure out which port your application is using by looking at the data from the traffic analyzer.

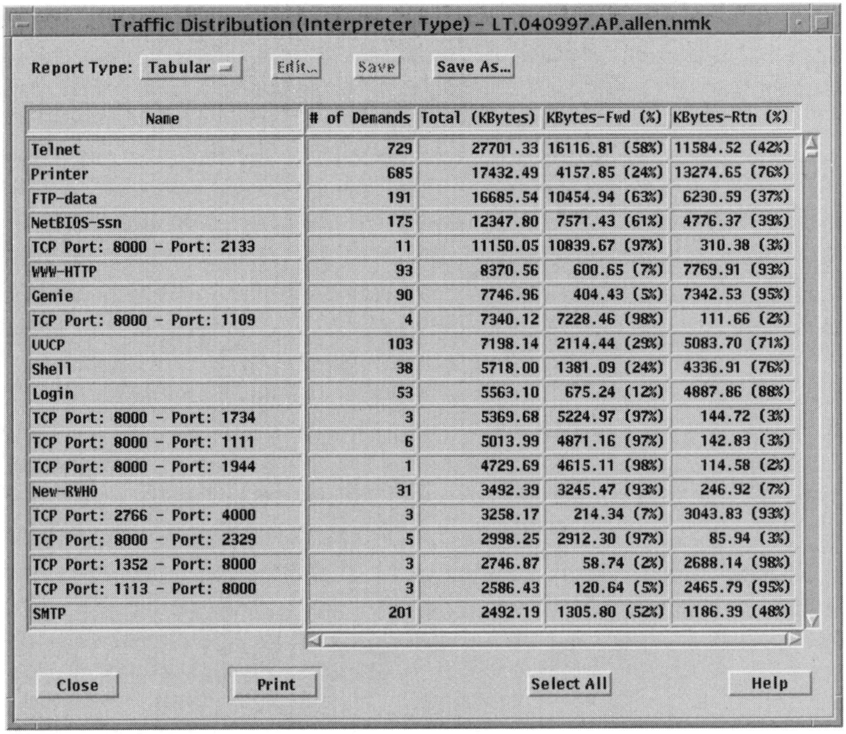

Figure 5-13
Example application
distribution chart
showing applications
by TCP port.

Traffic Distribution (Interpreter Type) – LT.040997.AP.allen.nmk

Report Type: Tabular   Edit...   Save   Save As...

Name	# of Demands	Total (KBytes)	KBytes-Fwd (%)	KBytes-Rtn (%)
Telnet	729	27701.33	16116.81 (58%)	11584.52 (42%)
Printer	685	17432.49	4157.85 (24%)	13274.65 (76%)
FTP-data	191	16685.54	10454.94 (63%)	6230.59 (37%)
NetBIOS-ssn	175	12347.80	7571.43 (61%)	4776.37 (39%)
TCP Port: 8000 – Port: 2133	11	11150.05	10839.67 (97%)	310.38 (3%)
WWW-HTTP	93	8370.56	600.65 (7%)	7769.91 (93%)
Genie	90	7746.96	404.43 (5%)	7342.53 (95%)
TCP Port: 8000 – Port: 1109	4	7340.12	7228.46 (98%)	111.66 (2%)
UUCP	103	7198.14	2114.44 (29%)	5083.70 (71%)
Shell	38	5718.00	1381.09 (24%)	4336.91 (76%)
Login	53	5563.10	675.24 (12%)	4887.86 (88%)
TCP Port: 8000 – Port: 1734	3	5369.68	5224.97 (97%)	144.72 (3%)
TCP Port: 8000 – Port: 1111	6	5013.99	4871.16 (97%)	142.83 (3%)
TCP Port: 8000 – Port: 1944	1	4729.69	4615.11 (98%)	114.58 (2%)
New-RWHO	31	3492.39	3245.47 (93%)	246.92 (7%)
TCP Port: 2766 – Port: 4000	3	3258.17	214.34 (7%)	3043.83 (93%)
TCP Port: 8000 – Port: 2329	5	2998.25	2912.30 (97%)	85.94 (3%)
TCP Port: 1352 – Port: 8000	3	2746.87	58.74 (2%)	2688.14 (98%)
TCP Port: 1113 – Port: 8000	3	2586.43	120.64 (5%)	2465.79 (95%)
SMTP	201	2492.19	1305.80 (52%)	1186.39 (48%)

Close   Print   Select All   Help

The chart shown in Figure 5-13 shows an application distribution
report generated by Make Systems' NetMaker XA from Network General Sniffer data. Once you know the port number used by the new
application, you will be able to distinguish the conversations created
by the new application from other conversations that may occur
between your client and the server.

Finally, you should make sure that the network conversations you
are collecting are between the network addresses you expect based on
the test bed you have diagrammed. In some cases you may discover
unexpected network conversations to other servers.

Determining Acceptable Quality of Service

The point of the application planning activities discussed in this chapter, and of the capacity planning activities discussed in Chapter 6, is to
project how an application will perform when it is implemented on
the enterprise network. But how will you determine what the results

mean—whether the predicted behavior of the application is acceptable? For example, one of the metrics you can get from the capacity planning phase is the predicted round-trip delay for application transactions running between various locations in the model. How will you evaluate these delays to determine whether the predicted response times seen by the users will be acceptable or not? You need to define a set of metrics for quality of service that you can use as goals, against which you will evaluate your application's predicted performance.

For purposes of this book, quality of service is defined in terms of application performance as perceived by the user; that is, response time and throughput. In some cases acceptable quality of service may be strictly a subjective attribute; long response times may simply be annoying and reduce users' productivities in terms of the number of transactions they can execute over time. In other cases long delays may cause more serious problems in the application. For example, if the client and application server or database server lose synchronization, the application may produce errors or crash. In such a case, your network's ability to meet acceptable quality-of-service goals may determine whether the application functions properly, or if it functions at all.

The critical measure for generating quality-of-service goals is the users' evaluation of the acceptability of an application's response, in terms of their ability to work with it. The user's reaction is definitely a subjective measure, but an important one. However, you may also be able to create more objective measures of acceptability (such as the actual time it takes for the user to complete a transaction), which can then be converted into a measure of productivity (such as the number of transactions the user could execute per hour). Another objective indicator is simply whether the application continues to function properly given standard network delays. If the application hangs, crashes, experiences errors that require the transaction to be reexecuted, or—in the worst case—handles the transaction improperly with resulting data corruption, then obviously it is not providing acceptable quality of service.

TESTING APPLICATION PERFORMANCE FOR QUALITY OF SERVICE As part of the application planning process, it is recommended that you use a WAN delay simulator as shown in Figure 5-12 to test varying amounts of round-trip delay and determine what the effect is on the application and on the user. Doing so lets you determine how much delay can be tolerated before the application response time becomes unacceptable to the user or to the application. These results then give you metrics that you can use to evaluate the delays predicted by the capacity planning model under various circumstances. In some cases, even without doing any capacity planning activities as defined in Chapter 6, the results may alert you to WAN environments in which the application will probably not function well. For example, if the known delay characteristics of some of your network's WAN circuits exceed your quality-of-service goals, you can predict that the application performance will not be acceptable when routing over those circuits. Clients communicating by overseas circuits to servers or databases located domestically often fall into this category.

Table 5.4 shows some common delays (tending toward the high end) that you might expect to see with various types of circuits in different environments. If your application traffic routes over multiple hops, the delays may be even longer. If your quality-of-service testing indicates that the application does not perform well if the delay is over 300 ms, for example, you can expect that you will have problems with clients located internationally (especially if there are multiple hops between remote client sites and the application server).

Note that if you do not have a WAN delay simulator, you may also be able to get some idea of acceptable quality of service by testing the application across actual enterprise WAN circuits with known delay characteristics. If that is not possible, you still may be able to determine a rough set of quality-of-service goals simply by making some educated guesses about the sorts of delays that are likely to produce unacceptable results.

To test application performance under various delay conditions, you capture data for the transactions in the benchmark using a traffic analyzer, as will be described in the next section, but with two differences. First, your knowledgeable user runs the set of benchmark application

TABLE 5.4

Network Delay by
Circuit Type

Network Environment (Circuit Type)	Common Round-Trip Delay per Packet
Satellite circuit	1000 ms
International circuit, multiple hops	500 ms
International leased-line circuit	250 ms
Domestic Frame Relay	100 ms
Domestic leased line	60 ms

transactions multiple times, using the WAN delay simulator to insert different delays onto the network. If you do not have a WAN delay simulator, the user would run the benchmark transactions across your actual WAN environment. Second, you do not need to save the data into files, because you will not need to use it for creating profiles. The data you observe and capture during this step is used only for determining acceptable quality of service.

STRATEGIES FOR TESTING DIFFERENT DELAYS Your strategy for testing the effect of different delays will depend on how much you know about the behavior of the network. If you know the delay characteristics of your various circuits, you may be able to start with your worst-case situation. If you do not know the characteristics of your network, then you can use trial-and-error testing to determine where the threshold lies, in terms of delay, between acceptable and unacceptable application performance.

Even if you have a good understanding of your network's performance characteristics, however, it may be a good idea to determine where the threshold lies between acceptable and unacceptable network delay. If the application you are testing has not yet been deployed on your network, its deployment in itself may change the performance characteristics of your network. Other factors may also have changed by the time the application is rolled out. Thus, it may prove to be very useful to know how much delay the application (or user) can tolerate before the application becomes unusable, even if that amount of delay seems beyond the range you anticipate from your existing network.

To determine where the delay threshold lies, you should start with a long delay that is certain to exceed the worst case on your network. For example, if you know the range of delays you typically see, you might start by doubling the longest delay you would typically see. You could also choose an arbitrary number; for example, you might start with a 1-second delay per packet (which roughly simulates the delay you might see across a satellite circuit). You then set the delay and run multiple benchmark transactions to observe the resulting application behavior and the user's perception of the application response. If the application response time at this delay is unacceptable, you can then halve the delay to 500 ms (which approximates the delay you might see on an international link with multiple hops). You could keep halving the delay until you reach a point at which the application behavior and the user evaluation of application response indicate that the delay allows acceptable application quality of service.

You should document the delays that you have determined to be acceptable in terms of your application's behavior. You will use these values in the capacity planning phase of your project to evaluate the results you get from modeling your capacity planning scenarios. Depending on the circumstances, you may set up different delay metrics (and thus different quality-of-service goals) for different circuits or routes on your network, especially if the reality of your network environment dictates that you must trade off what is ideal in terms of quality of service against what is possible.

WATCHING FOR TRANSPORT ERRORS   While you are testing the application to generate quality-of-service metrics, you should also keep an eye on the rate of errors that are detected by your data collection device. This information can be critical in helping you pinpoint problems with the application caused by the projected WAN environment. While NRP activities are concerned with the network's role in affecting quality of service, error rates you observe while carrying out these activities may also alert you to problems in the application itself or relative to the client or server configurations.

For example, a high percentage of retransmissions (5 to 10% of packets retransmitted) as reported by the traffic analyzer for certain application transactions indicates that there may be problems with the application. Excessive retransmissions could be caused by inadequate server capacity, problems with the transport protocol configuration (timers not set correctly), too much delay for the application to handle, or the design of the application. An inadequate server may not be able to accept data fast enough, the transport protocol may be timing out too soon, or the application may not be using network resources efficiently. This type of problem may also indicate that the application simply generates large volumes of data and saturates the circuit type being simulated, indicating that the bandwidth is simply not adequate to support the application.

A high error rate means that something about your application is not working correctly. Especially in the case of a high percentage of retransmissions, you should attempt to solve the problem before you continue on with your application planning activities. In particular, you should not attempt to collect data and create application profiles under these circumstances, because the profiles will contain excess data due to the retransmissions. Unless the problems cannot be solved, you probably do not want to use error-laden data to model your application performance. You should attempt to diagnose and resolve the problems before continuing on with application planning activities.

Capturing the Application Traffic Data

Capturing the data for the transactions in the application benchmark requires a highly coordinated effort between the knowledgeable user who executes the tasks in the benchmark and the person who monitors the data capture device and saves the captured data.

Once you have installed, configured, and tested your data collection devices and established your quality-of-service goals, you can begin capturing data. The actual data capture process involves the following steps for each activity in the benchmark:

- The person monitoring the data collection device begins the data capture and tells the application user when the capture interval is beginning.

- The application user begins executing a benchmark transaction; the person monitoring the data collection device records the start time of the data capture interval.

- The application user finishes the transaction or component activity and stops all use of the keyboard.

- The person monitoring the data collection device stops the data capture and saves the data to a file, or notes the end of the capture interval (if the data is saved automatically).

One of the participants, usually the person monitoring the data capture, must be responsible for recording the specifics of the transaction—the name of the transaction and the start and stop time of the transaction or of the capture intervals. This process is repeated for each transaction in the benchmark.

Table 5.5 shows an example of how information was recorded for a data capture session using a Network General Sniffer with programmed intervals of 3 minutes. The time notations indicate the time at which the Network General Sniffer saved the data from the interval into a file. Note that there are gaps between some of the transactions, during which no relevant data capture was performed. These gaps occurred because additional setup time was needed. Also note that the replication transactions spanned multiple capture intervals.

Running the Benchmark Multiple Times

The entire benchmark must be repeated for each test scenario, such as testing with or without a proxy server such as Citrix WinFrame. If you

TABLE 5.5

Application Data
Capture Record

Transaction	End Time
Initialize client	10:33
Open mail with password	10:36
Read mail (8 messages)	10:48
Read mail (enclosure)	11:21
Mail Replication (13 messages) (ended in error)	11:24, 11:27, 11:30, 11:33
Mail Replication again	11:42, 11:45, 11:48, 11:51
Access database (Company Address Book) and search	12:03

are testing a PeopleSoft version 6 application such as Financials, you may want to do the benchmark once with the native PeopleSoft client without caches loaded (in which case the templates get downloaded when needed), once with caches loaded (in which case the templates are already resident in the client), and a third time using the Citrix Win-Frame client and server.

Requirements for the "Knowledgeable" Application User

The user who performs the benchmark transactions is a critical element in the success of the data capture activity. This user should be thoroughly knowledgeable in the use of the application being tested, because you want each transaction to be executed smoothly and efficiently, without errors. Ideally the user who will be doing this testing should have an opportunity beforehand to become familiar with the benchmark so as to be able to do the transactions efficiently.

If the application being tested is still in development, it may be necessary to have one of the developers act as the user. It also will be critical to test the benchmark itself to ensure that the transactions work as expected and that the user knows how to execute a path through each transaction that will not generate errors due to application software bugs or incomplete functionality. As discussed earlier in the section on developing the benchmark, it is important that the benchmark transactions be repeatable: that any transaction behave exactly the same way each time it is executed.

The application user also needs to have a great deal of patience. Parts of the benchmark may have to be redone many times if problems arise in the data capture process, and the entire testing cycle will have to be repeated multiple times for different testing scenarios. The application user and the person monitoring the data collection device need to work together to coordinate the start and end of each benchmark transaction with the data capture intervals and the recording of the data (including the transaction identification information).

Application Profiling

Application profiling is the process of creating a representative statistical model (a profile) of application transactions based on the data captured in the previous step. These profiles will be used to represent the "typical" load that an individual application user would place on the network with a specific application transaction. You can then use these profiles in combination with the baseline model of your enterprise network to project what the load on the network would be if users were executing these transactions. You can in turn evaluate whether your quality-of-service objectives will be met under the conditions of the model.

For example, you could capture data for a General Ledger Edit activity and create a profile that statistically represents the "typical" traffic load this transaction will make on the network each time a General Ledger Edit is performed. You can then use this profile to load your network model to simulate one or more users doing this transaction with a predicted transaction rate.

Because you create profiles for individual discrete transactions, you can mix and match them to model the actual projected usage of the application within the baseline; for example, 25 employees at one location, each doing 10 PeopleSoft General Ledger Edit transactions and three Create Requisition transactions per hour during the business day. These network models can then be used for capacity planning purposes to predict bandwidth needs in order to meet quality-of-service goals, identify topology reconfigurations such as server locations, and so on. This is discussed in more detail in Chapter 6, "Capacity Planning."

Application Profile Data Reduction and Analysis

Once you have captured data for each transaction in your benchmark into files, you need to import the data into the performance management tool you will use to create the profiles. The way to do this task will depend on the tool you use. With Make Systems' NetMaker XA this task is done automatically, using the Interpreter tool; with Cisco's NETSYS Service Manager suite, it is done using the Performance Service Manager.

You will need to extract and calculate the following metrics (or have the performance management tool do so) from the data for each application transaction:

- The start and stop time of the conversation that represents the transaction
- The type of media network on which it was collected (Ethernet, Token Ring, FDDI, for example)
- The networking protocol used (typically IP for client/server applications such as SAP R/3, PeopleSoft, or BAAN IV)
- The average packet size for each direction of transfer, forward and return (calculated from the number of frames for each direction)
- The total number of bytes transferred for the forward and return directions
- The maximum bandwidth used (in either the forward or return direction) in Kbps (optional)

These requirements mean that your data collection device must be able to track the data by direction and distinguish the data going from client to server from that going from server to client. In turn, you need to establish which is the forward direction and which is the return direction, and do all your calculations consistently using this definition. Usually data is captured relative to a "source" and a "destination"; for example, the Network General Sniffer provides a source and destination for each conversation (see Figure 5-14). In your particular data set, if the source is the server and the destination is the client, then you would define the forward direction to be the traffic between server

Figure 5-14

Sample Network
General Expert
Analyzer output.

Local Client Peoplesoft Setup - GL testing
256K with 140ms Delay

Native Login

1stFrm	LastFrm	Protocol	ApplID1	ApplID2	Addr1	Addr2	Frms1	Frms2	Bytes1	Bytes2
13:00:16	13:01:20	NetBIOS-ssn	Port: 1202	Port: 139	[10.10.201.2]	[10.10.237.23]	71	65	4702	2610
13:00:22	13:00:26	TCP	Port: 1204	Port: 3700	[10.10.201.2]	[10.10.3.56]	16	15	2596	2802
13:00:26	13:01:11	TCP	Port: 1205	Port: 3700	[10.10.201.2]	[10.10.3.56]	131	192	21998	167511
13:01:06	13:02:22	TCP	Port: 1207	Port: 3700	[10.10.201.2]	[10.10.3.56]	16	16	2334	4042
13:01:20	13:01:53	TCP	Port: 1209	Port: 3700	[10.10.201.2]	[10.10.3.56]	232	429	12558	566688
13:00:15	13:00:16	NetBIOS-ns	Port: 137	Port: 137	[10.10.201.2]	[10.10.2.29]	1	1	50	62

Native Journal Query

1stFrm	LastFrm	Protocol	ApplID1	ApplID2	Addr1	Addr2	Frms1	Frms2	Bytes1	Bytes2
13:10:32	13:10:36	NetBIOS-ssn	Port: 1202	Port: 139	[10.10.201.2]	[10.10.237.23]	21	20	1412	780
13:10:36	13:12:14	TCP	Port: 1219	Port: 3700	[10.10.201.2]	[10.10.3.56]	387	625	50638	709333

Citrix Journal Query

1stFrm	LastFrm	Protocol	ApplID1	ApplID2	Addr1	Addr2	Frms1	Frms2	Bytes1	Bytes2
13:45:04	13:47:57	TCP	Port: 1251	Port: 1494	[10.10.201.2]	[10.10.3.55]	223	281	1728	43294

Native Journal Edit

1stFrm	LastFrm	Protocol	ApplID1	ApplID2	Addr1	Addr2	Frms1	Frms2	Bytes1	Bytes2
13:15:05	13:16:23	TCP	Port: 1219	Port: 3700	[10.10.201.2]	[10.10.3.56]	76	78	19936	34093
13:15:33	13:17:08	NetBIOS-ssn	Port: 1202	Port: 139	[10.10.201.2]	[10.10.237.23]	229	208	17591	18508
13:15:51	13:15:53	TCP	Port: 1222	Port: 3700	[10.10.201.2]	[10.10.3.56]	12	11	1812	1335
13:15:51	13:20:00	TCP	Port: 1223	Port: 3700	[10.10.201.2]	[10.10.3.56]	70	77	15166	32226
13:15:55	13:17:07	TCP	Port: 1224	Port: 3700	[10.10.201.2]	[10.10.3.56]	228	234	67778	73602

Citrix Journal Edit

1stFrm	LastFrm	Protocol	ApplID1	ApplID2	Addr1	Addr2	Frms1	Frms2	Bytes1	Bytes2
13:48:05	13:50:54	TCP	Port: 1251	Port: 1494	[10.10.201.2]	[10.10.3.55]	394	458	3033	56995

and client (source and destination) and the return direction to be the traffic between the client (destination) and the server (the source). When you apply these profiles to your network model, you need to know what data is going from server to client and what is going from client to server for the activity, in order to configure the profile correctly into the model as a network conversation.

The average forward packet size is calculated as the total number of bytes in the forward direction (for example, from server to client) divided by the total number of frames in the forward direction:

$$Average\ forward\ packet\ size = \frac{Total\ number\ of\ bytes\ forward}{number\ of\ frames\ forward}$$

The average return packet size is calculated as the total number of bytes in the return direction (for example, from client to server) divided by the number of frames:

$$Average\ return\ packet\ size = \frac{Total\ number\ of\ bytes\ return}{number\ of\ frames\ return}$$

For example, for the Citrix Journal Query shown in Figure 5-14, the average forward packet size would be calculated as Bytes1/Frms1, or 1728/223 = 7.75, and the average return packet size would be Bytes2/Frms2, or 43294/281 = 154.07. Note that these values do not include the overhead of approximately 60 bytes for an Ethernet IP frame.

The results you get for the number of bytes (forward and return) and the average packet sizes should be consistent over multiple executions of the specific transaction you are looking at. If you have time, you may want to have your user execute a particular benchmark transaction multiple times and verify that the data is consistent.

In addition, you will need to know (or decide on) a transaction rate for each transaction: the number of times the transaction will occur in a given time frame, as was discussed earlier in this chapter.

Building Application Profiles

Using your performance management tool, you can build application profiles for each transaction of interest. You can build a profile for every transaction in your benchmark, or you can start by just building profiles for the transactions that have the highest probability of occurring or that are of the greatest interest in terms of testing on your network. Other transactions may be interesting in terms of their network behavior but not occur frequently enough to be worth the trouble of building them into the projected network model. You may choose to start with a subset of transactions at first, and create additional profiles at a later time depending on the results of your initial analyses.

Figure 5-15 shows some sample profiles for transactions from the PeopleSoft version 6 Financials and Sales modules, created using Make

Figure 5-15

Example PeopleSoft application profiles.

Profile Name	Source Addr	Destination Addr	Bytes-Fwd	Bytes-Rtn	Trans Rate 1 per 5 min.	Kbps Fwd 5-min avg	Kbps Rtn 5-min avg
Native Peoplesoft Logon	Client	PS Server	62000	780000	0.0033	1.64	20.59
Native Peoplesoft Journal Query	Client	PS Server	82450	775811	0.0033	2.18	20.48
Native Peoplesoft Create Req.	Client	PS Server	140399	804532	0.0033	3.71	21.24
Citrix PeopleSoft Logon	Client	Citrix Server	13069	67887	0.0033	0.35	1.79
Citrix PeopleSoft Journal Query	Client	Citrix Server	19423	56389	0.0033	0.51	1.49
Citrix PeopleSoft Create Req.	Client	Citrix Server	13845	50919	0.0033	0.37	1.34

Systems' NetMaker XA Interpreter. Profiles were created for these transactions using both a native PeopleSoft client and a Citrix Win-Frame client.

You will use the profiles in your performance management tool to build your capacity planning scenarios, as will be discussed in Chapter 6, "Capacity Planning."

Capacity Planning as the Next Step

The results you have accomplished through your application planning activities may well be of interest in their own right—what amount of network delay will provide acceptable quality of service, or what volume of traffic each application transaction represents, for example—but the main value in terms of NRP is as input to the capacity planning process. The application profiles you have created and the information on how the application will be used will provide direct inputs into the capacity planning process for doing "what-if" modeling and analysis. The quality-of-service metrics you have developed will help you evaluate the results of that analysis, to determine whether your enterprise network will support your quality-of-service goals when the new application has been added to the existing network load.

The next chapter, "Capacity Planning," covers how to take the results from the baselining and application planning phases of your NRP project and use them to accomplish capacity planning.

CHAPTER 6

Capacity Planning

This chapter discusses in detail the techniques and processes of capacity planning.

Capacity planning is the process of analyzing enterprise network performance under possible conditions such as the introduction of new applications on the network, in order to determine future resource requirements. It uses network baseline data and application profile data to provide basic answers about network usage and the ability of the network to meet service-level objectives. It facilitates the development and validation of optimal settings for the network environment.

Capacity planning makes use of "what-if" analyses to look at network performance under conditions that don't necessarily exist in the present network. The intent is to be able to answer questions such as, "What if we add 32 users in Fresno accessing an SAP R/3 server in San Francisco over a 256K leased line, with each user doing one general ledger transaction every five minutes? Will it provide an acceptable per-packet response time? Will network usage on that circuit still be within a reasonable range to provide decent quality of service to the SAP R/3 users?"

The Objectives of Capacity Planning

The purpose of capacity planning activities is to analyze or predict how a network will perform, both under current conditions and when changes to traffic load (new applications or users) or network infrastructure changes are introduced. Capacity planning is the third of the three cycles that make up the complete Network Resource Planning (NRP) process (see Figure 6-1).

Capacity planning is the culmination of the NRP process. Through capacity planning activities, you can finally realize the objectives of

Figure 6-1

Capacity planning as a component of the NRP cycle.

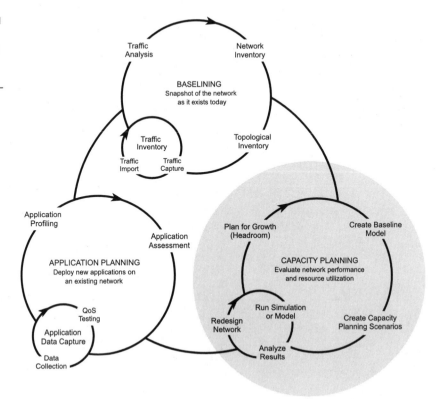

NRP: to ensure that distributed applications achieve an acceptable quality of service at minimum network cost. Capacity planning is essential whenever you contemplate making changes to a network— whether in response to complaints about performance, to reduce over- all telecommunications costs, or to add new applications or users. The "what-if" analyses you do in capacity planning let you predict how these changes will affect your network and whether the proposed changes will actually have the intended effects.

A Historical Perspective on Capacity Planning

Unlike the other two areas of NRP, "capacity planning" is a concept that has been in existence for a relatively long time. The idea of using simulation and modeling techniques for planning and designing net- works started within telecommunications companies to facilitate plan- ning for the growth of the telephone network. The goal was to ensure adequate telephone network capacity so customers would always be able to get a connection (dial tone). The same techniques have subse- quently been adapted to enterprise internetworks to plan for adequate capacity in terms of price/performance trade-offs.

Capacity Planning's Role in Network Resource Planning

Capacity planning takes the data collected in the two other NRP phases (baselining and application planning) and uses it to analyze the network's performance under various conditions you want to study. The earlier phases of NRP can help you uncover problem areas in your existing enterprise network: to locate bottlenecks, identify circuit utili- zation problems, and determine the conditions under which an appli- cation will provide acceptable quality of service. Capacity planning "what-if" analysis helps you locate possible problems in a hypothetical network that does not yet exist in reality but is based on your current network with various levels of changes in effect.

Capacity planning can be used to analyze various types of changes to a network, such as moving servers or hosts to new locations, mov- ing or adding geographic locations, redesigning the network back- bone, or changing routing protocols. The focus of this chapter, however, is primarily on the use of capacity planning to predict how additional workload added to the existing enterprise network will affect overall network performance. In this book, the workload of interest is the traffic created by one or more transactions from a new enterprise application. Characterizing the workload (profiling the application's transactions) is an important step that must have been done, using the application planning techniques discussed in Chapter 5, before the capacity planning analysis starts. As a secondary concern, the workload could also be due to existing applications, where capacity planning techniques are used to look at trends in terms of growth in users, locations, or volume of application transactions.

This chapter will focus primarily on using "acceptable quality of service," in terms of application response time, as the metric for evaluating the results of various capacity planning scenarios. The goal of the capacity planning analysis will be to determine whether you can guarantee that quality of service. You do this by aggregating the additional workload due to the application on top of the baseline model of your existing network, and then analyzing the results using a performance management software tool that can do network simulation or modeling.

Alternatively, depending on your objects, you may elect to focus just on utilization (percentage of capacity used) rather than quality of service (application response) as the criterion for evaluating your capacity planning scenario results. This option follows from the techniques described in this chapter, but will not be discussed as an end in itself.

For any networked client/server application, quality of service is affected by three components: the behavior of the client, the behavior of the network, and the behavior of the server. It is important to note that this book focuses strictly on the role of the enterprise network in affecting quality of service, specifically in terms of network delays as they contribute to application response times. It does not deal with other issues that will affect end-to-end application quality of service, such as the performance of the client and server, or the design of the application. The definition of acceptable quality of service as used in this book, along with a method for converting what is often a qualitative or subjective valuation into a quantitative metric, is discussed at length in Chapter 5, "Application Planning."

Unlike Chapter 4, "Baselining the Network," and Chapter 5, "Application Planning," this chapter does not deal with data collection. Capacity planning techniques are purely analytical and make use of the data collected in the first two cycles of the NRP process. If additional data is found to be needed for specific capacity planning activities, you would go back and collect it using the techniques defined in one of the previous chapters.

The Requirements for Capacity Planning

Because capacity planning is an analytical process, it depends on the existence of data about the usage of your network, which is used to build the baseline model of the network. You must also have data about the applications you are studying: the traffic each one will generate (application profiles), the location of clients and servers, the number of users, and so on. Finally, you need a performance management tool that can use the data you supply to do "what-if" analyses or network modeling.

Baseline Data

The first requirement is that baseline data be available for your network, or at least that portion of the network that you plan to include in your capacity planning scenarios. Baselining is described in detail in Chapter 4, "Baselining Your Network." The data must include topology data (a network "map") that provides a model of the physical network showing the relative location of critical elements such as routers, local area networks (LANs), and circuits.

Your baseline data must also include at least one to two full days of usage-based data, and optionally application-based data, collected from the enterprise network. The data must span the time periods of interest to your study. This could range from an 8-hour business day (weekday), if significant activity happens only during those hours, to a full 24-hour period if your business is international or if significant activity happens during off hours. Usage-based data provides information about the volume of traffic for each leased-line circuit or Frame Relay permanent virtual circuit (PVC) in the network. Application-based data provides specifics about the applications that produce the traffic on the network, including a list of application types, the hosts that are communicating over the network, and the duration and volume of individual network conversations. The baselining process is all discussed in detail in Chapter 4.

Application Profiles

In order to create an additional "workload" representing a new (proposed) application, you must have application profiles for all the application transactions of interest. An application profile is constructed by looking at the traffic created by a specific application transaction, most commonly between a client and the application or database server. Your workload may include multiple profiles if you want to include more than one application transaction in your model. Application profiles are typically created for application transactions that are believed to have a high probability of occurring over the network (that is, are done relatively frequently) or that may generate a high volume of data when they occur (such as report generation or data replication). The methodology for creating application profiles is discussed in detail in Chapter 5, "Application Planning."

Application Usage Projections

If you are using capacity planning to model how a new enterprise application will behave on your network, you need to know how the application will be deployed and used in order to manipulate the workload on your network model. If you have followed the process laid out in this book, you would have researched and documented this information while you were undertaking the application assessment stage of the application planning activities described in Chapter 5. The exact information you need to know depends, of course, on the objectives of your NRP study and the questions you are attempting to answer.

Assuming you are looking at the effects of adding a typical two- or three-tier client/server enterprise application to your network, you will need to know the following:

▪ The location of the application servers and clients by country, city, or network address (LAN segment, closest router name, or whatever is sufficient to identify the locations relative to the elements on your baseline network topology map). This information is required so that you can allocate the additional workload from the new application to the correct circuits in your network topology map.

▪ The number of users at each location that will be running the application transactions. This information is used to create the workload volume attributable to the new application on any given circuit or LAN (between a given location and the application server).

- The frequency of use for each application transaction (in terms of one transaction every *x* seconds, if possible). This quantity is also used when creating the workload volume attributable to the new application.

- The test bed environments—specifically the scenarios that were used to create the application profiles. This information is needed to determine what capacity planning scenarios you should test. For example, if application profiles were created for a PeopleSoft application using a Citrix WinFrame client as well as a native PeopleSoft client, then you would need to create capacity planning scenarios to test both circumstances.

These are all elements that are needed to create capacity planning scenarios that model the deployment of a new enterprise application. The more closely these values approximate the actual deployment situation, the more realistic and useful the results will be from the "what-if" analyses performed using the scenarios.

Network Modeling Tool

The final requirement for capacity planning is the availability of a performance management tool that can do the analysis required for a "what-if" scenario. There are a number of tools available from various vendors that you can use. These include NetMaker XA from Make Systems, Inc.; the NETSYS Service Manager suite from Cisco Systems, Inc.; and the Optimal tool suite from Optimal Networks, and they are discussed in some detail in Appendix B, "Tools for Network Resource Planning." Whatever tool you choose, it must provide the following capabilities:

- The tool must be able to run a "what-if" analysis using analytical modeling techniques, discrete-event simulation, or the two techniques in combination. The pros and cons of each of the two types of analyses are discussed in some depth later in this chapter. Note that for the types of scenarios typically associated with Network Resource Planning as discussed in this book, a tool that can do analytical modeling is recommended.

- The tool must be able to create network conversations in the network model; that is, to add additional traffic onto the model that represents the conversations that a new application would add on the network.

■ The tool must be able to calculate and output the per-packet response time (or latency) for each network conversation as a result of the modeling or simulation.

The Capacity Planning Cycle

The goal of capacity planning as a component of Network Resource Planning is to look at possible enterprise application deployment scenarios to see how the network will behave under those conditions. Capacity planning methodologies do not require the collection of network data beyond what was collected during the baselining and application planning stages of NRP. The tasks comprised in the capacity planning cycle, as shown in Figure 6-2, depend on the network data collected in the other NRP phases.

The steps in the capacity planning cycle are

■ Create the baseline model to represent existing network usage.
  ▪ Start with the topology inventory created during the baselining phase.
  ▪ Identify the usage-based data sets (collected in the NRP baselining phase) that will provide the data for the model.

Figure 6-2
The capacity planning cycle.

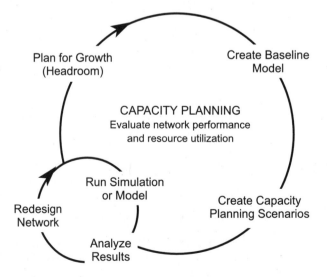

- Decide on the type of baseline model to use: worst-case, hybrid, or average, by traffic volume or by percent utilization of WAN circuits.
- Select the actual data points from your data set and import into a performance management tool that supports modeling or simulation.

- Create capacity planning scenarios.
  - Start with the baseline model created from usage-based data.
  - Use the information from the application usage scenarios (locations of users, number of users, transaction frequencies) to determine where and how to load the application profiles onto the baseline model.
  - Add the application profiles generated in the previous step to the baseline model to represent the additional traffic created by the applications under study.

- Run the model or simulation.
  - Use the performance management tool to run the model or simulation to completion.

- Analyze the results.
  - Look at the amount of delay for the target transactions in comparison to the quality-of-service goals established in the application planning phase.
  - Look at circuit utilization, especially for circuits where quality-of-service goals are not being met.

- Change the network design (if needed, depending on your objectives).
  - Identify modifications to the network infrastructure that will alter capacity usage of the network's resources. A redesign can include increasing or decreasing capacity, relocating application elements such as servers among existing network sites, or changing communications technology (moving from leased lines to Frame Relay circuits).
  - Modify the capacity planning scenarios to reflect these modifications.

- Plan for growth.
  - Assess known application development or deployment plans in terms of projected network impact.
  - Assess business conditions and plans in terms of their impact on the network from projected additional users, new sites, and other effects of the plans.
  - Use ongoing baselining techniques to watch usage trends over time, especially related to Internet and intranet usage.

Baseline Model Creation

For most of the capacity planning scenarios discussed in this chapter, baseline models are created using the existing network topology model and the usage-based data collected during the baselining phase of the NRP cycle. A baseline model created in this manner can be augmented with additional workload demands and can be redesigned in terms of circuit changes (size and type). These baseline models are not as useful for testing topology redesigns or redundancy because of the problem of determining how to redistribute the existing traffic (the usage-based data). The issues involved in topology redesign and redundancy planning are beyond the scope of this book, although they will be discussed further in the section on network redesign later in this chapter.

Figure 6-3 shows an existing network topology model as discovered using the Optimal Surveyor tool from Optimal Networks. For NRP purposes, capacity planning scenarios can be used to model different locations, among the existing enterprise network sites, for new application users and the associated new application servers and to redesign the network in terms of bandwidth between locations. However, the techniques discussed in this chapter assume that the network topology will *not* change from what existed when the baselining was done.

Figure 6-3

Network topology map. (© Optimal Networks.)

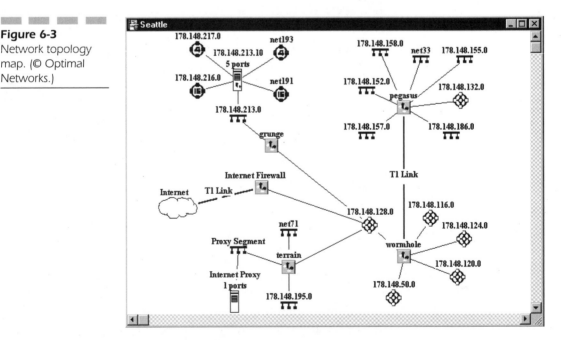

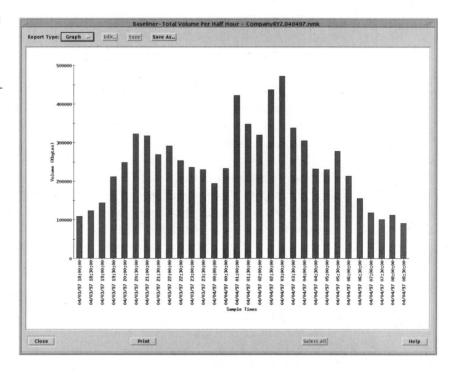

Figure 6-4
System volume chart.
(© Make Systems,
Inc.)

Figure 6-4 shows a view of usage-based data. A system volume chart such as this shows the total volume of data (in kilobytes) on the network over a given time period (15 hours, in this case). In this particular example, this data represents network activity for the business day in Asia, but it was collected at a location within the United States and therefore occurred during the night in local time. This data is useful for determining which hours to include in the data set you will use to create your baseline model, especially if the model will be built using some sort of average of volume or utilization. You will want to be sure that the samples over which you average include the data that represents the network conditions you want to model but does not include periods that might skew the baseline away from a valid representation of those conditions.

Making Assumptions

Creating the baseline model is probably the most critical step in the capacity planning process in terms of the validity of the results you get. Specifically, the assumptions you use in selecting the usage-based data for the model are critical to determining how well your results will represent what will actually occur on your network when your "what-if" scenario becomes implemented in reality.

In developing the baseline model, you are creating a snapshot in time of the usage of your network, in terms of either utilization (percentage of capacity used) or total volume of data. For planning purposes you need to decide whether this snapshot should represent a worst-case situation, an average situation, or something in between. How you elect to create your baseline model will depend on your NRP objectives and on the trade-offs you want to make in terms of maximizing performance (specifically, guaranteeing quality of service) versus costs. If it is critical that you maintain quality of service for the new application, even under peak load conditions, and cost is a secondary factor, then a conservative baseline model (based on peak utilization or volume) might be appropriate. If cost is a significant factor and you can tolerate occasional degradations in level of service, then a baseline based on average utilization or volume would be appropriate, allowing you to ensure quality of service under most conditions.

A very conservative model, based on peak utilization or volume, can lead to overcapacitation: excessive bandwidth capacity that is rarely used, leading to low usage under average utilization and volume conditions and high WAN transmission costs. Using average utilization or volume can lead to undercapacitation: insufficient bandwidth to handle loads at peak times, leading to saturated circuits and poor network performance. Unless your situation is unusual, you will probably want to create a baseline model that falls somewhere between these two extremes.

QUALITY OF SERVICE VERSUS COST   The goal of NRP is to ensure that distributed applications achieve an acceptable quality of service at minimum network cost. In deciding how to create the baseline model, you must decide how you will define "acceptable" quality of service versus "minimum" network cost.

In some situations, these goals may turn out not to be in conflict:; your network may support your quality-of-service goals (as established using the methods discussed in Chapter 5, "Application Planning") at costs that you consider reasonable and acceptable. However, in other situations you may need to trade off quality of service against cost. The monthly transmission costs of the network (leased lines, Frame Relay PVCs, and, in the future, public ATM) directly affect the bottom-line operating costs for an IT organization. Even a small percentage decrease in monthly transmission costs can produce significant savings, because the cost savings are realized month after month. In such a situation, the costs of capacitating the network to guarantee the highest levels of service may not be justified, especially if peak load conditions happen very rarely or not during mission-critical operations.

Increasing capacity to solve a performance problem often seems to be the obvious solution. However, it may not be the best solution, and it can lead you to pay for capacity that you rarely—in some cases never—use. Because network behavior is only one of the factors that affect application response time and throughput, adding bandwidth may not even solve the performance problems. If an application is performing poorly because of inadequate client or server capacity or inherent application design problems, adding bandwidth will not solve the problems; it may even make them worse. For example, if an application server is unable to process the data stream as fast as packets arrive, speeding up the arrival rate of packets by adding a higher-speed circuit will not help and, in fact, is likely to cause an increased rate of errors and retransmissions as the application server is even less able to keep up. For these reasons, it is important to understand the existing usage of the network and the behavior of the application of concern before implementing costly network capacity changes.

Baseline Model Creation Strategies

A network baseline model is a snapshot of a network's usage at a given point in time. When you create a model, you create a snapshot that represents the network under the conditions you want to test (average usage or volume, peak usage or volume, or something in between). You select the data for your baseline depending on your objectives for your planning, on the weight you give to cost versus guaranteed quality of service, and on the assumptions you make about the usage of your network. You can create models based either on utilization (percentage of capacity used) or on volume of usage (total bytes in a given sample period).

THE BASELINE AS AN ABSTRACTION FROM REALITY   The baseline you create for capacity planning purposes is indeed a "model" of the network. It is an abstraction from reality that represents the network in some way that meets your capacity planning goals: the "normal" network or the "worst-case" network, for example. In most cases, rather than simply using an actual baseline sample taken at a specific date and time (say, the values representing the usage and volume on the network on Tuesday at 11:05 A.M.), you select or generate data for each WAN circuit individually to build a model with the characteristics you want.

For example, if you want to create a baseline model that represents the worst-case usage of your network, you could select the one five-minute sample for each circuit that represented the highest utilization or volume on that circuit during the day, even though the peak samples occurred at different times of day on each circuit—say between 10:50 and 10:55 A.M. on circuit A, between 1:35 and 1:45 P.M. on circuit B, and so on. The result is a time-independent model that did not actually happen in reality, but models the condition, "What if every circuit on the network just happened to experience the maximum usage at the same time?"

Alternatively, you might construct your model by taking the average of all of the actual utilization values over a given time period (the 8-hour business day, a 24-hour period, three 8-hour days during the week, or whatever) and create your model that way. At any actual given time on your network, the values you would observe will vary somewhat from the average, but the model still represents a good hypothetical model of "normal" network behavior.

If these models are too extreme, you can construct a model using a "peak average" (called a *merged peak*), created by taking a number of peak values (the top 5, the top 12, or the top 24, for example) and averaging over just those samples to create a merged-peak model. Such a model has the advantage of allowing for the effects of possibly anomalous or nonrepeatable peak values while still modeling usage that tends toward peak usage. Depending on the number of samples you use to create your average, you can decide how conservative (how much toward the worst case) you want your model to be. This model is probably the most useful and is recommended for many situations.

Of course, it is also possible to select an actual set of samples for all circuits from a specific point in time on your network and use that as your model, if it meets your needs—especially if your network behavior is shown to be very consistent over time.

BASELINE MODEL EXAMPLES   The three figures in this section show three different types of baseline models based on utilization, created from the same set of sample data. In this example, the baseline data was collected over a 12-hour period (from 6:00 A.M. to 6:00 P.M. on a business day) with a sample interval of five minutes. Twelve hours of data were collected because the network under study spanned the continental United States, and data collection was done in the Central Time zone. Thus, data collection started at 7:00 A.M. for sites in the Eastern Time zone and ended at the equivalent of 4:00 P.M. in the Pacific Time zone.

The first example, Figure 6-5, shows peak utilization for selected WAN circuits. This model was created by selecting the single highest sample out of the 144 samples collected for each circuit during the 12-hour period. This models a completely worst-case scenario but has the drawback that this level of utilization may reflect anomalies (nonrepeatable occurrences).

Figure 6-6 shows merged-peak utilization values for the same WAN circuits shown in Figure 6-5. The utilization value for each circuit was calculated by averaging the top 12 samples (one hour's worth) out of the 144 usage-based samples taken for each circuit. These 12 samples had the highest total utilization after summing usage in both directions (forward and return). Comparing this model to the peak utilizations shown in Figure 6-5, it can be seen that averaging across multiple samples results in utilization values that are significantly lower than the single-peak values. This result supports the idea that the peak values may be overstating what would be more "normal" peak usage. This conclusion is supported further by the average circuit utilization values shown in Figure 6-7, again for the same WAN circuits as shown in Figures 6-5 and 6-6.

Figure 6-5
Peak utilization for selected circuits.

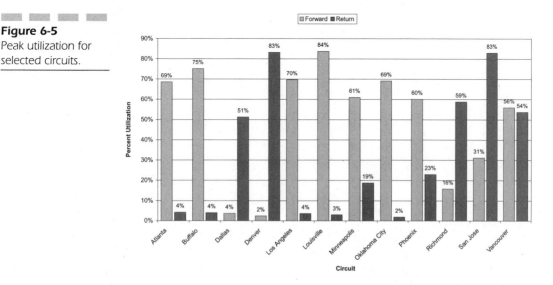

Figure 6-6
Merged-peak utilization for selected circuits.

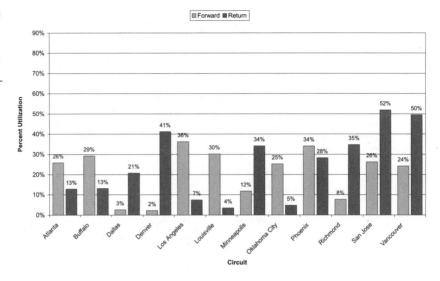

Figure 6-7
Average utilization for selected circuits.

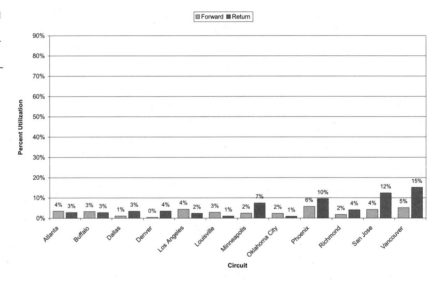

The utilization values shown in Figure 6-7 were created by averaging all 144 samples taken during the 12-hour business day for every circuit. The figure indicates that levels of peak utilization must be interspersed with significantly longer periods of much lower utilization on each circuit. Because of the long sampling period, this baseline model strategy incorporates several hours of low activity for each circuit, probably reflecting the hours before or after normal working hours at the location where the circuit terminates. To create a more accurate average usage baseline model for this particular network, you would probably need to create the average for each circuit using the eight hours representing the main business day for that location, based on its time zone or the most active hours.

CHOOSING THE RIGHT BASELINE MODEL CREATION STRATEGY Figures 6-5, 6-6, and 6-7 effectively illustrate how different baseline model creation strategies can create baseline models with dramatically different characteristics. The results of a "what-if" scenario will be significantly different depending on which baseline creation strategy you choose to use.

The key to creating a good baseline model is the validity of the data on which it is based. Because the baseline model is created from usage-based data you have collected during the baselining phase of the project, it is critical that you understand how well that data represents the reality of your network.

You have several strategies to choose from in creating a baseline model. The strategy you use depends both on your capacity planning objectives and on your understanding of your network usage data.

First, you need to make sure that the usage-based data you plan to use was collected during "active" periods on the network. If there are patterns of usage around business events or cycles, you want to take those into account so that your data reflects the most active day of the week, month, or quarter, depending on your objectives.

If your data shows great variation in usage—especially if there are dramatic spikes—you need to understand what causes those spikes before you decide how to incorporate their existence into your model. If the spikes are legitimate, repeatable network events, then you need to make sure that your baseline model does not attenuate their effects too much. If the spikes represent anomalies that can be eliminated by "fixing" whatever situation is causing them (for example, changing the time of a backup to a nonbusy hour), then you may want to choose a baseline model that does attenuate their effects. Again, your understanding of your network's behavior and of how well your data reflects that behavior is critical to creating a valid baseline model.

CREATE THE BASELINE FROM THE APPROPRIATE ACTIVE PERIODS You need to make sure to select the data for your baseline from times at which the network is doing activities relevant to your NRP goals. For example, if the application you are studying will be used only during normal business hours and from locations within the continental United States, then you would want to create your baseline model based on data during the 12 hours of each weekday that represent business hours across the United States. If you are creating a baseline model based on average usage, you would not include the other 12 hours of each day, because the reduced usage during those "off" hours would result in a baseline that underrepresents the average usage during the business day. Even if you are creating a baseline model using a merged-peak or peak strategy, you still probably would not want to include the "off" hours, although it is unlikely that the peak samples would occur during those times on any circuit.

Figure 6-8 shows an example of total system volume over a 24-hour period for an enterprise network, in half-hour increments from 4:30 P.M. to 6:00 P.M. the following day. Clearly, the volume of usage during business hours is quite different from that seen during "off" hours. Thus, in such a case you would probably want to use data from the most active hours of the business day to create your baseline model. In particular, if you were going to create a model based on average usage, you definitely would not want to include the low-volume "off" hours, because the model would then seriously underrepresent the usage during the more active business day.

On the other hand, in some cases, backup or batch traffic that occurs during "off" hours might skew the average in the opposite direc-

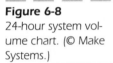

Figure 6-8
24-hour system volume chart. (© Make Systems.)

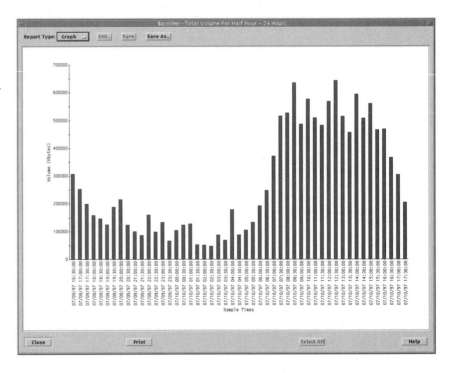

tion (overrepresenting the average usage) on some backbone circuits, even though it would normally have no effect on business traffic occurring during the day. In the same way, if you are using peak usage data, you want to make sure that the peaks you select occur during times when they could affect the new application traffic. You would want to include "off" hour traffic only if you are interested in the behavior or effects of a backup or of batch traffic. In that case you would create your baseline from usage-based data taken during time periods when that activity would typically occur.

You also want to make sure to select data from days of the week that represent the most active days, based on the business cycles of your organization. Depending on the goals of your capacity planning activities, you might want to select usage-based data from the middle of the week if those are the most active days. Or you may create your baseline based on the end of the week, end of the month, end of the quarter, or any other days when enterprise network usage might be particularly high based on the business cycles and uses of the network.

EVALUATE YOUR RESULTS CRITICALLY The validity of your baseline model as a representation of your actual network behavior is critical to the reliability and usefulness of the results from your capacity planning activities. When you document the results of your capacity planning activities, you must be sure to document the assumptions you used to build the baseline model so that the results can be understood in the correct context. For example, if you used a peak usage baseline model and the capacity planning results show that every circuit needs to be upgraded, it is critical that you understand the assumptions behind the peak usage model in order to understand the possibly extreme results. In such a case, the model based on peak usage may need to be challenged, and additional analysis may need to be done using a less conservative model to see how the results compare.

In general, if the results of your capacity planning activities are not what you expect, or if they do not make sense based on your knowledge of the characteristics of the network, you should definitely reexamine the assumptions and methods you used to create your baseline model. As a network manager you probably have a basic "understanding" of your network and can probably tell when results make sense and when they do not. If you were using a peak usage model, you should probably reevaluate the peak samples to make sure that they represent legitimate activity and that they were taken from relevant time periods. For a model based on averages, you need to ensure that the data used to compute the average spanned the appropriate time periods. Basically, your capacity planning results are only as good as the assumptions on which they are based, so you should look at those assumptions with a critical eye.

Appendix A, "Baseline Model Creation Strategies," discusses in detail the strategies for creating baseline models as well as the advantages and disadvantages of each strategy.

The Benefit of Creating Multiple Baseline Models

Each strategy for baseline model creation has its strengths and weaknesses, and the validity of an individual baseline model is highly dependent on the validity of the baseline data used to create it. The use of multiple baseline models of the same type, created using data from different time periods (multiple days, for example) is a good technique for checking the validity of the results you get from any one model. If the results are consistent (within 5 to 10%) day to day, the model is probably a valid representation of the network, given the assumptions for that strategy.

However, it may also be valuable to create multiple baseline models using several different strategies and comparing the results from the different methods. For example, you could create baseline models using the peak usage strategy, the merged-peak usage strategy, and the average usage baseline strategy and compare the resulting circuit utilizations for each model type. This would give you a good idea of the range of variation in your network between peak activity, averaged peak activity, and "normal" or average activity. Although it might take a lot of effort to set up these models (especially if your performance management tool cannot do the average calculations for you), comparing the results can give you a very good idea of exactly the trade-offs you might need to make in terms of the transmission costs for capacitating your network versus application quality-of-service guarantees.

Creating Capacity Planning Scenarios

A capacity planning scenario is the description of the predicted usage of the network by an application (usually an application planned to be added to the network) in terms of the location of application users and application or database servers, the number of users at each location, and the frequency with which each user will execute the application transactions under study. The scenario is implemented on top of a network baseline model by using a performance management tool to add network conversations that represent the new application traffic between locations on the network. The network conversations to be added are based on the application profiles created for specific transactions a user would perform using the application, as defined during the application planning phase of the NRP project. The information (number of users, locations, and so on) that defines the application usage is also investigated and documented during the application planning phase (see Chapter 5, "Application Planning").

A capacity planning scenario can describe an application in any phase of deployment—in the preimplementation phase, the rollout and validation phase, or in the life cycle management phase (see Chapter 2, "The Network Resource Planning Process").

Requirements for Creating Capacity Planning Scenarios

In order to create a capacity planning scenario (that is, to add network conversations to your baseline model to reflect the new application traffic), you need to make several assumptions about how the new application will be deployed and used. This information ideally will have been investigated and documented, if possible, during the application planning phase of your NRP project, as discussed in Chapter 5.

LOCATION OF APPLICATION-RELATED SERVERS AND CLIENTS You need to determine the location of each proposed (or existing) server in terms of the LAN (the IP subnet address), the closest router, or, at a minimum, the city and country in which it will be located. This information is required in order to identify the server end points for the network conversations to be added to the model.

You also need to know the location of the proposed application clients by LAN (IP subnet address), closest router, or city and country. As for the servers, this information is needed to identify the client end points for the network conversations you will be adding to the model.

If there are multiple server locations, you need to know which client locations will use which server locations so that you can allocate the new conversations between the correct end points.

FREQUENCY OF USE PER USER OF APPLICATION TRANSAC-TIONS For each transaction to be used in the capacity planning scenario, you must know the frequency of use in terms of the number of application transactions an individual user would be expected to perform within a given time frame. The transactions are those defined in the application planning phase of the NRP project, for which application profiles were created (as discussed at length in Chapter 5).

For example, if you will be adding conversations based on an application profile of a General Ledger journal edit transaction, then the frequency of interest would be how often any one user would execute a journal edit transaction. If a normal user could be expected to do a journal edit once every five minutes, then the transaction rate in transactions per *second* would be 0.0033 transactions per second (1 transaction/5 minutes, or 1/300 seconds).

DURATION OF TRANSACTION ACTIVITY You must know the actual duration of the transaction activity, as measured during the application planning phase of the project. This information is important when predicting the user transaction rate, because it puts a lower limit on the transaction rate a user can achieve. The time value used to calculate the transaction rate must not be less than the actual duration of the activity within the environment where the activity will occur. For example, under ideal conditions (running over a LAN), it might be possible for a user to do one transaction every two minutes. However, in a given WAN environment, the actual measured duration of the activity (the duration of the conversation due to the activity) might be five minutes, so the maximum transaction rate (the fastest possible rate at which a single user can execute the transaction) must be based on five minutes rather than two minutes.

THE NUMBER OF USERS AT EACH LOCATION Finally, you must know the number of predicted simultaneous network conversations for every location (site) to be modeled. These numbers are calculated based on the total number of users that could possibly use the application simultaneously at a given location.

For example, if a particular location is projected to have five users for the new application, then the possible number of simultaneous conversations would be 5. In reality, all five users might not normally be expected to use the application at the same time, so five simultaneous users would constitute a "peak activity" scenario. If the new application is a financial application such as General Ledger, and you are modeling end-of-month or end-of-quarter activity, modeling all five users simultaneously might be an appropriate scenario. Otherwise, you may decide to use a lower number of simultaneous users or reduce the frequency of use per user.

For a new application, you may be able to predict its usage in terms of the business functions the application will be providing, rather than as a function of the number of users. For example, given the volume of business at a certain location, you may be able to predict a certain number of order entry transactions each day, based on the volume of orders that the site currently processes by whatever method is in use prior to the new application's implementation. You can then use this to calculate a number of simultaneous users and a frequency-of-use metric for a given time period that may be independent of the number of users that could potentially use the application.

EXAMPLE APPLICATION USAGE SCENARIO Figure 6-9 shows a portion of an application usage scenario for three modules of a proposed SAP R/3 implementation. This chart shows the client locations in terms of city and state as well as the router. This usage scenario includes distributed application servers, so the column titled "Region" shows the

Figure 6-9

Sample application usage scenario for SAP R/3 modules.

Router	Office Name	State	Region	# Employees	FI (GL) Users	FI (AP) Users	HR Users
rtr829	Knoxville	TN	Norfolk	20	4	2	0
rtr850	New Orleans	LA	Norfolk	20	4	2	0
rtr862	Norfolk	VA	Norfolk	60	12	7	1
rtr818	Raleigh	NC	Norfolk	10	2	1	0
rtr863	Richmond	VA	Norfolk	35	7	4	1
rtr819	Roanoke	VA	Norfolk	55	11	7	1
rtr864	Wilmington, DE.	DE	Norfolk	30	6	4	1
rtr823	Winston-Salem	NC	Norfolk	10	2	1	0
rtr883	Appleton	WI	St. Louis	9	2	1	0
rtr886	Davenport	IA	St. Louis	20	4	2	0
rtr807	Des Moines	IA	St. Louis	17	3	2	0
rtr857	Fresno	CA	St. Louis	15	3	2	0
rtr888	Madison	WI	St. Louis	36	7	4	1
rtr805	Memphis	TN	St. Louis	50	10	6	1
rtr889	Milwaukee	WI	St. Louis	18	4	2	0
rtr806	St. Louis	MO	St. Louis	65	13	8	2
rtr882	Akron-Canton	OH	Hartford	5	1	1	0
rtr866	Boston	MA	Hartford	50	10	6	1
rtr875	Cincinnati	OH	Hartford	30	6	4	1
rtr876	Cleveland	OH	Hartford	40	8	5	1
rtr918	Columbus	OH	Hartford	35	7	4	1
rtr877	Dayton	OH	Hartford	30	6	4	1
rtr867	Hartford	CT	Hartford	50	10	6	1
rtr868	New Haven	CT	Hartford	5	1	1	0
rtr843	North Jersey - Sales	NJ	Hartford	85	17	10	2
rtr870	Portland ME	ME	Hartford	5	1	1	0
rtr869	Providence	RI	Hartford	20	4	2	0

location of the application server that the client site will home to. The remaining columns show the total number of employees at each site and the projected number of users for each of the application modules.

Note that the information as just described assumes that the network activity of interest is between clients and servers in a two- or three-tier client/server application. If you are looking at traffic between servers (a subject not really covered in any detail in this book), you still need to know the locations of the end points of the network conversations between the servers, plus information that will let you apply the server profile conversation data with the appropriate frequency on the relevant circuits.

Scenario Assumptions That Affect Capacity Planning Outcomes

The assumptions you use to load network conversation data onto your baseline model will have a big effect on the outcome of your capacity planning activities. When you obtain and document the results of your capacity planning analyses, you need to document the assumptions that underlie each scenario carefully. The results are only as valid as the assumptions that went into them.

NUMBER OF SIMULTANEOUS USERS The number of simultaneous users you project for each location in your model is an important assumption, because it directly affects the volume of traffic that will be added on the circuits for each location. Traffic attributed to simultaneous users is added to the network in an aggregated way. For example, if you specify the simultaneous number of users to be 10, then the load added to the network (in bits per second) will be ten times the load for a single user. If the *actual* number of users *at any one time* will never be greater than 5 (even if there are 10 employees at a location who use the application), then your projection for usage due to the new application on that circuit will be twice as high as what will actually occur, and the results in terms of needed capacity would be overstated.

TRANSACTION RATE PER USER The transaction rate (number of transactions per user) is also an important assumption that can cause invalid results if it is projected erroneously. The transaction rate is used as a multiplier for calculating the network load based on the traffic profile created for the transaction in question. The network load in one direction (in bits per second) attributable to a single user for a given transaction and transaction rate is calculated as follows:

$$Load = (Number\ of\ bytes\ in\ one\ direction) \times \left(\frac{8\ bits}{byte}\right) \times (transaction\ rate\ in\ seconds)$$

The number of bytes in any one direction is the number of bytes determined by the application profiling process for the transaction in question. The load is calculated for each direction separately. From this equation it can be seen that the transaction rate determines the network load that a single user will be assumed to add to the network. Again, if the predicted transaction rate (frequency of use) is too high, the load added to the network will be too high, and your results will be wrong. Combining overestimates for both transaction rates and simultaneous numbers of users can result in network loads attributed to the new application that far exceed reality and could lead to capacity planning results that could cause overcapacitation of the network, and thus to excessive transmission costs.

Using Multiple Scenarios

Ideally, it is a good idea to create multiple capacity planning scenarios using worst-case and "normal case" estimates, and compare the two. If you do not have high confidence in your estimates for frequency of use (transaction rates) or number of simultaneous users, you may want to test several variations of a possible normal or worst-case scenario. You may also want to create scenarios specifically for special business events such as month-end, quarter-end, and year-end close, as well as to simulate a crisis situation that would generate extraordinary network traffic demands, such as a natural disaster for a gas, electric, or telephone utility, or the Hong Kong stock market slide in October 1997 for stock brokerages. Again, in these cases the validity of the results is only as good as the validity of the assumptions on which the results are based.

Using a Performance Management Tool to Create Scenarios

In order to create the capacity planning scenarios for analysis, you must have a performance management tool that has the ability to create a "network conversation" within the network model (your baseline model). The data you need to create a network conversation comes from the application profiles you created using the techniques discussed in Chapter 5, "Application Planning." You need the following data for each application transaction you will be using in your scenario:

■ The direction of flow for the data (from client to server or from server to client)

■ The type of LAN the data was collected on (Ethernet, Token Ring, or FDDI, for example)

■ The networking protocol used (typically IP for client/server applications such as SAP R/3, PeopleSoft, or BAAN IV)

■ The average packet size, in bytes, for both the forward and return directions

■ The average size, in bytes, of the data for the complete transaction, for both the forward and return directions

■ The average duration of the transaction, for both LAN and WAN environments, if possible

■ The transaction rate for a single user

Figure 6-10 shows some of this data for a set of PeopleSoft application profiles, as discussed in Chapter 5.

You should be able to input these values into the appropriate area of your performance management tool to create a profile for the transaction. Exactly how this is done will depend on the tool you are using. Figure 6-11 shows a panel within Make Systems' NetMaker XA Visualizer tool that performs this function, using one of the transactions shown in Figure 6-10. With some tools, such as those that do discrete-event analysis, additional data beyond that in the list above may be needed, such as packet size variation and packet and conversation interarrival times. This additional data may also be needed for future analytical models that support ATM.

Figure 6-10

Sample application profile. (© Make Systems, Inc.)

Profile Name	Source	Destination	Bytes-Fwd	Bytes-Rtn	Trans Rate 1 per 5 min.	Kbps Fwd 5-min avg	Kbps Rtn 5-min avg
Native Peoplesoft Logon	client	server	62000	780000	0.0033	1.64	20.59
Native Peoplesoft Journal Query	client	server	82450	775811	0.0033	2.18	20.48
Native Peoplesoft Create Req.	client	server	140399	804532	0.0033	3.71	21.24
Citrix PeopleSoft Logon	client	server	13069	67887	0.0033	0.35	1.79
Citrix PeopleSoft Journal Query	client	server	19423	56389	0.0033	0.51	1.49
Citrix PeopleSoft Create Req.	client	server	13845	50919	0.0033	0.37	1.34

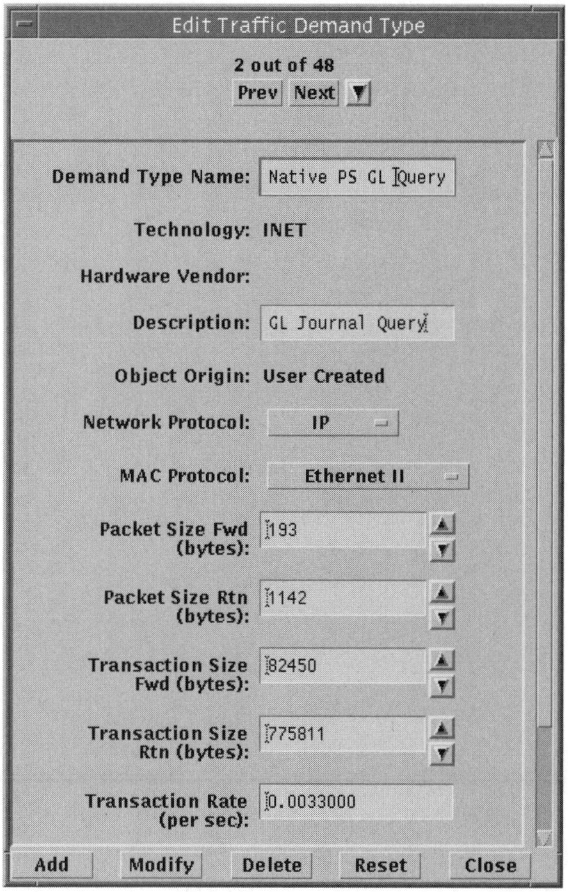

Figure 6-11
Application profile
creation within
NetMaker XA.

Once the transaction profiles are configured into the performance management tool, you then use the tool to configure a network conversation for each transaction, using the profiles to represent the transaction characteristics for the application and specifying the end points (location of clients and server). The performance management tool will create a network conversation between the client and server that is based on the profile (the single-user application activity characteristics) multiplied by the number of simultaneous users at that location. The end points for the network conversations can be LANs (identified by IP subnet address), or actual hosts if your performance management tool supports the ability to model servers and client workstations. Figure 6-12 shows an example of how this is done using Make Systems' NetMaker XA Visualizer tool.

Figure 6-12
Adding a conversation based on a traffic profile with NetMaker XA.

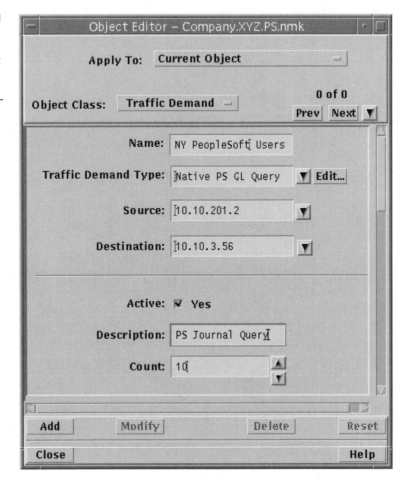

CREATING CONVERSATIONS BETWEEN THE CORRECT SOURCE AND DESTINATION When creating the network conversations, it is very important to specify correctly which end point is the source and which is the destination. The application profile dictates which end point (the client or server) is considered the source and which is considered the destination, based on the way the profile was created. It is important to be consistent in how you model these flows. In many cases the volume of data will be very different from client to server than from server to client. Often there is a much larger volume of data flowing from the server to the client than in the other direction. If your application transactions are characterized by this type of unequal data flow, it is important that the flows do not get reversed.

Otherwise, you will produce results that capacitate the model incorrectly.

Once you have created all the conversations arising from your new application, you now have a model of your network that includes the baseline traffic (existing network activity) and the additional traffic due to the new application. This capacity planning scenario can now be used as the basis for analysis to answer various questions, such as "What kind of per-packet response rate can I expect for the new application transactions under these conditions? Is the existing bandwidth sufficient to support a reasonable quality of service for users of the new application? Will any circuits become saturated under these conditions?"

If you are deploying multiple new applications at the same time, you may want to add conversations representing transactions from all the new applications, to see what the aggregate effects might be on the behavior of your enterprise network. You may also elect to study the effects of each new application separately.

Running the "What-If" Analysis for Capacity Planning

Once you have built your network baseline model and loaded new application traffic based on the capacity planning scenario you want to test, you are ready to use a performance management tool to run a "what-if" analysis of your scenario.

There are two basic types of analyses you can run: an analytical modeling analysis, and a discrete-event simulation analysis. Performance management tools that do "what-if" analysis are based for the most part on one or the other of these techniques, so it is important that you understand the benefits and drawbacks of each type of analysis before you select your performance management tool. Some performance management tools use a hybrid analysis model; for example, using analytical modeling for queueing but simulation for routing. The two basic types of analysis were discussed earlier in this book, in Chapter 2, "The Network Resource Planning Process," to help you determine how to select the appropriate tool for your needs.

It is not the intention in this book to discuss the theory or mathematics of these two methods for "what-if" analysis. However, it is important to understand the basics about the two methodologies in order to determine which methodology is right for meeting your capacity planning objectives. This also provides a context for evaluating the strength and validity of the results you obtain.

Basically, the type of "what-if" analysis you choose will determine the amount of time it takes to obtain results from the analysis. It also determines the size of the network (number of components) you can analyze, the level of detail with which you can manipulate the processes or models within the tool, and the level of detail in the results returned from the simulation or modeling effort. For the types of capacity planning scenarios described in this chapter, analytical modeling techniques (or a hybrid model) will generally be more useful than a discrete-event simulation technique, because of the need to model enterprise networks that could have tens or hundreds of network locations and users.

Discrete-Event Simulation

Discrete-event simulation is a technique that simulates the movement of traffic through the network by "following" events through the network. Using a packet as an event, a discrete-event simulation runs each packet through a group of processes that define different types of devices and traffic sources (bridges, routers, switches, servers) on the network. As packets continually "run" through this process, the simulation should eventually be able to converge to a single value for the effects that the packet traffic has on such metrics as average queue delay, per-packet response time through the system, or device utilization. The simulation must be able to run for a long enough period of time that the behavior of the devices you are simulating can stabilize; you do not want to base your results on the transient behavior of the devices as you start up the simulation.

THE STRENGTHS OF DISCRETE-EVENT SIMULATION The benefit of discrete-event simulation is that you can get a very detailed and accurate look at the behavior of your network (assuming that you can get your results to converge in a reasonable amount of time), because you are actually simulating the function of the network, process by process and packet by packet. Because discrete-event simulation tools also let you control the process models (such as the traffic flow into and out of the various devices), you can look at the effects of very specific manipulations, such as protocol flow control, changes in queue or buffer sizes, queuing priorities, or other very discrete configurations.

For example, if you were testing the performance of an application and wanted to look at the effects of varying the protocol windowing (the number of packets that you can send before an ACK is required) a discrete-event simulation analysis would be appropriate, because it would let you control each packet. You could manipulate the model of the receiver to change its windowing and then see exactly what effects this change has on how efficiently packets are handled.

THE DISADVANTAGES OF DISCRETE-EVENT SIMULATION
The drawback with discrete-event simulation is that it requires a significant amount of computational power—at least one CPU cycle per process per packet. Running a small simulation on a network of around 10 sites and a few hundred conversations could take several days, based on certain assumptions. Because of this limitation, discrete-event simulation is probably not the best choice for doing "what-if" analyses on the types of capacity planning scenarios this book describes, which mostly deal with much larger enterprise networks and traffic sets.

Analytical Modeling

Analytical modeling uses a set of formulas that describe a network's behavior (modeling such things as router output queues and traffic flows), to solve for unknowns such as bandwidth utilization and packet latency through the network. Parameters such as the average packet sizes, the number of packets per second, and the assumed arrival time between packets and between conversations are used in today's analytical modeling algorithms.

Ideally, you should get similar results for the metrics of interest, such as packet latency or bandwidth utilization, to those you would get from the convergence results of a discrete-event simulation using the same capacity planning scenario, assuming that everything could be configured the same. In the case of analytical modeling, the tool uses an equation to model what happens to the packets as they go through the processes on the network and then solves the equation, rather than "watching" the progress of each packet.

THE STRENGTHS OF ANALYTICAL MODELING The strength of analytical modeling is that it is computationally fast, and therefore can be used to model the behavior of large enterprise networks. You can use analytical modeling to predict packet latencies or bandwidth utilization on a large number of network components (WAN circuits,

LANs, routers, hosts, and so forth) in a network at the same time. This capability lets you analyze capacity planning scenarios that model the deployment of a new application with hundreds of client sites, with tens of users at each site—exactly the types of scenarios described in this book.

THE DISADVANTAGES OF ANALYTICAL MODELING   A disadvantage of analytical modeling is that a number of simplifying assumptions are required in order to use equations to model the network behavior. Thus, the model may not be able to account for all the complexities that a network device or application might exhibit. This means that the results may not be quite as accurate (precise) as the results of a discrete-event simulation. However, as a rule the modeled results will approximate the actual results to a degree that is quite sufficient for most capacity planning purposes.

The accuracy of any results, regardless of the method used, must be understood in the context of the accuracy of the assumptions that went into creating the baseline model and the capacity planning scenario. In many cases these assumptions, such as the characteristics of "typical" baseline network usage, the characteristics of a "typical" application activity, the projected number of users, and the frequency of use, are projections based on best guess estimates, which in themselves lack accuracy. Thus, a high level of accuracy in the computational techniques used for the simulation or modeling analysis is in a sense "wasted" by being applied to data that is not necessarily very accurate.

Another drawback to analytical modeling is that you typically do not have control over the model's equations used within a given performance management tool. For example, you may feel that the queueing model for the behavior of the queue at the output of a specific router is not correct, but you may not be able to change the model. Most of the time you are dependent on the vendor's expertise built into the product you are using.

Performance Management Tool Requirements

The first requirement in a performance management tool is that it can perform one of the types of "what-if" analyses described in the preceding paragraphs. It is very important that you understand what type of analysis the tool you have chosen does, because this determines the types of "what-if" analyses you can run. Ideally, you should understand before you purchase it how the performance management tool will support your NRP goals. However, if you do not have a choice as to the performance management tool available, then an understanding of the type of analysis your tool supports (analytical, discrete event, or a hybrid) will help you determine whether you can create workable scenarios that can be analyzed effectively.

As discussed earlier, not all tools will support a "what-if" analysis on a large enterprise network with tens or hundreds of sites and many users. If you must use a tool that is not optimal, you may need to revise your capacity planning objectives to focus on smaller, more narrow scenarios. For example, if you must use a tool that does only discrete-event simulation, you could create a scenario that models a small number of specific client locations (or even just one) at a time, carefully selected so that the results of the simulation can help you understand what impact the application you are studying might have on other locations with similar characteristics.

Regardless of the type of "what-if" analysis the tool can perform, as a result of its simulation or modeling analysis it must be able to calculate and report on the following:

- The routing of the network conversations as simulated by the performance management tool: how the conversation gets from point A to point B. This must include each component (hosts, routers, switches, LANs, WAN circuits, and even concentrators if the performance management tool supports them) through which the conversation passes.
- Bandwidth utilization for all network components within the model (WAN circuits, LANs, routers, switches, and hosts). Some performance management tools may support a subset of these network components.
- Per-packet response time (in both the forward and return directions) for each network conversation (typically, the conversations related to the new application you are studying).

The next few sections discuss how the performance management tools calculate these metrics.

Calculating the Route on a Per-Packet Basis

In a real network, a packet's route from a source to a destination is determined by the router or switch, based on the address of the destination and a set of routing tables, which tell the router or switch which inter-face to use to forward the packet on toward the destination. If the net-work segment associated with that router or switch interface does not directly connect to the destination, then when the packet reaches the next router, the route determination is done again based on that router or switch's routing tables, and so on for every "hop" the packet makes until it reaches the destination. This process is repeated for each packet in the conversation.

In general, all packets between a given source and destination will always take the same route, based on the routing tables of the devices along the path. The configurations of the routing tables do not nor-mally change unless a network component in the route changes.

Changes to the route of the packets could be due to changes to the routing protocol used by the routers or switches, changes in circuit size, or connectivity changes (adding sites or routes or physical changes to the network topology). However, it is unlikely that these changes would occur in the middle of a network conversation.

Routing changes could also occur because of a failure of a compo-nent in the path. In that case the routers or switches in the path would either converge to a new route for the destination, using their routing tables, or else designate the destination as unreachable because there is not a secondary route available. If such a failure occurs in the middle of a network conversation, then once the routing tables have con-verged to a new route, the subsequent packets will take a different route from the source to the destination than the packets did prior to the failure.

Routers or switches calculate a route through the network based on the routing protocol that is being used in the enterprise system. For example, for an IP packet–based network the protocol might be RIP (Routing Information Protocol), OSPF (Open Shortest Path First), IGRP (Internet Gateway Routing Protocol), or BGP (Border Gateway Proto-col). IPX networks use a RIP-like protocol, and networks running DEC-net can use DECnet Phase IV routing. Many networks use multiple routing protocols (IGRP and IPX-RIP, for example), and individual interfaces on one router can run different routing protocols. The algo-rithms for the various routing protocols are different (for example, OSPF requires an "OSPF Cost" for each interface, RIP requires a hop count for each interface), so each router or switch must be configured correctly based on the routing protocols it is using. These configura-tions are usually static within the router or switch and do not change dynamically. They usually must be manually reconfigured to change.

SIMULATED ROUTING USING A PERFORMANCE MANAGE-MENT TOOL The performance management tool, whether it uses analytical modeling or discrete-event simulation, must be able to simulate the process of determining the route through the network in the same way as the routers or switches do it, packet by packet. This means that each routing component within the network model must be configured with the correct routing protocols and routing protocol metrics, exactly as the devices in the real network are configured. Depending on the performance management tool you are using, the router or switch configurations can be learned during a network "discovery" process (as discussed in Chapter 4, "Baselining the Network"), imported using the router configuration files, or input manually.

In addition to calculating the route for every packet individually, the performance management tool must also be able to simulate the failure of a router, switch, WAN circuit, or LAN; calculate a new route; and reconfigure the simulated routing tables as the real routers or switches would as they converge to a new route.

You need to ensure that the performance management tool you have available (or plan to purchase) can support all the routing protocols that you plan to use in your real enterprise network, including any customizations you may have made to the routing protocols. Most tools support hop-based routing (similar to RIP) and SPF (Shortest Path First) routing similar to OSPF, but those may not be sufficient for your needs. For example, if your network uses IGRP (which is similar to, but not exactly like, generic hop-based routing), you must be able to "configure" IGRP for the router and router interface components within your network model, or else the routes calculated by the performance management tool will not be correct.

Calculated Bandwidth Utilization

Bandwidth utilization is the ratio of the total traffic load on a circuit to the full capacity of the circuit. The performance management tool calculates WAN circuit utilization based on the various traffic "demands" that impact each leased line or Frame Relay PVC.

For NRP purposes, an individual traffic demand is the amount of bandwidth needed by a network conversation. In a capacity planning scenario, the total traffic load on a circuit is made up of a combination of usage-based baseline traffic, representing the traffic demands that already exist on the network, plus the new traffic demands resulting from the new application you are studying. The issues around loading traffic data into the capacity planning model were discussed in some detail earlier in this chapter.

The percentage utilization for each WAN circuit is calculated using the following equation:

$$\% \text{ utilization } = \frac{\sum (avg. \text{ bps for each traffic demand})}{speed \text{ of the media (bps)}} \times 100\%$$

The traffic demands are the conversations attributable to the new application and any usage data representing baseline usage of that circuit. Which packets get placed onto which circuits is a function of the route that the performance management tool calculates to get the conversation traffic from its source to its destination. The route is calculated by routing the packets of the conversation through the network from source host to destination host using a particular routing algorithm, such as RIP or OSPF for IP packet traffic. The routing components in your network model must have been configured correctly for these protocols, and the performance management tool must support the appropriate route calculation algorithms. If these conditions are not met, the calculations for bandwidth utilization for the different network components will be wrong.

Reporting Utilization Values

The utilization figures for WAN circuits need to be reported in both the forward and return directions, because most WAN links are full-duplex (that is, each direction is effectively an independent circuit requiring an independent utilization calculation). For example, a 56Kbps circuit really has 56Kbps capacity in each direction, and the utilization in one direction does not directly affect utilization in the other direction.

The bandwidth utilization for a LAN is calculated and reported in the same way as for a WAN circuit, except that the utilization is reported as a percent of total LAN bandwidth. Because LANs are typically not full-duplex (conversations in either direction share the same capacity), direction is not an issue. This characteristic may change in the future with full-duplex Ethernet cards and new LAN switches.

The performance management tool can also calculate utilization for a router or other internetworking device. Router performance is typically reported as at least two metrics. One is the forwarding rate in packets per second (pps), calculated as how many packets per second the router is forwarding compared to its capacity (the maximum throughput the router can achieve). The other is the percentage of the backplane used, in megabits or gigabits per second (Mbps or Gbps).

Per-Packet Response Time

The per-packet response time is calculated by a performance management tool as the sum of all the delays in the forward route of a packet as it makes it way from the source host to the destination host, plus all the delays in the return path as the packet makes it way from the destination host back to the source host. The results can be reported as separate forward and return delays or response times, which can be summed to create a round-trip delay (RTD) in seconds or milliseconds.

It is important to note that the response time calculated in this way is strictly the delay due to the network—it does not take into account additional processing delays within either the client or the server (see Figure 6-13). The RTD calculated in this fashion by the performance management tool can be used to evaluate whether your quality-of-service goals are being met, as determined during your application planning activities, because the metrics you generate for acceptable quality-of-service goals (as defined in Chapter 5) are also in terms of the network component of the round-trip delay.

However, the *acceptability* of the quality of service as judged by the user *does* include the performance of the other components (client and server). Thus, it is important that the behavior (in terms of added delay) of the application client and server components in your application planning test bed be very similar to the behavior of those same components as they would be deployed in the real enterprise network. Otherwise, the same network RTD that allowed acceptable quality of service in your test bed environment might produce unacceptable quality of

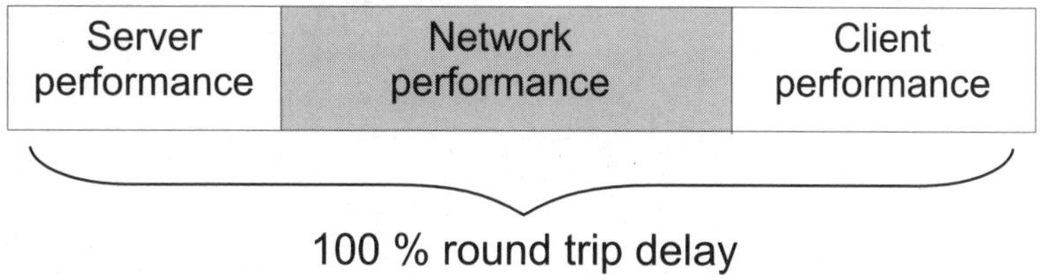

Figure 6-13
The components of quality of service.

| Server performance | Network performance | Client performance |

100 % round trip delay

service under actual network conditions. For example, if you tested your application with a small test database running on a dedicated test database server, the server process response times it returned might be dramatically different from those you will see when the application is making requests to a fully deployed corporate database being shared by multiple applications. In that case, the server performance component could degrade dramatically and overwhelm the effects of the acceptable network performance component.

Calculating Response Time

For most of the discussions in this section we will discuss per-packet response time in terms of separate forward and return delays. The components of (or contributors to) per-packet response time in a given direction include the characteristics of the network devices in the route of the packet (circuit types/sizes and LAN types) and congestion in the path (the inability of an internetworking device to forward the packet immediately). Congestion is usually caused by an output buffer or queue in an internetworking device needing to hold the packet for some amount of time beyond what it would normally take to insert the bits onto the circuit (transmission time).

The diagram in Figure 6-14 shows the source of significant potential delays in a packet's progress from a client to a server across a WAN. In this case the direction from client to server is considered the forward direction. The forward delay is calculated as

$$Forward\ delay = D_1 + D_2 + D_3 + D_4 + D_5 + D_6 + D_7$$

Figure 6-14

The components of a forward delay.

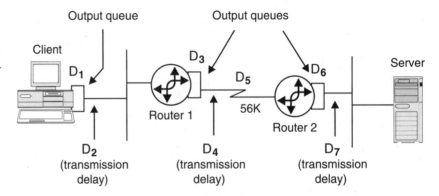

The significant components of the delay are as follows:

- A possible queue delay coming out of the client workstation if the LAN has high utilization, shown as D_1 in the diagram.

- Transmission delay per packet, which is a function of the packet size and the characteristics of the type of media the packet is being forwarded onto (also known as insertion delay), shown in the diagram as D_2. Assuming the LAN is a 10Mbps Ethernet, the transmission delay per packet would be calculated as

$$D_2 = \textit{(packet size in bytes} \times \textit{8 bits/byte)/10 Mbps}$$

- A possible queue delay at the output of Router 1 if the WAN circuit has high utilization, shown in the diagram as D_3

- Transmission delay per packet due to insertion of the bits onto the 56Kbps circuit, shown as D_4 in the diagram, and calculated for packets as

$$D_4 = \textit{(packet size in bytes} \times \textit{8 bits/byte)/56 Kbps}$$

- Propagation delay for each bit in the packet as it travels between Router 1 and Router 2 (because bits cannot move faster than the speed of light), shown in the diagram as D_5

- A possible queue delay at the output of Router 2 if the destination LAN has high utilization, shown in the diagram as D_6

- Transmission delay per packet due to insertion onto the destination 10Mbps Ethernet LAN, shown as D_7 in the diagram and calculated for packets as

$$D_7 = \textit{(packet size in bytes} \times \textit{8 bits/byte)/10 Mbps}$$

The values D_1 through D_7 are the most significant contributors to the network delay in the forward direction. There may also be delays at the input buffers to each device (client, routers, and server), but these delays are usually orders of magnitude less than the delays on the output queue buffers of the same devices and therefore are normally not significant.

It is also possible to have delays within the routers or switches for processing the packet through the device. Here again, router or switch processing delays are not usually significant, because specialized tasks such as policy, encapsulation, and priority queuing are dealt with by dedicated processors within the device.

As discussed previously, delays within the client workstation or server due to application processing are not accounted for within the calculations of forward and return delay as shown in Figure 6-14. However, these delays can be very significant and will need to be investigated separately if they are found to be a significant factor in overall application end-to-end response time.

DISCRETE-EVENT SIMULATION RESPONSE TIME CALCULATION   A performance management tool that does discrete-event simulation models the length of each queue in the system, and therefore it can calculate how many packets are in the queue and how long a packet will have to wait before it can get out (the average wait in queue) at each point in time as the packet moves through the network. The tool can also predict when packets might be lost because the queue length has been exceeded and packets start to be discarded from the queue. A discrete-event simulation needs to run enough packets through the network model that the average wait time can converge to the average queue delay for the packets of the network conversation. Once this convergence has happened, the transmission delay is calculated as shown previously.

ANALYTICAL MODELING RESPONSE TIME CALCULATION   With an analytical modeling performance management tool, the calculation of the average wait in queue is done using a queuing model (a mathematical equation) for each output queue or buffer shown in Figure 6-14. A popular queueing model used for an output buffer of a router is the *M/G/1* model, used for modeling networks that use packets for transport. Inputs to the equation are the average packet size for each network conversation and the number of packets per second for each conversation. The *M/G/*1 queue model assumes a Poisson distribution for the arrival of packets into the queue and for the arrival of conversations to the device.

New queueing models are being developed and tested for ATM edge devices and backbone switches.

Analyzing the Results
of the "What-If" Analysis

Once you have run your "what-if" analysis (simulation or model), you need to evaluate the results to determine whether the predicted behavior of the network meets your objectives. First, you will want to look at the per-packet response times, in both the forward and return directions, for each packet in the conversations you're concerned about (typically those related to the new application you are adding to the network). In this analysis you look at the predicted values for response time and compare them to the network delays that you determined were acceptable in order to meet the quality-of-service goals you established during your application planning activities. If any of the per-packet response times exceed (or are close to exceeding) the acceptable quality-of-service goals, then you will need to determine which components within the conversation's route (round trip) are causing the problem. The components (LANs, WAN circuits, routers) at which excessive delays occur are known as bottlenecks.

DETERMINING THE LOCATIONS OF BOTTLENECKS   In order to determine where the bottleneck exists in getting a particular conversation through the network, you must be able to trace the route of that conversation through the model from source to destination and back. The first concern is to make sure that the routing was successful—that it is possible for a conversation to go from source to destination. You should look for predicted failures in routing because of a routing loop or a routing boundary (for example, where the conversation route needs to go from a RIP-based network to an IGRP-based network) where route redistribution was not set up correctly within the network model.

Assuming that routing is working correctly, you can then look at the utilization of the various resources within the route: LANs, WAN circuits, or other internetworking devices. This analysis can help you identify network components where predicted high utilization might be causing significant queue delays at the outputs of certain routers or switches and thus affecting the per-packet response times.

Even if your initial analysis shows that per-packet response times are not a problem, you still may want to look at predicted resource utilization. It may be that some resources are predicted to have high utilization, although not so high as to cause the per-packet response times to exceed your quality-of-service goals based on the assumptions you've made in creating your model. However, this result might point out areas of your network that you should watch carefully. On the other hand, the utilization analysis may also point out areas with very low utilization, indicating that you may be paying for more capacity than you really need.

THE RELATIONSHIP BETWEEN RESPONSE TIME AND UTILIZATION The amount of delay you will see in a network is directly related to utilization. The utilization of a specific resource (a LAN, WAN circuit, router, switch, or host) has a direct effect on the average delay of the queue that handles that resource. Queue or buffer delay in turn is typically the major contributor to excessive delay in a network. When utilization of a WAN circuit or LAN is high for a long time (five minutes), then packets needing access to that resource have to wait. The length of this wait depends on how high the utilization is on the affected resource and how long it stays high. Basically, if you observe more network delay than can be explained by the electrical characteristics of the network, that delay is probably because high utilization of some network resource causes a bottleneck somewhere along the route of the conversation.

Note that the degree of utilization that will cause problems will be different depending on the capacity of the resource, as shown in Figure 6-15. For example, 80% utilization of a 56K circuit may cause problems, whereas 80% utilization of a T1 circuit may not be an issue because the remaining 20% capacity is still quite adequate in terms of the actual amount of available capacity that it represents.

Another source of delay can be processing time within a router due to functions such as filtering, encapsulation, or router traffic accounting or even router software bugs. Excessive delays of this type are usu-

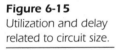

Figure 6-15
Utilization and delay related to circuit size.

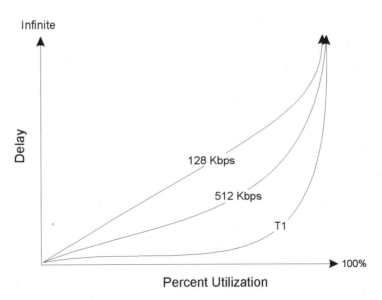

ally considered bugs and are normally fixed by the router vendors so that they do not remain a bottleneck. Still another source of delay may be a process delay on the client or sever, as has been discussed previously. The techniques in this book can point out the existence of this type of performance problem, but this book does not deal with how to analyze or solve such problems.

ANALYZING PER-PACKET RESPONSE TIME In order to analyze per-packet response time, you must be able to get reports from your performance management tool that show the average forward and average return predicted response times on a per-packet basis, as is shown in Table 6-1. By adding the forward and return delays, you can get an estimate of the total round-trip delay for each packet of the network. Remember that this is just the portion of the round-trip delay that is attributable to the network; it doesn't include delays at the client or server.

The estimated round-trip delay per packet can then be compared to the network round-trip delay that you determined to be acceptable for your quality-of-service goals during your application planning activities. If any of the estimated round-trip delays exceed your quality-of-service goals, you need to do further analysis to find the network components that are causing the problem.

You may find situations in which the predicted forward or return per-packet delays are reported as infinite. This can occur if the simulation or model cannot support the load of the conversations—in other words, if the conversations require more bandwidth than is available at some point on the route. For example, this could happen if the conversations require 100Kbps but, at one place in the route, only 56Kbps of bandwidth is available. Some performance management tools will then

TABLE 6.1

Per-Packet
Response Times

Demand	Fwd Delay (msec)	Rtn Delay (msec)	Source	Destination	Type	Count
Site A Create Req	9.63	9.31	10.10.63.0	10.10.2.0	Native PS Create Req. C->S	14
Site A Journal Query	9.24	9.39	10.10.63.0	10.10.2.0	Native PS Journal Query C->S	28
Site B Create Req	2.65	14.15	10.10.42.0	10.10.2.0	Native PS Create Req. C->S	1
Site B Journal Query	2.61	14.42	10.10.42.0	10.10.2.0	Native PS Journal Query C->S	3
Site G Create Req	4.28	8.34	10.10.48.0	10.10.2.0	Native PS Create Req. C->S	12
Site G Journal Query	4.25	8.48	10.10.48.0	10.10.2.0	Native PS Journal Query C->S	25
Site D Create Req	43.31	58.57	10.10.53.0	10.10.2.0	Native PS Create Req. C->S	1
Site D Journal Query	43.01	59.4	10.10.53.0	10.10.2.0	Native PS Journal Query C->S	2
Site E Create Req	11	27.57	10.10.208.0	10.10.2.0	Native PS Create Req. C->S	1
Site E Journal Query	10.9	31.34	10.10.208.0	10.10.2.0	Native PS Journal Query C->S	1
Site F Create Req	4.81	12.03	10.10.12.0	10.10.2.0	Native PS Create Req. C->S	2
Site F Journal Query	4.61	13.68	10.10.12.0	10.10.2.0	Native PS Journal Query C->S	3

report the delay to be infinite and consider that all of the conversations have failed going across this saturated resource. In this case, you will need to redesign your network model using the performance management tool to provide adequate bandwidth before any further analysis can be done. Network redesign is discussed later in this chapter.

ANALYZING THE ROUTING OF NETWORK CONVERSATIONS If any of your network conversations show predicted per-packet response times that exceed the delay that is acceptable in terms of your quality-of-service goals, you now need to analyze the routes of those conversations.

To analyze the routing of these conversations, your performance management tool must provide a report that includes all the components (LAN, WAN circuits, routers, switches, hosts) through which the conversation travels, based on the routing protocols that are operating in those components. The report must report the delay that each component adds to the total delay. Ideally, the report should break each component's delay down into queue delay and transmission delay. If it does not, you can calculate the transmission delay using the formula discussed earlier in this chapter (see Figure 6-14) and then subtract it from the total delay at the output of the device to determine the queue delay. The performance management tool must also report the propagation delay between any two components.

FINDING THE CAUSES OF EXCESSIVE DELAY Usually you will find that one or two related components will be the cause of the excessive delay. Typically, you will discover a high queue delay at the output of a router or switch, which will be caused by high utilization on the WAN circuit or LAN that is the next component in the route.

If any of the routes are reported as "no route available," you should carefully analyze those route failures. You need to determine whether there are routing loops or problems with redistribution at a boundary, such as where a RIP network interfaces with an IGRP network. The performance management tool may be simulating a problem that actually exists in your network, but your model may also be incorrect, so you should verify your model and the router configuration data you used as inputs. It is also possible that no physical route exists between the source and destination for a particular conversation—most likely because of a problem in creating your model. If you find any of these types of problems, you will need to reconfigure your network model before you can rerun the simulation or model.

Once you have identified the components that are showing excessive delays, you need to document their names or identifiers within the network model so that you can keep track of them. Then you can analyze the utilization of those components.

ANALYZING THE UTILIZATION OF NETWORK COMPONENTS Once you have identified the components that are showing excessive delays, you need to analyze the utilization of those components.

To analyze the predicted utilization of the components in your network, your performance management tool must be able to report on the percent utilization for each network component (both forward and return if needed), and also how much (what percentage) of that component each individual network conversation uses. These features will let you determine what conversations (applications) are the most responsible for utilization on that component. For example, if a particular WAN circuit is 30% utilized in one direction, 20% of that traffic might be due to baseline traffic and 10% might be due to the new application conversations you are studying.

If the utilization of any one component is over 100%, then all network conversations through that component are failing. There are two reasons for this to happen. One is, of course, that the predicted load (or demand) exceeds the capacity of the component. The other reason is that the model is configured incorrectly. If the circuit size or LAN type is found to be incorrect when validated against the actual network, you will need to reconfigure your network model to solve these problems and then rerun the simulation or model.

FINDING THE CAUSES OF BOTTLENECKS To analyze the cause of the utilization problems (the bottlenecks), you need to understand the breakdown of the traffic using the network component. Is the utilization high because the baseline traffic was already causing high utilization and the new application traffic pushed it over the edge? Or is the new application traffic causing the high utilization?

Carefully document which components are causing bottlenecks, because these components will be the targets of your network redesign. Make sure you include the reports that show the current utilization of these components by network conversation as a guide to how to redesign the component. For example, if a WAN circuit is 95% used in one direction, a first redesign effort might be to double the bandwidth of the circuit.

Checking Your Assumptions

Analyzing the results of your "what-if" analysis will provide insight into where problems may arise as you deploy your new application. At this point, however, it is important to check and verify the assumptions that you used to set up your baseline model and capacity planning scenarios. In particular, if the results are somewhat extreme (if all circuits need to be significantly upgraded, for example), you will need to verify that your assumptions were realistic. To some degree, you probably have a feeling about whether the results of your "what-if" analysis makes sense, given what you know about your network and given the specifics of the problem areas you have uncovered.

Specific areas you should check in your assumptions are the following questions:

■ Did you use a "peak utilization" or "peak volume" baseline model? Are you still comfortable with that assumption?

■ How realistic is your estimate of the number of users that could be using the application at one time at one location? Was it a worst-case estimate? How likely is that scenario in reality?

■ Is your estimate of frequency of use (the transaction rate per user) of the new application too high? Will users realistically be doing that many transactions, especially in relation to your estimate of the number of simultaneous users?

If your utilization analysis shows that baseline usage is responsible for most of the utilization, you should check and verify the assumption you made in creating your baseline model. If your utilization analysis shows that your new application is responsible for most of the high utilization, you will want to examine the assumptions you've made about number of simultaneous users and the frequency of use for the new transactions to make sure that these values are realistic.

In particular, if you set up a worst-case baseline model and then created a worst-case scenario in terms of number of simultaneous users and frequency of use for transactions, the result may be a rather exaggerated projection of load on the network. At this point, you may want to scale back one or more assumptions and rerun the "what-if" analysis to see how the results might change. It is often very valuable to model both a worst-case scenario and a "more realistic" or "normal" scenario and compare the results of the two. This comparison is valuable for understanding what might happen as network traffic grows.

Once you are happy with your assumptions and are sure that the results of your "what-if" analyses are valid, you are ready to redesign your network to attempt to meet your quality-of-service goals.

Redesigning the Network

The uses of capacity planning in the overall NRP process are to predict how additional workload added to the existing enterprise network will affect overall network performance, and to ensure that distributed applications achieve an acceptable quality of service at minimum network cost. Because the focus is on the existing network, the discussion of network redesign found in this section is limited to changing the capacity or type (from leased line to Frame Relay, for example) of the network resources (WAN circuits) that have been identified as causing failure to meet quality-of-service goals for the new application traffic. This limited definition of network redesign is sufficient for the purposes of NRP as defined in this book, because the goal is to determine how to deploy enterprise applications onto the existing enterprise network at minimal cost (that is, with the minimum of changes).

In reality, the NRP process, and specifically the results of the baselining activities, may demonstrate the need for a network redesign beyond simply changing circuit speeds and types—particularly if this is the first time the enterprise network has experienced this type of scrutiny. However, the NRP process as defined in this book does not adequately support network redesigns that involve topology changes or technology changes beyond changing leased lines to Frame Relay.

Network Design beyond the Scope of This Book

There are a number of legitimate and potentially important types of network design problems that capacity planning ideally should be able to address. However, many of those problems are beyond the scope of this book and are not as yet adequately supported by the techniques discussed here. Such design problems include

■ changing the network topology, such as adding or removing network hub sites or adding circuits for redundancy. This would require a complete, end-to-end application-based traffic matrix for the entire enterprise network (or the portions to be redesigned).

- Changing technologies, such as from public Frame Relay to public ATM. (Changing from leased lines to public Frame Relay is supported, however, if there are no topology changes.) Support for ATM will require different queueing algorithms (or models) than those supported in most performance management tools available at the time this book was written. In addition, unlike leased-line circuits or Frame Relay, modeling ATM will require knowledge of the application-based traffic, because of the way ATM does the transition from packet data to cell data.

- Adding new network locations with new network users. Like other topology changes, this requires a complete end-to-end traffic matrix.

- Moving server farms or other major network resources. This change also requires a complete end-to-end traffic matrix.

- Moving significant numbers of users to new locations within the existing network. This change also requires a complete end-to-end traffic matrix.

It is theoretically possible to accomplish any of these tasks using capacity planning techniques similar to those discussed in this book. However, for most of these network design tasks, which involve topology changes in the network, the process of gathering sufficient application-based data to create a valid network model would be extremely difficult and extremely expensive, making it basically impossible for all practical purposes today.

The network design goals just listed all require capturing extensive end-to-end application-based traffic data. In order to move parts of the network around, add new circuits, move servers, and so on, you would need to be able to isolate the specific traffic going from source to destination for every user (client) and application within the network to be redesigned. For example, if you wanted to model moving an application server, you would need to be able to reroute the portion of each client's traffic that is created by that particular application going to that application server. Doing so would require using a traffic analyzer to capture application-based traffic between every client and the existing application server, in order to determine which conversations are related to use of that application. Depending on the number of sites affected by this change, the information needed can be difficult or even impossible to obtain at the level of detail required.

Obstacles to Collecting an End-to-End Traffic Matrix

Collecting an end-to-end traffic matrix requires collecting every conversation that crosses the WAN from every host to every other host that will be affected by the redesign, as well as all broadcast traffic. This means a data collection device, such as a traffic analyzer or RMON2-compatible probe, must collect every byte of data that crosses the WAN during the collection interval and archive it in the form of a network conversation. The barriers to accomplishing this are significant.

First, depending on the topology of the network, a large number of collection devices might be required, because the traffic needs to be collected simultaneously at all locations during the collection interval. Thus, a collection device would need to be placed at every location (WAN circuit or backbone LAN) at which traffic can enter or exit the portion of the network to be redesigned. The cost of purchasing, installing, and maintaining a large number of data collection devices could be prohibitive in terms of most network management budgets.

Second, assuming you could place the required number of collection devices, most data collection devices in use today (at the time of writing this book) lose some of the data that passes by, because of router updates or broadcasts that are not archived or because the data collection device simply runs out of space to store all the data it is receiving. This is especially likely on busy WAN circuits or backbone LANs. In order to get an idea of how much data is lost, you need to validate the application-based data against usage-based data (collected from the routers). When the data collected by a traffic analyzer or RMON2-compatible probe is validated against the usage-based (router-based) data collected at the same time, it typically turns out that between 20% and 50% of the application-based data is lost by the collection devices available today.

This does not mean that collecting application-based data is not a worthwhile activity. As discussed in Chapter 4, "Baselining the Network," application-based data can be collected at a few limited key points within the enterprise network to provide valuable information about how the network is being "used" by different applications (an application inventory or application distribution). The collection devices of today are good at saving "most" of the bytes of "most" of the "significant" network conversations. The resulting data provides a heuristic for all the network traffic and is very good for the purposes outlined within Chapter 4 for application-based traffic, but it is *not* sufficient for determining an application's exact utilization of the enterprise network by network conversation for the purposes of creating a baseline model.

Even if you could collect every byte of every conversation on your network, there are still barriers to creating a valid capacity planning scenario for a network redesign. For one thing, the application-based data sets (the traffic matrix) would be huge and difficult to work with. In addition, you have the problem of determining whether the application conversations you have collected represent "typical" usage of the application and are thus appropriate for use in redesigning the network infrastructure.

For these reasons, the capacity planning scenarios discussed in this chapter all assume that the network infrastructure does not change and that the only variables are the addition of new application traffic not included in the existing baseline and the ability to manipulate the capacity or configuration of existing network resources. Note that you *can* model changing the location of servers and clients for a *new* application as long as the locations are all existing network sites, and that the traffic that they represent is all new traffic not included in the existing network baseline.

Redesigning the Network to Meet Quality-of-Service Goals

In order to redesign a capacity planning scenario, you need to have a documented list of the network resources (WAN circuits, for the most part) that are preventing your quality-of-service goals from being met. This information should be documented as part of the results of running the model or simulation on your initial capacity planning scenario.

Redesigning the network is now just an exercise in using your performance management tool to "change" or reconfigure the circuit sizes in your model so that they have sufficient bandwidth that quality-of-service goals can be met for those circuits.

The following examples show the results of running a scenario that added traffic for a new application, redesigning the scenario to increase bandwidth on selected circuits, and running the scenario again. For this scenario, acceptable quality of service is considered to be a round-trip delay of less than 100 ms for a packet transiting all circuits in the path of the new application conversation.

Figure 6-16

Baseline utilization for client locations.

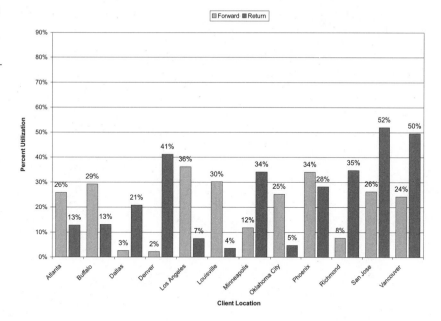

Figure 6-16 shows the baseline utilization on a set of 128K circuits between proposed client locations and a centrally located application server. The utilization represents existing traffic before conversations due to the new application are added. Note that two of these circuits (San Jose and Vancouver) already show utilization at or greater than 50%.

Figure 6-17 shows the average per-packet round-trip delays predicted by the modeling analysis for the conversations due to the new application after the new application traffic was added to the baseline traffic shown in Figure 6-16.

Figure 6-18 shows the utilization on those circuits predicted by the modeling analysis after the addition of the new application traffic. Some sites show a much larger increase than others, depending on the number of new application users at the different sites.

As shown in Figure 6-17, there are four sites (Minneapolis, Phoenix, San Jose, and Vancouver) where the predicted round-trip delay exceeds 100 ms, the quality-of-service goal. Figure 6-18 shows that for these four sites circuit utilization is also predicted to rise above 80%. These four sites were redesigned to use a 256Kbps circuit using the NetMaker XA performance management tool, as shown in Figure 6-19, and the modeling analysis was run again. The results are shown in Figures 6-20 and 6-21. Now, all four circuits show per-packet round trip delays within the acceptable range for quality-of-service (less than 100 ms) and utilization below 50%.

Figure 6-17
Predicted round-trip
delay for application
conversations.

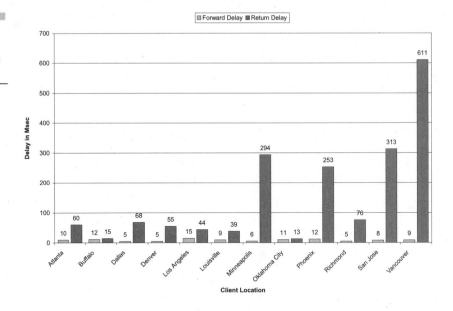

Figure 6-18
Circuit utilization
after addition of
application traffic.

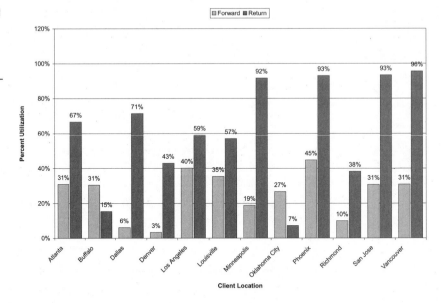

Deciding How to Redesign

Deciding how much bandwidth is enough is not always simple. You
need to provide enough bandwidth to provide the quality of service
needed for the new application traffic as well as to allow for a certain

Figure 6-19
Redesigning a WAN circuit using the NetMaker XA Object Editor. (© Make Systems.)

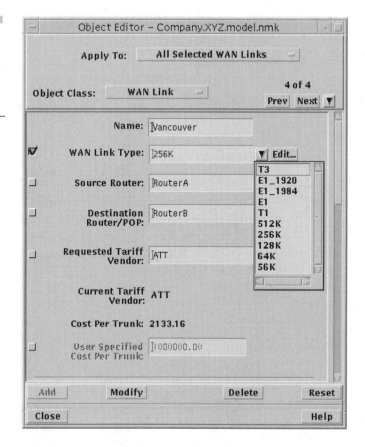

amount of "headroom" (additional capacity for predicted growth). For the purposes of redesigning your capacity planning scenarios, doubling the capacity is a good place to start if the original circuit is 256Kbps or below (56Kbps, 64Kbps, or 128Kbps circuits). In the example in Figure 6-21, doubling the bandwidth from 128 to 256Kbps solved the capacity and quality-of-service problems. However, if the circuit is above 256Kbps, then doubling may not be appropriate. Doubling the bandwidth may be more than is needed to meet quality-of-service goals, and the cost of twice the bandwidth can be significantly more expensive for larger circuit sizes. In addition, not all possible circuit speeds are available from the carriers.

The cost of different circuits is not always straightforward. In some locations, the cost of a T1 circuit (1.544 Mbps) may be only slightly more than the cost of a 512Kbps circuit for three times the capacity. This depends on the end points of the circuit and the vendor involved (such as AT&T, MCI, Sprint). Once you have decided on the circuit

Figure 6-20
Predicted per-packet
round-trip delay after
redesign.

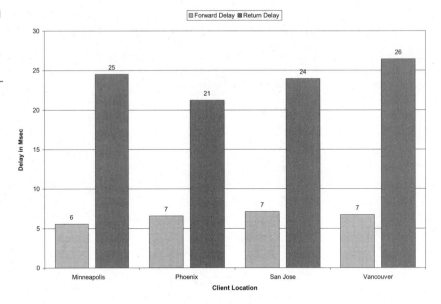

Figure 6-20
Predicted per-packet
round-trip delay after
redesign.

Figure 6-21
Circuit utilization after
redesign to 256Kbps
circuits.

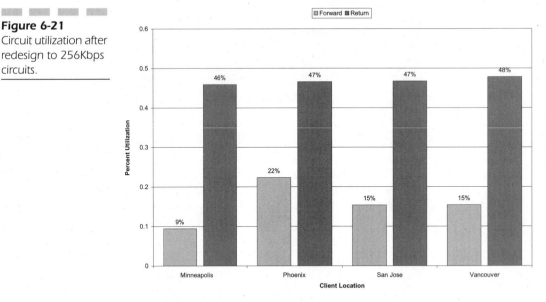

sizes required to meet your quality-of-service requirements, you will
then need to investigate the costs (tariffs) of available circuits that will
meet your needs. You may decide to install a higher-capacity circuit
than is strictly called for by your quality-of-service needs if it offers an
attractive price.

Frame Relay Design: A Special Case

The methodology outlined in this chapter can help you meet the network design goal of migrating from leased lines to Frame Relay technology, as long as the end points of the new Frame Relay circuits do not differ from those of the original leased-line circuits. In other words, the technology can change as long as the topology stays the same, for the reasons discussed earlier. This is possible because the bandwidth available on a leased line of a given size is the same as that on a Frame Relay circuit of the same size. The difference is that a Frame Relay circuit is tariffed differently, with a Committed Information Rate (CIR) and an excess burst size capability.

A Frame Relay circuit is priced (tariffed) on the assumption that it is not normally used to full capacity. Frame Relay circuits are tariffed not just relative to the total bandwidth, but also depending on the CIR. The CIR defines the throughput that is "guaranteed" and is generally for an information rate less than the full capacity (port speed) of the circuit. For example, a 256Kbps Frame Relay circuit might have a CIR of 128Kbps. The circuit can be used up to its full capacity (256Kbps), but when usage exceeds the CIR for a certain length of time (usually one second or less), the excess packets are marked "discard eligible" (DE) at the entry to the public Frame Relay network or *cloud*. Packets marked DE can be discarded within the public frame relay network if there is not sufficient capacity within the cloud. The benefit is that Frame Relay is less expensive than a leased line for the same total bandwidth, but it comes at the expense of being guaranteed only some portion of the total bandwidth. The price of a Frame Relay circuit varies with the CIR and port speed.

A second difference between Frame Relay and leased lines is that delay within the public Frame Relay network is typically greater than that of a leased line. For example, if the per-packet round-trip delay for a leased line can be as much as 60 ms, the per-packet round-trip delay for a 256Kbps Frame Relay circuit with a 128Kbps CIR might be as much as 100 ms. Thus, additional delay for frame relay may need to be configured into your model, using your performance management tool to account for this difference. A Frame Relay circuit can have more delay because packets may make multiple hops within the Frame Relay cloud, whereas a leased line is guaranteed to be a single hop from end point to end point.

The fact that, with Frame Relay, bandwidth is guaranteed only up to the CIR may affect your capacity planning goals. If your scenarios are not quite worst-case scenarios (that is, they are based on an average or merged-peak baseline strategy), you might choose to design your circuits so that your quality-of-service goals can be met within the CIR rather than within the total bandwidth (port speed) available for the Frame Relay circuit. Alternatively, if you have run multiple scenarios to determine the relationship of needed circuit capacity to your quality-of-service goals, you might choose to purchase a CIR that allows your quality-of-service goals to be met under most (but not all) circumstances within the CIR.

Projecting Growth

When deciding whether you need to add capacity to the WAN circuits on your network, you need to look beyond the traffic demands that your current and near-term new applications will make. You also need to plan for future capacity based on the predicted growth of your network in terms of applications, new users, and increased usage by existing users. This planning can be a major challenge.

If you underestimate the rate of growth of your network, you may find yourself repeating your capacity planning exercises in the near future. Depending on the type of circuits you have in place, adding capacity can be disruptive and expensive, especially if you have service contracts in place that require renegotiation. On the other hand, you want to avoid paying for too much capacity that you really do not need as of yet.

Traffic tends to grow quickly in today's networks, and breakthroughs in applications and technology (for example, the swift and dramatic rise in Internet use with the advent of browser-based World Wide Web technology) can accelerate change beyond the best-laid plans. Realistically, you cannot expect to predict with much accuracy beyond six months in the future. However, there are certain areas at which you can look to help you predict the growth of your network.

Some of the more predictable sources of network growth are new applications that are in the planning or development process or the addition of new sites and users due to growth of the overall business. The growth of intranet or Internet traffic can be much more difficult to predict. Usage may start off slowly, but as users become more comfortable with Internet technology, the frequency of use may increase dramatically. In many cases, users can download applications directly off the Internet, and some products, such as multimedia e-mail or those based on push technology (PointCaste and similar products, for example), can saturate network resources if their use is not controlled. Internet and intranet use can be extremely difficult to predict.

Regardless of the source of traffic growth, the regular use of the baselining techniques described earlier in this book (collecting both usage-based and application-based traffic) can help you identify trends in network usage. These trends may be helpful in predicting the sorts of unplanned, evolutionary growth caused by such things as increasing e-mail, Internet, and intranet usage.

Capacity Planning in the Future

Today's performance management tools are excellent for analyzing and redesigning networks in terms of capacity to meet quality-of-service requirements for new applications. In the future, performance management tools will need to evolve to support the additional redesign goals, such as topology redesigns, that cannot be effectively or accurately modeled today. As network technologies evolve, NRP processes and techniques will also evolve to handle the new technologies and greater complexity of the networks of the future. The next chapter, "The Future of Network Resource Planning," looks at this possible evolution.

CHAPTER 7

The Future of Network Resource Planning

As networks evolve, the need for Network Resource Planning (NRP) will not only continue—it will become even more critical. NRP, as already defined, is a software-supported set of processes that ensure that distributed applications achieve an acceptable quality of service at minimum network cost. The need to provide acceptable quality of service at minimum cost will not become obsolete in any foreseeable future, and the use of software tools and processes to determine how to achieve these goals will become even more critical as networks increase in complexity. NRP processes include

- Documenting the current network topology and configuration
- Creating a baseline of current network utilization and application distribution

- Testing network behavior to assess quality of service for specific applications
- Profiling traffic demands to document the behavior of existing and future applications
- Modeling network behavior to predict performance under specified conditions, such as worst-case traffic loads
- Redesigning the network to resolve problems or to meet quality-of-service goals

The technology, components, and complexity of enterprise networks will change, as will the performance management tools used for NRP. However, the processes listed here, and described in the rest of this book, will still be needed.

NRP as a Requirement as Enterprise Networks Evolve

The evolution of enterprise networks and the applications they support will make NRP necessary for designing the wide area networks (WANs) of the future. According to GartnerGroup:

- 80 percent of user applications will rely on network computing architectures by 2002.
- By 2000, 20 percent of major network-centric applications will experience severe performance problems because of users' failure to understand network/application interactions.
- Unless major reengineering efforts are undertaken, 80 percent of today's enterprise WANs will not be "network computing ready."

Individual machines are getting faster, and the speed of the local area networks (LANs) to which they connect are also increasing dramatically. Applications are getting larger and requiring more bandwidth. Increasingly, WANs are not keeping pace with the needs and capability of these network elements.

As a result of these trends, NRP will be critical. According to GartnerGroup (1997), "Due to the increasing complexity of network infrastructures, more staff will be needed to plan and design networks, or the ability to maintain functional environments will be at risk." Further, the "back of the envelope" type of planning will become inadequate, and reliance on bandwidth overprovisioning as an approach to network design will become ineffective. GartnerGroup states bluntly that without thorough baselining and the characterization of applications, no network design process will be successful. They predict that computer-aided network planning tools, and the processes that surround their use, "represent the only hope out of this design dilemma for end-user organizations."

NRP as presented in this book outlines a network management strategy that meets the GartnerGroup's challenge, both today and on into the future.

The Evolution of the NRP Cycle

The basic definition of NRP as discussed throughout this book will not change. The activities that define the NRP cycle (Figure 7-1) will still be

Figure 7-1
The NRP cycle of activities.

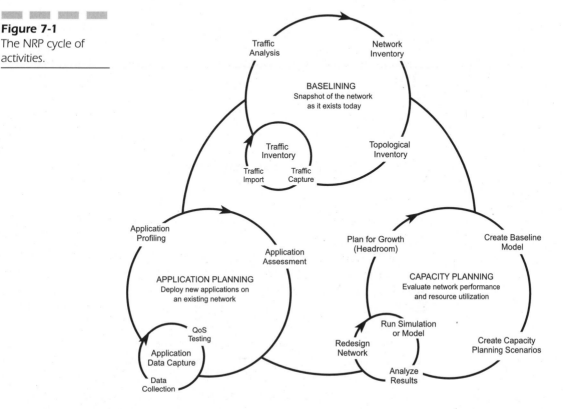

needed. NRP will continue to include baselining, application planning, and capacity planning activities, and the activities within each of these cycles will still be performed. However, the implementation and execution of the various NRP activities will need to adapt as networking technologies within the enterprise network change, and as network performance management and design tools change over time.

The following sections look at each of the three areas of the NRP process and examine the ways in which the process will evolve over time.

Baselining

Baselining is the process of documenting the current network in order to understand what is available and how it is typically being used. This includes developing an accurate rendering (topology map) and characterization of the network infrastructure as well as obtaining snapshots of network activity or traffic flow. Because it provides a picture of the "typical" use of the network, the baseline provides the foundation from which all further planning activities can be undertaken. While the baseline for any given network will change over time as the network evolves, that baseline provides a starting point against which the effects of proposed changes can be analyzed. Although network technology will change and evolve, the need for baselining will remain.

As illustrated in Figure 7-2, baselining activities include four basic tasks: network inventory, topological inventory, traffic inventory, and traffic analysis. The need for these four activities will continue, but the details of how they are done may change.

Network Inventory

The network inventory is a collection of all the known network elements (routers and their configurations, WAN circuits and circuit speeds, LANs) to be tracked and referenced throughout the network planning cycle. This stage will still be needed in order to evaluate the results of a network "discovery."

Today, network documentation is often kept on many different systems, maintained by different people or organizations, and presented in different formats that can be difficult to correlate. For example, the responsibility for tracking telecommunications circuits is frequently

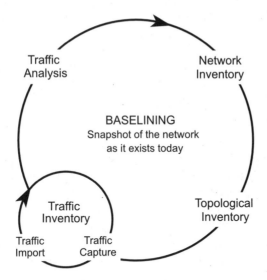

Figure 7-2
Baselining cycle
of activities.

BASELINING
Snapshot of the network
as it exists today

Traffic
Analysis

Network
Inventory

Traffic
Inventory

Topological
Inventory

Traffic
Import

Traffic
Capture

quite separate from the group that tracks PCs within an organization. In the future, these tasks may evolve to be an integral part of the baselining system. For example, network diagrams, addressing information, software inventory information, and circuit information may all be maintained within the same platform (or software) that is used to archive and analyze the baseline traffic data.

Topological Inventory

The topological inventory provides a visual representation (layout or network map) of the network, built by importing topology data from routers into a performance management tool of choice. The data includes all routers, LANs, and network connections.

The need for this information remains unchanged, but the discovery and import capabilities of the performance management tools will need to evolve to incorporate new devices, technologies, and concepts. Examples of new devices will be Asynchronous Transfer Mode (ATM) edge devices, ATM backbone switches, ATM private virtual circuits (PVCs), ATM and Frame Relay switched virtual circuits (SVCs), and ATM Virtual Paths (VPs). New LAN media types will include Gigabit Ethernet and ATM. Virtual LANs (VLANs) are an example of a new concept that will need to be supported by a discovery or import process.

Performance management tools will need to be able to build network models as completely as possible. Therefore, discovery and import capabilities must evolve to provide topological information to a very detailed level. For example, it will be important to discover all of the configuration on an ATM edge switch, not just its existence.

Traffic Inventory

The traffic inventory uses usage-based traffic data obtained from internetworking devices and, if available, application-based data captured with RMON2 (Remote Monitoring)-compatible probes or traffic analyzers. This data is then imported into the appropriate performance management tools for analysis. Both the traffic capture and import capabilities will need to change in the future.

Usage-based data will need to include data from ATM edge devices and backbone switches. Therefore, the methods for gathering this data will need to evolve to provide measurements in terms of cells as well as bytes.

The data collection devices used for capturing traffic will need to evolve to capture and output more information about network conversations. For example, in the future it will become important to record not only the average packet size for a particular network conversation but also the packet size variation and packet arrival time variation. This additional data will be necessary in order to model "native mode" conversations going through segmentation and reassembly (SAR) to cross an ATM environment. Also, data collection devices will be needed to collect data from ATM environments or new LAN environments such as Gigabit Ethernet. Data collection devices may also need to collect traffic for new types of services such as voice or video, which will increasingly be found in the same environments as legacy data is today.

Traffic import capabilities will need to support the import of new parameters such as packet size variation and arrival time variation, so that these parameters can be used to model network conversations. They will also need to handle other types of traffic, such as voice or video traffic, to enable modeling of a complete network environment.

Traffic Analysis

Traffic analysis uses the capabilities of the performance management tool to analyze usage-based data to determine network utilization and available capacity. Application-based data is also analyzed to generate a list of the major applications transiting the network, how they behave (throughput), and how they use network resources (bandwidth utilization). These basic functions will not change. However, the types of applications will evolve, and some of the metrics may also change; for example, cells will have to be used instead of bytes in ATM as the basis for calculating utilization.

A major difference will be the emergence of voice and video as new application types, especially in ATM networks. For ATM environments (or for traffic that is destined for an ATM environment) there are four types of applications (or service classes) to consider:

- *Constant Bit Rate (CBR) applications:* voice and fax
- *Variable Bit Rate—real time (VBR-rt) applications:* video, video conferencing, and document retrieval
- *Variable Bit Rate—non–real time (VBR-nrt) applications:* database retrieval and high-speed LAN/WAN traffic
- *Unspecified Bit Rate (UBR) or Available Bit Rate (ABR) applications:* electronic mail, file transfers, and all other data transfers in existence today

It may become important to be able to do traffic analysis around these five types of ATM service classes and to quantify how much bandwidth each service is using, because most traffic in the future may be "touching" an ATM environment.

Application Planning

Application planning activities focus on characterizing the demands that new applications are likely to make on the network or that existing applications will make as users are added or an application server is moved. This information can then be used to build on the baseline model to predict how the network will support the application. Application planning will continue to be important, and perhaps even play an expanded role in NRP processes, as networks evolve into the future.

Application planning methodologies require that a representative set of application transactions be measured to determine what demands the application is likely to make on the network. The application transactions can also be measured to create metrics for assessing how well the network will support the application's quality-of-service

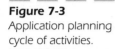

Figure 7-3
Application planning
cycle of activities.

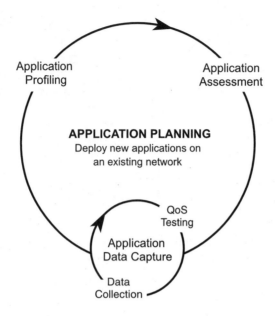

goals. These measurements are documented and analyzed to create a "profile" of the application, which can then be superimposed on the baseline model to simulate how the new application load will affect the network.

The three tasks comprised in an application planning activity, as shown in Figure 7-3, are application assessment, application data capture, and application profiling. Although the basic nature of these tasks is not likely to change in the foreseeable future, the scope of these activities will need to expand to take into account data types and technologies not supported today.

Application Assessment

Application assessment is the process of identifying how an application will be deployed and used on the enterprise network. This includes determining where the application's users and servers will be located, how many users will be at each location, and how frequently these users are expected to do various application tasks. It also involves deciding which application transactions are representative of the way the application will be used by users (clients) on the network. These transactions (or a subset of them) form a benchmark, which is used to generate the traffic data that will become the basis for application profiles.

Finally, application assessment includes defining and understanding the network environment in which the application will run when it is deployed, including the existing application distribution and how the introduction of the new application may affect that distribution.

These tasks will still be required as NRP evolves. However, the applications being studied may be voice or video as well as legacy data. This will make such issues as predicting the location of users and the frequency of use much more complicated. For example, a multipoint video conference conversation is based on the probability of a "client" joining the video conference. Predicting the number of clients is really predicting the probability of the number of users joined to the conference at any given point in time. For this type of traffic, the definition of frequency of use or transaction rate will need to be expanded to include the probability of activity at a given point in time and the transaction rate during active periods. This refinement will also be helpful in more accurately representing traffic due to today's legacy data.

Application Data Capture

Application data capture is the process of collecting traffic data that corresponds to the target transactions that make up the application benchmark. You may also want to test the application to quantify quality-of-service goals for application response time and throughput. The data capture itself is done by using a traffic analyzer to collect the appropriate data that corresponds to the application transactions in the benchmark, as executed by a knowledgeable user as part of the data collection process.

Application data capture will continue to be critical to application planning, but it may need to change in the future in several ways. First, the definition of quality of service will need to expand to incorporate additional components. Also, the data capture devices will need to be able to capture data in new environments, such as ATM or Gigabit Ethernet, and record additional information to allow the modeling of conversations in that environment.

The definition of quality of service in terms of application performance as perceived by the user (response time and throughput) will still remain valid for the types of application planning activities described in this book. However, the factors that make up quality of service will expand. Quality of service is affected by three components: performance of the server, performance of the network, and performance of the client. In this book, the examination of quality of service has been limited to the performance of the network component only. Specifically, it has focused on the amount of network delay that can be tolerated while still providing acceptable quality of service from the user's point of view.

Analyzing client and server performance is also possible today but currently requires separate processes and tools and is not well integrated with tools that look at network performance. In the future that situation should change. It should become possible to analyze and incorporate client and server performance contributions to quality of service for an application within the same tools and processes used to quantify the network performance.

In terms of the network component of quality of service, testing will need to include additional factors beyond round-trip delay, such as *jitter*, caused by cell delay variation (CDV) in ATM networks. Jitter can have a dramatic effect on quality of service for voice and video conversations because of loss of synchronization.

Data collection devices will need to evolve to record more information about network conversations, such as the packet size and arrival time variance in addition to average packet size. Data collection devices will also need to be fully developed to capture data about network conversations in ATM environments (SVCs) and other new types of LAN or WAN environments.

Application Profiling

Application profiling is the process of creating a representative model (known as a profile) of the traffic characteristics of a set of application transactions based on the data captured during the data capture task. The profiles will be used to represent the "typical" load that an individual application user represents in terms of traffic demands.

Application profiles will need to evolve to record more information about an application transaction so that it can be modeled in an ATM environment and its behavior can be described more completely. For example, the profile will need to include packet size variance and packet arrival time variance for the conversation. The profile may also need to include a probability of the transaction being active and a transaction rate to apply when the transaction is active. For an ATM environment, the profile may need to include metrics such as peak cell rate (PCR), sustained cell rate (SCR), and maximum burst size (MBS), in addition to the required bits per second.

Performance management tools may evolve to provide "canned" profiles for voice and video conversations where the required metrics—frames per second, cells per second, or ATM Quality of Service (QoS) metrics—are known.

Capacity Planning

The purpose of capacity planning as defined in this book is to analyze and predict how a network will perform, both under current conditions and when changes to traffic load (new applications or users) or network infrastructure changes are introduced. Capacity planning uses baselined network data and application data to provide basic answers about network usage and the ability of the network to meet quality-of-service objectives in possible enterprise application deployment scenarios. This principle will not change, although the underlying network technologies and planning methodologies will.

The tasks in the capacity planning area, as shown in Figure 7-4, are creating a baseline model, creating capacity planning scenarios, running the "what-if" scenarios, analyzing the results, redesigning the scenarios if necessary, and planning for growth. These activities will continue to be important. However, the way these activities are done, the data involved, the modeling techniques, and the interpretation of the results may change in significant ways as enterprise networks evolve in the future.

Figure 7-4
Capacity planning
cycle of activities.

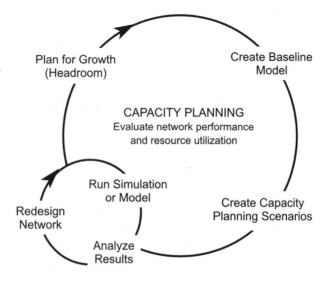

Plan for Growth
(Headroom)

Create Baseline
Model

CAPACITY PLANNING
Evaluate network performance
and resource utilization

Run Simulation
or Model

Redesign
Network

Create Capacity
Planning Scenarios

Analyze
Results

Creating the Baseline Model

The first step in capacity planning is to create one or more baseline models that represent the existing usage on an enterprise network. These models are the basis for the capacity planning scenarios. There are two ways in which baseline model creation will change in the future. One is that it will become possible to obtain an end-to-end application-based traffic matrix and make use of that data during baseline model creation. The other change will be in the ability to apply more statistical methods to the creation of baseline models.

Initially, performance management tools will develop the ability to infer an end-to-end traffic matrix based on usage-based data plus some amount of correlated application-based data from the same network. Eventually, when data collection devices become widespread, it may become possible to collect true end-to-end traffic matrices. The availability of complete end-to-end traffic data will enable the explicit allocation of existing application traffic instead of the inferred allocation of that traffic based on its inclusion in usage-based traffic data.

The second area of change will involve the increasing use of statistical methods to aid in developing different types of baselines within performance management tools. Today a baseline might be created by averaging volume from the 12 time periods that showed the highest volume over a business day. In the future it may be possible to create a baseline model that represents a certain percentile usage—for example, for 80% of the time the overall utilization of the network is below the level used for the baseline model and for 20% of the time it is higher than that level. This feature will require the ability to apply some statistical analysis to baseline data.

Creating Capacity Planning Scenarios

A capacity planning scenario is the description of the predicted usage of the network by an application (usually an application you are planning to add to the network) in terms of the location of application users and application or database servers, the number of users at each location, and the frequency with which each user will execute the application transactions under study. The scenario is implemented on top of a network baseline model by adding network conversations that represent the new application traffic based on the application profiles created during the application planning phase of the NRP project. This process will not change.

The difference in this area is that the application profiles will have to change to incorporate additional factors. Also, the way the number of users and transaction rates are defined may also change because of multipoint applications and the need for better definition of network conversations involving legacy data. Both of these issues were examined in the discussion of application planning earlier in this chapter.

Running the Model or Simulation

The techniques for both simulation and modeling used within performance management tools in the future will have to change to accommodate new networking devices and traffic types. For analytical modeling, new queueing models are currently being developed and tested by various software vendors to model devices in ATM environments. The tools will also need to output ATM QoS metrics after a simulation or model is run.

QoS for ATM is specified by at least three parameters:

- *Cell transfer delay (CTD):* the time from the insertion of the first bit of the cell to the exit of the last bit of the cell, from source to destination, including both propagation delay and processing delay for each ATM device along the route

- *Cell delay variation (CDV):* a measure of the standard deviation of the arrival of cells, which may be reported as a certain level of jitter (packets or cells arriving out of synchronization)

- *Cell loss ratio (CLR):* the ratio of lost cells to the total number of transmitted cells (the sum of cells received plus cells lost)

Not all classes of service (CBR, VBR-rt, VBR-nrt, UBR, and ABR) use all QoS parameters. However, the model or simulation will need to output the relevant values for conversations (SVCs or PVCs) that transit ATM environments and that have required QoS metrics. The other outputs of a simulation or model—utilization, routing, and round-trip delay (RTD) per packet—will still be needed as well. These metrics will continue to be important because many, if not most conversations will start and end in native mode (packet, voice, or video) rather than ATM (cells).

Figure 7-5 shows the elements involved in moving voice, video, or legacy data traffic from a native environment through an ATM environment. Data coming from a non-ATM packet-based environment will need to go through segmentation and reassembly (SAR) to put the data

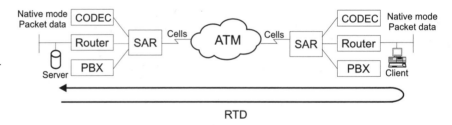

Figure 7-5

Traffic flow through
an ATM environment.

into cells and again to move it back into packets on the other side. The
concept of round-trip delay is still the same, however, regardless of the
processes that are involved in the path of a packet.

Analyzing Results

The analysis of the modeling and simulation results will become much
more complicated as the models themselves are changed. Both the data
used by the models or simulations and their outputs will be more complicated. The meanings of today's outputs—utilization, routing, per-
packet RTD—are fairly straightforward, and network management
staff can relatively easily determine what the results mean in terms of
the performance of their network and the effect on quality-of-service
goals. In the future, with parameters such as jitter and probability of
cell loss, it may be much less obvious what a given set of results means.
Thus, more intelligence will need to be built into the performance
management tools to aid in interpreting the results for the performance management tool user.

Redesigning the Network

The basic process of network redesign will not change. Capacity planning scenarios will still be modified to reflect changes to the network
based on analysis of the results of a model or simulation, and then the
simulation or model will be rerun. However, the scope of the types of
redesigns that are possible should broaden considerably.

   In Chapter 6, "Capacity Planning," network redesign is limited to
changing the capacity or type (from leased line to Frame Relay, for
example) of the network resources (WAN circuits). Network redesigns
involving topology changes or technology changes beyond changing
leased lines to Frame Relay were not discussed.

For example, redesigns that would involve changing the network topology, adding new sites, moving major network resources such as server farms, or moving existing users to different locations within the network are not supported by the capacity planning techniques discussed in this book, because these types of redesigns require an end-to-end traffic matrix for the entire network (or at least the portion that is being redesigned), and the barriers to collecting an end-to-end traffic matrix today are significant. Without complete end-to-end application-based traffic for the entire network, it is extremely difficult to determine the amount of existing network traffic that is caused by specific applications; therefore, it is not possible to know how to reallocate that traffic relative to the network topology. (These issues are discussed in detail in Chapter 6.)

In the future, it should become possible to collect (or at least infer heuristically) complete end-to-end traffic matrices for enterprise networks. Once a complete matrix of application-based traffic data is available, it will become possible to support network redesigns that involve topology and technology changes or the relocation of existing resources and users.

Another area of network redesign that is not supported today is redesigns involving ATM, because the modeling and simulation techniques available today do not, for the most part, support the analysis of ATM cell-based traffic. However, as models that support ATM devices and environments become available (they are currently in development), these types of redesigns will also become available.

Planning for Growth

The factors to be considered in planning for growth—projecting the addition of new applications, new users, and new sites—will basically remain the same. However, the types of applications, and the technology available for meeting network growth needs, will change—such as the move to ATM, the adoption of browser-based and Java-based thin clients for enterprise applications, new types of network devices, and so on. However, at the same time as networks grow in complexity, data collection tools should increase in sophistication and analytical techniques. Thus, you should be able to get better and increasingly complete data on the usage and usage trends of your existing network. However, accurately projecting network growth will undoubtedly continue to remain much more "art" than science and require a great deal of intuition, prescience, and luck.

The Continued Role of NRP

As networks evolve, NRP will not only continue to be important—it will become critical to the development of functional enterprise networks. Organizations that master and apply the basic concepts and philosophies of NRP will have the best chance of moving forward into the next millennium with a minimum of network-related capacity problems. The authors hope that this book has provided useful insights into the use of data collection and performance management tools to gain truly useful information about the performance of today's enterprise networks. The adoption of NRP processes can significantly help smooth the deployment of enterprise applications such as SAP R/3, BAAN IV, PeopleSoft, and other enterprise client/server applications.

The second part of this book contains case studies about three organizations—Lucent Technologies, the 3M Company, and AlliedSignal—that have undertaken NRP projects. These case studies should provide valuable insight into the issues that arise during an NRP project as well as a look at the types of results that can be obtained by using NRP techniques.

References

GartnerGroup (1997). *GartnerGroup Symposium/ITExpo97,* Lake Buena Vista, FL, October 6–10, 1997.

Case Studies

The following case studies show how three large organizations are using Network Resource Planning (NRP) methodology within their organizations.

Two of these case studies, based on projects done at Lucent Technologies and the 3M Company, describe complete NRP projects that encompassed all three phases: baselining, application planning, and capacity planning.

The third case study, from AlliedSignal, illustrates the use of baselining methodology to monitor performance of the network.

CHAPTER 8

Lucent Technologies

Lucent Technologies, headquartered in Murray Hill, New Jersey, designs, builds, and delivers a wide range of public and private networks, communications systems and software, data networking systems, business telephone systems, and microelectronics components. Bell Labs is the research and development arm for the company. Lucent Technologies is an organization of approximately 100,000 employees. The CIO organization is responsible for managing the Lucent Technologies global network infrastructure. At the time of writing this book, the CIO Enterprise Architecture group had undertaken an evaluation of a proposed deployment of the PeopleSoft HRMS application.

Project Background

Lucent Technologies had several concerns about the deployment of Enterprise Resource Planning (ERP) applications on its current network, particularly within one of the geographic regions of its worldwide network environment. To address these concerns, Lucent Technologies decided to use Network Resource Planning techniques to ascertain the performance characteristics of the existing network, including the applications currently in use at the various sites. In addition, Lucent Technologies wanted to understand the potential traffic demands that would be added to the network by the proposed new PeopleSoft application and to use this information to redesign the network to support both current and future needs. Finally, Lucent Technologies used this project to evaluate whether to purchase the NetMaker XA software for ongoing network planning activities. This chapter describes the process and results of this NRP project.

Lucent Technologies hired an outside consultant to assist with the NRP project, but Lucent Technologies personnel were involved at every step so that they could evaluate the performance management tools used for the project in preparation for undertaking future planning activities on their own.

The performance management tools used for this case study were the NetMaker XA suite of performance management tools along with several Network General WAN Distributed Server Sniffers (DSSs). During the baselining phase the NetMaker XA tool suite was used to discover the network topology, collect usage-based data from the routers, and to create the baseline model. Network General WAN DSSs were used to capture application-based traffic data on key circuits between the region under study and the region where the centralized application resources were expected to be located. As part of the application planning phase, application profiles were created for the PeopleSoft HRMS module that was to be deployed on the regional network. Capacity planning techniques were used to create "what-if" scenarios that projected future network throughput and performance of the new application planned for deployment. This case study did not address redesign of the network, but the data gathered for this project could be used for a redesign effort.

Lucent Technologies' worldwide network environment, at the time of the project, was divided into five major geographic regions. Of these, the project focused on one specific region, known in this case study as Region A. The Region A network included both factory sites and sales and business offices. The needs of the factory sites and the business sites are different, so the design requirements for these types of sites will also be different.

The Region A network was organized as a spoke-and-wheel topology, using TCP/IP as the network protocol. Four main hub sites in Region A connect to a second regional backbone (Region B) through fractional T1 circuits: Site3, Site5, and Site6 connect to Backbone Site1, and Site4 connects to Backbone Site2, as shown in Figure 8-1. Site6, Site3, and Site4 were also interconnected, creating a Region A backbone network.

Most of the remote sites connect directly to one of the four Region A hub sites through leased lines, although a few remote sites connect indirectly through another remote site. For the most part, there was no redundancy in the tail circuits. Some circuits also carried voice, but that was not within the scope of this project. Many of the applications used at the Region A sites had servers located in main Region B data centers.

Figure 8-1

Network diagram of Lucent Technologies' Region A hub sites and Region B backbone.

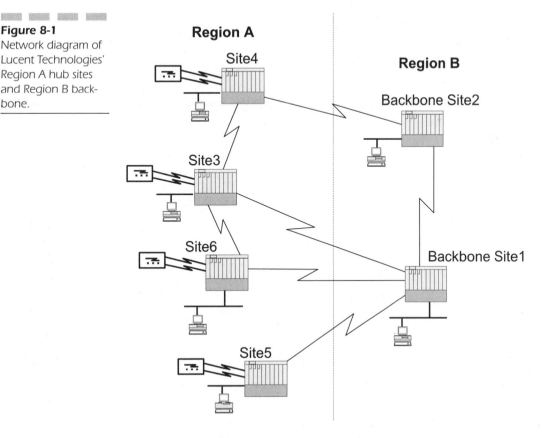

Lucent Technologies' Objectives

The focus of the NRP project was primarily on the proposed People-Soft HRMS application deployment. Given the need to determine the potential impact of the new application, the following objectives were identified:

▪ To understand the characteristics of the existing applications on the network, including which applications are being used and the usage by the most critical (top N) applications

▪ To identify any existing performance bottlenecks within the Region A network

▪ To characterize a proposed new application (PeopleSoft HRMS) and to understand the traffic demands it would make on the Region A network if it were deployed

▪ To evaluate the NetMaker XA suite of tools

Project Tasks

To accomplish the identified objectives, the following tasks were performed. Three of the tasks fall into the area of baselining, one of the tasks is in the area of application planning, and one task is in the area of capacity planning.

Baselining:

▪ Identify the Region A network and relevant portions of the Region B network (Backbone Site1 and Backbone Site2) to generate a physical inventory of the network components.

▪ Collect usage-based data and identify and document current network utilization.

▪ Collect application-based traffic using WAN Network General Distributed Server Sniffers (DSSs) installed on the Region B side of the four circuits that connect the Region A network to Region B. Identify and document the application mix.

Application planning:

▪ Monitor the PeopleSoft HRMS application being developed, using a Network General Sniffer to identify application traffic characteristics, and create traffic profiles of the HRMS activities.

Capacity planning:

■ Build a valid baseline model of the network using the NetMaker XA tool suite.

■ Create "what-if" scenarios that incorporate the new PeopleSoft transaction traffic according to the defined deployment strategy (number of users and transaction rates) to predict network operation under full application deployment. Identify any network changes required to support the new network load.

These tasks underwent some modifications, as noted in the following sections.

Project Overview

The project was set up and organized through various conference calls that identified the project objectives, the schedule, the equipment, and who would participate. Lucent Technologies used existing network diagrams and knowledge of the location of key data centers and application servers to identify collection points. Once the collection points were identified, Lucent Technologies decided that the project would need four Network General Sniffers to collect application-based data on the four Region A–to–Region B circuits. The project schedule was created, and the project began.

The first step was to generate a network inventory. Often the network inventory step is completed as part of reviewing the network drawings and gathering needed information to prepare for a project. This was the case at Lucent Technologies.

Prior to launching the discovery processes, the Lucent Technologies project personnel obtained the needed SNMP access, and prepared a list of router addresses that specified the area of interest (Region A). The discovery and validation of the Region A network and a selected portion of the Region B network, using the NetMaker XA Discovery tool, were completed on the first day.

The next step was creating the traffic inventory. This involved collecting usage-based data from routers and application-based data using Network General Sniffers. Both usage-based and application-based data needed to be collected at the same time. This coordination was necessary in order to correlate the usage information to the type of applications utilizing the network. The collection of both usage-based data and application-based data began after the discovery was completed. The data collection was done from within Region B during hours that corresponded to the business day in Region A.

Usage-based data was collected for approximately two weeks from the routers using the NetMaker XA WAN Baseliner tool. Collecting application-based data using Network General Sniffers for traffic inventory was more difficult, for various reasons; therefore, correlated usage-based and application-based data was available for only part of the two week period. Network General worked with Lucent Technologies to fix the problems, and Lucent Technologies was able to collect three consecutive days of correlated usage-based and application-based data samples. Collection was done for 15 hours to capture the Region A business day for each of the three days. The usage-based and application-based data from these three days was used for all subsequent analyses.

A Network General Sniffer was installed on the Site6–to–Backbone Site1 circuit, but the application-based data for this circuit was compressed by the routers, and the Network General Sniffer was unable to decode the compressed data, so no usable application-based data was collected for the Site6–to–Backbone Site1 circuit.

The next step in the project was to capture the application-specific traffic that would be needed for the application planning phase of the project. Two Lucent Technologies groups (the CIO Enterprise Architecture group and the Data Planning and Information Platform group) worked together to acquire the needed pieces for the application planning phase of the project. The Data Planning and Information Platform group provided a benchmark for the PeopleSoft application (HRMS transactions with probabilities of usage), a test bed, and two knowledgeable HRMS users to execute different parts of the benchmark. The CIO Enterprise Architecture group provided the Network General Sniffer to capture the application traffic. Application-based data was captured for every PeopleSoft HRMS transaction that Lucent Technologies identified as being important to understand.

This data was used to create the application profiles that would be used to build "what-if" scenarios for the PeopleSoft application when the project was ready for capacity planning activities. The Data Planning and Information Platform group also provided the application deployment plan, which provided the intended location of the People-Soft server and the projected number of users per site.

In the capacity planning phase, the first step was to create a baseline model of current network usage to use as the basis for capacity planning scenarios. This task required reviewing the usage-based data collected during the baselining phase and selecting a set of samples that represented "typical" usage patterns on the network.

Once the baseline model was created, capacity planning scenarios were created by loading the application profiles for the PeopleSoft HRMS transactions onto it based on the application deployment plan (locations, numbers of users, frequency of use by a single user). The scenarios were then run through the modeling analysis to predict the level of circuit utilization that would occur when the PeopleSoft HRMS application was deployed.

Project Results

For this project most of the techniques within the NRP baselining, application planning, and capacity planning areas were used. The results and analysis of the data collected for this project are discussed in the following sections.

Usage Results

The second baselining task in the list given earlier was to collect usage-based data using the NetMaker XA tool suite and to identify and document current network utilization.

Reviewing and comparing circuit utilization from the usage-based data is a crucial step in the baselining process. The analysis of circuit utilization was done for the circuits between Site3 and Backbone Site1, between Site5 and Backbone Site1, between Site4 and Backbone Site2, and between Site6 and Backbone Site1. The charts shown in this section were representative of the utilization levels seen on Lucent Technologies' network at the time of the project.

The first analysis, shown in Table 8.1, compares the Site3, Site5, and Site4 circuits using averages of 30-minute Kbyte quantities for the data collected during the 10-hour period that corresponded to the business day in Region A. These were the largest-capacity circuits in the system at the time of the project and carried almost all the data between Region B and Region A. The direction of data flow was primarily from Region B to Region A on all three circuits; a high amount of Internet traffic was seen on these circuits, probably because of users accessing

TABLE 8.1

Average Total Volume (Forward and Return) per Half-Hour

Circuit	Average Total Volume per Half-Hour
Site3 to Backbone Site1	30,000 Kbytes/30 min
Site5 to Backbone Site1	20,000 Kbytes/30 min
Site4 to Backbone Site2	25,000 Kbytes/30 min

information from Web sites in Region B. This pattern was especially striking in terms of the data on the Site3 circuit, where as much as 90% of the traffic was from Region B Backbone Site1 to Site3. The Site3 and Site5 circuits were 256Kbps circuits. The Site4 circuit was a 320Kbps circuit, whereas the Site6 circuit was a 64Kbps circuit. The Site4 circuit was a larger circuit, but data volume was less than on the Site3 circuit. Of these three circuits, the Site5 circuit was the least utilized.

The Site3–to–Backbone Site1 circuit was most highly utilized in total volume and percent utilization (other than Site6). These results were consistent with the complete set of usage-based data that was collected over the two week data capture period.

The next analysis was to compare the morning percent utilization to the afternoon percent utilization. The average percent utilization was also compared to the total number of samples. The following tables show this information for the Site3–to–Backbone Site1 (Table 8.2), Site5–to–Backbone Site1 (Table 8.3), Site4–to–Backbone Site2 (Table 8.4), and Site6–to–Backbone Site1 (Table 8.5) circuits. The significant data flow was from Backbone Site1 to Site3, from Backbone Site1 to Site5, from

TABLE 8.2

Average Percent Utilization (Five-Minute Samples), Site3 to Backbone Site1, 256K Circuit

Time of Day	Average Percent Utilization	
Morning	40%	About one-quarter of the samples are 60–70%.
Afternoon	50%	About one-third of the samples are 60–70%

TABLE 8.3

Average Percent Utilization (Five-Minute Samples), Site5 to Backbone Site1, 256K Circuit

Time of Day	Average Percent Utilization	
Morning	15%	About three-quarters of the samples are *below* 30%. A few samples are over 80%.
Afternoon	25%	About three-quarters of the samples are *below* 30%, with 3 non-consecutive samples over 50%.

TABLE 8.4

Average Percent
Utilization (Five-
Minute Samples),
Site4 to Backbone
Site2, 320K Circuit

Time of Day	Average Percent Utilization	
Morning	25%	Three samples are above 65%.
Afternoon	25%	Three samples are above 65%.

TABLE 8.5

Average Percent
Utilization (Five-
Minute Samples),
Site6 to Backbone
Site1, 64K Circuit

Time of Day	Average Percent Utilization	
Morning	85%	About three-quarters of the samples are above 80%.
Afternoon	80%	About one-half of the samples are above 80%.

Backbone Site2 to Site4, and from Site6 to Backbone Site1. All average and peak utilization numbers were of concern only for these directions of data flow. The Site3–to–Backbone Site1 circuit was highly asymmetrical—used primarily in only one direction. All percentage utilization figures were five-minute averages, collected over a 10-hour period corresponding to the Region A business day. Each sample equals one five-minute average.

Traffic Analysis Results

The third task within the area of baselining was to understand the characteristics of the existing applications on the network, including which applications are being used and the usage of the top N applications. To do this, the project personnel collected application-based traffic using Network General WAN DSSs installed on the Region B side of the four circuits that connect the Region A network to the Region B network, to identify and document the application mix.

Through this analysis, Lucent Technologies wanted to identify the top three applications that represented the largest portion of network utilization. Based on Lucent Technologies' areas of interest, this study focused on the three types of applications: intranet traffic, Internet traffic, and electronic mail.

The three circuits included in the analysis are Site3 to Backbone Site1, Site4 to Backbone Site2, and Site5 to Backbone Site1. The Site6–to–Backbone Site1 circuit is not included because the data over that circuit was compressed at the time of capture, and the Network General Sniffer could not decode it.

The data shows that the bulk of the traffic was Internet traffic rather than electronic mail and intranet traffic. Internet traffic accounted for 30–40% of the network conversations and 20–40% of the total volume for each sample (five-minute samples collected using a Network General Sniffer). Intranet traffic was much less, representing less than 7% of the total conversations and averaging about 10% of the total volume in the samples where it was represented.

Electronic mail consisted of two separate electronic mail transport protocols, referred to in this case study as Transport 1 and Transport 2. Together, electronic mail represented about 10% of the total conversations on all circuits and less than 10% of the total volume for any sample where electronic mail was represented. For the most part, Transport 1 mail represented the majority of the volume in any one sample.

The results in Tables 8.6 through 8.8 show each application of interest broken down by the number of network conversations on each one of the three circuits. "# of Conversations" is the conversations attributable to the particular application over the 10-hour period. "Total Conversations" is all conversations on this link over this 10-hour period. "Avg. Percent Vol./Sample" is the average percentage of bytes for this application over the total number of bytes on the circuit, during any five-minute sample period where the application of interest was active.

TABLE 8.6

Intranet Application Results

Intranet Applications	# of Conversations	Total Conversations	Average Percent Vol./Sample
Site3 to Backbone Site1	297 (7%)	4388	25%
Site5 to Backbone Site1	199 (4%)	5468	12%
Site4 to Backbone Site2	93 (1%)	6740	8%

TABLE 8.7

Internet Application Results

Internet Applications	# of Conversations	Total Conversations	Average Percent Vol./Sample
Site3 to Backbone Site1	1403 (32%)	4388	20%
Site5 to Backbone Site1	2333 (43%)	5468	36%
Site4 to Backbone Site2	2421 (36%)	6740	34%

TABLE 8.8

Electronic Mail
Application Results

Electronic Mail	# of Conversations	Total Conversations	Average Percent Vol./Sample
Transport 1 Mail			
Site3 to Backbone Site1	164 (4%)	4388	3%
Site5 to Backbone Site1	419 (8%)	5468	8%
Site4 to Backbone Site2	103 (2%)	6740	6%
Transport 2 Mail			
Site3 to Backbone Site1	165 (4%)	4388	3%
Site5 to Backbone Site1	340 (6%)	5468	1%
Site4 to Backbone Site2	201 (3%)	6740	1%

The average was calculated using the first 20 samples collected starting at an hour that corresponded to midday in Region A, where this application was active.

Application Planning Results

The application planning task involved monitoring the PeopleSoft HRMS application being developed and using a Network General Sniffer to identify application traffic characteristics. Traffic profiles of the HRMS transactions were created using this data.

Application-based data was collected while a knowledgeable user executed the benchmark activities. This data was used to create People-Soft HRMS transaction profiles, which were later used within the area of capacity planning. The analysis done in this phase of application planning used a benchmark developed by Lucent Technologies personnel in the Data Planning and Information Platform group as a guide to the transactions that were going to be important for the PeopleSoft HRMS user community. Table 8.9 shows each activity in the benchmark and the estimated rate at which a typical user would perform this activity.

The benchmark was used as a guide during the application capture session. The test bed environment included a 90 MHz Pentium client, a server with the PeopleSoft HRMS database, a Citrix server, and a Network General Sniffer to capture the network conversations created by

TABLE 8.9	Transaction	Frequency
PeopleSoft HRMS Benchmark	**Administer Personnel**	
	—Hire Employee	15% of workforce
	—Update Personal Information	2 per employee per year
	——Address	
	——Name	
	——Phone	
	——Family Status	
	—Update Job Information	8 per employee per year
	——Promotion	
	——Transfer	
	——Leave of Absence	
	——Terminate	
	——Retire	
	——Rehire	
	——Change Employee Class/Type	
	——Salary Change	
	—Track Citizenship	1% of workforce
	—Track Additional Pay	2 per employee per year
	—Track Skills, Training, Education	6 per employee per year
	Plan Careers	
	—Create/Update Plan	10% of workforce
	—Review Employee Progress	10 per plan per year
	Recruit Global Employee	
	—Create Job Req	15% of workforce
	—Record Application Information	10 per Job Req
	—Identify Qualified Candidates	2 per Job Req
	—Track Applicant Activities	3 per candidate
	—Search/Select Candidate	1 per Job Req
	Track Global Assignments	
	—Assign Employee to Assignment	2% of workforce
	—Identify Related Requirements	3 per Assignee per year
	——Visa	
	——Dependents	
	——Permits	
	—Track Employee Movement	3 per Assignee per year
	—Complete Assignment	1 for each Assignee
	Logon/Logoff	3 per user per day

Figure 8-2
Test bed
environment.

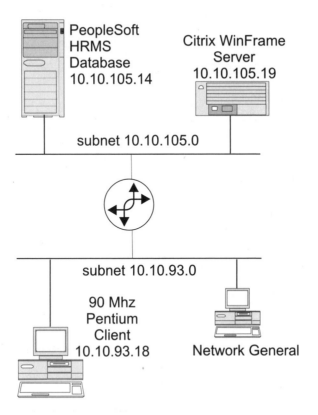

the benchmark transactions. The client was located on a different sub-network from either the PeopleSoft HRMS database or the Citrix Win-Frame server. Figure 8-2 shows a diagram of the test bed environment (with IP addresses changed to fictitious addresses).

The data for the benchmark was captured using three different client configurations:

■ Native PeopleSoft (the standard PeopleSoft user interface) without caches loaded on the client

■ Native PeopleSoft with caches loaded on the client

■ Citrix WinFrame client

The results of the data capture for each HRMS transaction were thoroughly reviewed to determine which transactions should be used to create application traffic profiles. The key points that were considered in deciding which transactions to include for the capacity planning scenarios were

■ The frequency with which a transaction was likely to occur (see Table 8.9)

TABLE 8.10

PeopleSoft Data
from Network
General Sniffer, by
Activity

Login

	1stFrm	LastFrm	Protocol	Addr1	Addr2	Frms1	Frms2
HRMS Native No Cache	14:43:49	14:43:51	TCP-TNS	[10.10.105.14]	[10.10.93.18]	44	26
HRMS Native No Cache	14:43:53	14:44:39	TCP-TNS	[10.10.105.14]	[10.10.93.18]	1340	747
HRMS Native with Cache	11:05:22	11:05:24	TCP-TNS	[10.10.105.14]	[10.10.93.18]	44	26
HRMS Native with Cache	11:05:26	11:05:43	TCP-TNS	[10.10.105.14]	[10.10.93.18]	419	242

Login to Citrix

	1stFrm	LastFrm	Protocol	Addr1	Addr2	Frms1	Frms2
Login to Peoplesoft	13:09:11	13:11:54	TCP	[10.10.105.19]	[10.10.93.18]	174	129
Login to Citrix	13:09:11	13:09:11	UDP	[10.10.105.19]	[10.10.93.18]	2	1

Logout

	1stFrm	LastFrm	Protocol	Addr1	Addr2	Frms1	Frms2
Native HRMS no Cache	11:00:09	11:03:10	TCP-TNS	[10.10.105.14]	[10.10.93.18]	1101	573
Native HRMS with Cache	11:51:08	11:51:08	TCP-TNS	[10.10.105.14]	[10.10.93.18]	7	5

Hire Employee

	1stFrm	LastFrm	Protocol	Addr1	Addr2	Frms1	Frms2
Native HRMS no Cache	9:59:42	10:00:00	TCP-TNS	[10.10.105.14]	[10.10.93.18]	638	333
Native HRMS no Cache	10:00:02	10:04:57	TCP-TNS	[10.10.105.14]	[10.10.93.18]	8962	4574
Native HRMS no Cache	10:05:08	10:07:39	TCP-TNS	[10.10.105.14]	[10.10.93.18]	498	268
Native HRMS with Cache	11:10:10	11:14:48	TCP-TNS	[10.10.105.14]	[10.10.93.18]	660	375
Native HRMS with Cache	11:15:09	11:17:21	TCP-TNS	[10.10.105.14]	[10.10.93.18]	142	79
Citrix	13:35:10	13:40:00	TCP	[10.10.105.19]	[10.10.93.18]	1620	1538
Citrix	13:40:02	13:41:23	TCP	[10.10.105.19]	[10.10.93.18]	286	276

▨ The quantity of data that was sent to accomplish the transaction (see Table 8.10)

Based on these criteria (frequency and volume of data) the following transactions were selected as best representing PeopleSoft HRMS transactions for the purposes of creating application traffic profiles:

▨ Hire Employee transaction using native PeopleSoft with caches loaded.

▨ Hire Employee using the Citrix WinFrame client.

▨ Login to native PeopleSoft with caches loaded.

Table 8.10 shows an example of the data captured by the Network General Sniffer for a subset of the transactions that were chosen to represent PeopleSoft HRMS usage. The client is shown in Table 8.10 as "Addr2" (10.10.93.18), the servers are shown as "Addr1". The address 10.10.105.14 was the PeopleSoft database server. Address 10.10.105.19 was the Citrix WinFrame server. The transactions that are in the foregoing list are those that were used to create the application profiles for three transactions shown in Table 8.11.

The source address shown in Table 8.11 was the server side of the conversation in all cases, either the PeopleSoft HRMS server or the Citrix WinFrame server. The destination address was the Pentium client,

TABLE 8.11

PeopleSoft
Application Profiles

Transaction	Source Address	Destination Address	Bytes Forward	Bytes Return	Average Kbps Forward	Average Kbps Return
HRMS Login	10.10.105.14	10.10.93.18	357226	36121	9.53	0.96
Citrix, Hire Employee	10.10.105.19	10.10.93.18	204811	94710	5.46	2.53
Native, Hire Employee	10.10.105.14	10.10.93.18	159514	100564	4.25	2.68

which had the ability to run either the native PeopleSoft client or the Citrix WinFrame client. "Bytes Forward" was the number of bytes from the server to the client. "Bytes Return" was the number of bytes from the client to server. The "Average Kbps Forward" and "Average Kbps Return" were calculated as the number of bytes (forward or return) multiplied by 8 and divided by five minutes. The HRMS Login, Citrix Hire Employee, and Native Hire Employee activities took at least five minutes to complete during the benchmark testing.

APPLICATION ASSESSMENT The next step in application planning is to identify the locations where the application will be deployed and the number of users that might use the application. This information is used in the capacity planning phase to build capacity planning scenarios. Table 8.12 shows the proposed locations of the PeopleSoft server and the PeopleSoft HRMS clients (many of these are remote sites not shown by name in Figure 8-1). The "Possible # of HR Users" shows the total number of HR staff users at each location. The capacity planning scenarios also require information on the frequency of use of the application by a single user in a given amount of time. For this project, that information was provided along with the benchmark, as shown in Table 8.9.

Capacity Planning Results

Many of the activities up to this point have been in preparation for capacity planning. Through the analysis of the usage-based data, Lucent Technologies was able to identify the set of samples that would represent the existing network load (the baseline model). Through the analysis of the PeopleSoft HRMS application-based data,

TABLE 8.12

Planned PeopleSoft
Deployment Chart

City, Country (Client/Server)	Possible # of HR Users
Site4, Region A (Server)	N/A
Site8, Region A (Client)	1
Site6, Region A (Client)	6
Site9, Region A (Client)	5
Site3, Region A (Client)	2
Site10, Region A (Client)	3
Site11, Region A (Client)	3
Site12, Region A (Client)	1
Site5, Region A (Client)	4
Site13, Region A (Client)	3
Site14, Region A (Client)	2
Site15, Region A (Client)	3
Site4, Region A (Client)	5
Site16, Region A (Client)	2
Site17, Region A (Client)	5
Site18, Region A (Client)	6

Lucent Technologies was able to determine which transactions best represent the most likely user activity as already discussed. At this point, Lucent Technologies was prepared to model the impact the proposed PeopleSoft deployment would have on the existing network.

Several tasks were to be accomplished during the capacity planning phase of the project. The first was to build a valid baseline model of the network. The second was to create "what-if" capacity planning scenarios that incorporated the new PeopleSoft transaction traffic profiles according to the defined PeopleSoft deployment strategy (number of users and transaction rates). Finally, a modeling analysis was run for the capacity planning "what-if" scenarios to predict network operation under full application deployment.

CREATING THE BASELINE MODEL   The baselining steps identified how the network was behaving at the time of data capture. Creating the baseline model involves determining which specific set of usage-based data represents the network behavior in order to create a snapshot of the network. In creating the baseline model, Lucent Technologies was interested in planning against the worst case. Each day's data set was loaded into the model and then compared, looking for the busiest day. The next step was to identify the busiest hour or half-hour. Although Lucent Technologies was able to correlate only three days of usage-based data and application-based data, those three days were representative of patterns seen within the entire usage-based data set captured. Of those three days, the day with the highest volume was used for all the analysis in this section and to build the baseline model. The data shown in Figure 8-3 was used.

Figure 8-3 shows the total aggregate number of bytes (cumulative, both forward and return) by half-hour averages for all the Region A sites. Based on this data, Lucent Technologies decided to use the peak hour, which was the traffic collected during the hour between 22:30 and 23:30 (Region B time), as the baseline traffic for the capacity planning scenarios. This hour was determined to have the most network activity and represent the worst case of the system behavior.

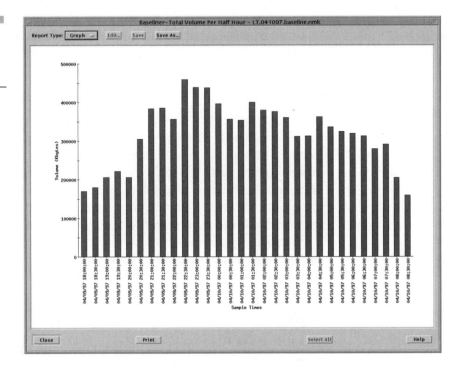

Figure 8-3
System usage chart. (© Make Systems, Inc.)

BUILDING THE CAPACITY PLANNING SCENARIOS Using the location information of the proposed deployment plan to map the transaction conversations, three scenarios were built. Two of the three scenarios were chosen to compare the Citrix WinFrame client versus native PeopleSoft client network behavior. The Hire Employee transaction was chosen because of the comparatively large amount of data transferred across the network and the high probability for this type of activity to occur. The Login transaction was chosen for one of the scenarios because of the high number of potential users who could attempt to log in simultaneously.

Scenario 1 assumed that one PeopleSoft HRMS client at each site was doing a Hire Employee transaction using the native PeopleSoft interface simultaneously (within the same five-minute sample period).

Scenario 2 was similar to Scenario 1 but used the Citrix WinFrame client communicating to the Citrix server. The Citrix server was assumed to be at Site4, colocated with the PeopleSoft HRMS database.

Scenario 3 was the Login scenario. It assumes that for any site with more than five employees, two will log in simultaneously, with one user per site logging in at the other locations.

Using the application profiles shown in Table 8.11, project personnel imported the profiles and created network conversations within the baseline model, using NetMaker XA. The location and number of users, as shown in Table 8.12, were used to define the conversations for each of the scenarios. All conversations were created between Region A Site4, where the PeopleSoft server was proposed to be located in these scenarios, and the various other client sites in Region A.

HIRE EMPLOYEE SCENARIO, CACHE LOADED For this scenario the native PeopleSoft Hire Employee application profile was used to add network conversations to the baseline model. A modeling analysis was run using the NetMaker XA Planner tool and the NetMaker XA Analyzer tool in the interval analysis mode. The interval analysis mode ran the model for every five-minute period from 22:30 to 23:30 local (Region B) time. A sample of the modeling results is shown in Table 8.13.

After the model was run, the results showed that three circuits were predicted to be at saturation (100% utilized), which would have a severe impact on transaction response time for users of these circuits. The circuits were

- Backbone Site1 to Site3
- Site4 to Site3
- Site6 to Site9

TABLE 8.13

Simulation Statistics, Hire Employee Scenario, Native PeopleSoft (Cache Loaded)

	(from 22:30:00 to 22:35:00)		(from 22:35:00 to 22:40:00)		(from 22:40:00 to 22:45:00)		(from 22:45:00 to 22:50:00)	
	(Avg)	(Max)	(Avg)	(Max)	(Avg)	(Max)	(Avg)	(Max)
Per-demand round-trip delay (ms)	154.622429	1737.518509	180.047683	2393.766024	160.864048	1866.076192	Infinite	Infinite
Per-demand forward delay (ms)	55.547410	317.001043	59.718442	372.136655	51.840741	269.109950	Infinite	Infinite
Per-demand return delay (ms)	99.075020	1664.421142	120.329242	2325.745156	109.023307	1794.332755	Infinite	Infinite
Average packet delay (ms)	152.331445	1664.421142	187.075882	2325.745156	134.926914	1794.332755	Infinite	Infinite
Average WAN link utilization	34.908%		37.414%		35.364%		39.554%	
Minimum WAN link utilization	4.343%		3.457%		2.986%		3.424%	
Maximum WAN link utilization	97.73%		97.586%		96.505%		100.128%	

The predicted response times on a per-packet basis can be found in Table 8.13 for a sample of modeling runs. Applications transiting these circuits could have as much as two seconds of round-trip delay per packet. This scenario required about 300 packets to be transferred for each Hire Employee transaction. At a two-second-per-packet round-trip delay, this type of transaction could take as much as 10 minutes.

HIRE EMPLOYEE SCENARIO, CITRIX WINFRAME For this scenario, the Hire Employee application profile for Citrix WinFrame was used to add network conversations to the baseline model as discussed previously. The same type of modeling analysis was run using the Net-Maker XA Planner tool and the NetMaker XA Analyzer tool in the interval analysis mode. The interval analysis mode ran the model for every five-minute period from 22:30 to 23:30 local (Region B) time.

The results of running this model again showed that the same three circuits were predicted to be at saturation (100% utilized): Backbone Site1 to Site3, Site4 to Site3, and Site6 to Site9.

Applications transiting these circuits could have as much as two seconds of round-trip delay per packet. Compared to the previous scenario, the Citrix WinFrame scenario sends considerably more (although smaller) packets to transfer the same data, thus creating the possibility of a much higher total transaction response time.

LOGIN SCENARIO The Login application profile was used to add network conversations to the baseline model to create this scenario. The model was then run using the NetMaker XA Planner tool and the Net-Maker XA Analyzer tool, in the same manner as the other two modeling analyses. Again, the modeling analysis ran for every five-minute interval from 22:30 to 23:30 Region B local time.

After this analysis was run, the three circuits already mentioned were predicted to be at saturation (100% utilized). In addition, the circuits from Site6 to Site3, from Site5 to Backbone Site1, and from Site3 to Site17 were also at saturation. The additional circuits were saturated because the PeopleSoft (native mode) login activity uses more bandwidth than either the Hire Employee scenario using Citrix WinFrame or the Hire Employee scenario using native PeopleSoft with caches loaded.

Project Conclusions

Lucent Technologies' first objective was to understand the characteristics of the existing application mix on the Region A network. During the consulting engagement, Lucent Technologies personnel decided to focus on Internet, intranet, and electronic mail applications (Transport 1 and Transport 2) for detailed analysis.

The following conclusions emerged from the analysis of these three applications:

- Internet traffic was responsible for 20 to 40% of the volume of data on the Site3–to–Backbone Site1, Site5–to–Backbone Site1, and Site4–to–Backbone Site2 circuits, which are the main backbone circuits back to Region B.

- Internet traffic was also responsible for 30–40% of the network conversations (sessions) on these same three circuits.

- The other two applications produce significantly less volume of data and number of conversations. The order of usage of these other applications was intranet, Transport 1 mail, and Transport 2 mail, with intranet responsible for the most volume of the three. Even so, the number of intranet sessions and volume of data was an order of magnitude less than those of Internet traffic at the time of this analysis.

Lucent Technologies' second objective was to identify performance bottlenecks within the Region A network. During the NRP project it was decided to focus on the following circuits: Site3 to Backbone Site1, Site5 to Backbone Site1, Site4 to Backbone Site2, and Site6 to Backbone Site1. At the time of the project, these four circuits carried most of the data from Region A to Region B and vice versa. While the other Region A circuits were important, bottlenecks on those other circuits did not have the same impact as bottlenecks on these four.

The following conclusions emerged from the analysis of these four circuits:

- The circuit from Site3 to Backbone Site1 was the most heavily used, both in volume of data and capacity used (percentage of utilization).

- Of the usage-based data analyzed, the circuit from Site3 to Backbone Site1 averaged 70% usage, with many peak values above 70% and some peaks at saturation (100% used).

- The circuit from Site6 to backbone Site1 was the highest-utilized circuit in the entire Region A network. This circuit was close to saturation most of the time (for entire business day), possibly causing performance problems for the network users at the factory located at Region A Site9. Currently this circuit is a 64K circuit with compression.

■ The circuits from Site5 to Backbone Site1 and from Site4 to Backbone Site2 have less volume of data and capacity used (percentage utilization) than the Site3–to–Backbone Site1 circuit. In the days analyzed, the volume of data for the Site4–to–Backbone Site2 circuit averaged about two-thirds the volume of the Site3–to–Backbone Site1 circuit. The Site5–to–Backbone Site1 circuit averaged about one-half the volume of the Site3–to–Backbone Site1 circuit.

Lucent Technologies' third objective was to characterize a proposed mission-critical application, PeopleSoft HRMS, and to understand the additional demand it would make on the Region A network if it were deployed to many key sites. During the project it was determined that it was also important to understand the demand Citrix WinFrame would make on the network when used with PeopleSoft HRMS. The interest in Citrix WinFrame was based on a belief that it could give PeopleSoft users better performance than using the native PeopleSoft HRMS clients.

The following conclusions emerged from the analysis of PeopleSoft HRMS as a proposed new, mission-critical network application:

■ Assuming that the PeopleSoft HRMS databases and the Citrix WinFrame server are colocated on the same LAN, the network bandwidth needed by the clients (for both Citrix WinFrame clients and native PeopleSoft HRMS clients) was low (10Kbps per session at most). Citrix WinFrame clients need more bandwidth than native PeopleSoft clients by a small percentage (1–3 Kbps).

■ In addition to needing more bandwidth, the Citrix WinFrame client data was sent in small packets, has no windowing (every packet must be acknowledged), and therefore requires more network time to do the same corresponding activity as the native client.

■ PeopleSoft recommends the Citrix WinFrame solution for WAN environments with many circuits in the range of 64K to 128 Kbps. The WAN environment within Region A of the network, at the time of the project, had many circuits that were within the suggested range. Because of the discrepancy between the observed network behavior and the PeopleSoft recommendation, more testing and verification of user perception of performance should be done. Additional testing similar to this project should be repeated, either in a WAN environment with a circuit of 64K to 128Kbps or in a simulated WAN test environment. In addition, there should be investigations to determine whether the Citrix WinFrame server can be more optimally configured.

■ Regardless of the client chosen (native PeopleSoft or Citrix Win-Frame), the overwhelming performance issue for this proposed application is the existing congestion on many critical circuits within the Region A network. This issue should be addressed, in order to deliver acceptable performance to PeopleSoft HRMS users.

Many changes have been made in Region A, and continue to be made, based in part on the results of this study as well as on other types of analyses of Lucent Technologies' business needs and other network issues. In addition, as a result of this NRP project, Lucent Technologies has subsequently applied this NRP methodology to testing many other applications.

9

The 3M Company

The 3M Company, headquartered in St. Paul, Minnesota, is well known as the manufacturer of everyday items such as Post-it® Notes, Scotch™ brand tape, and Thinsulate™ material in winter clothing. 3M has successfully put science and technology to work in adhesives, ceramics, coated abrasives, microstructured surfaces, fasteners, and optics. 3M products are used in health care, construction, dental and orthodontic, office, photographic, and electrical applications. As an organization, 3M literally spans the globe with a large number of locations and a variety of networking needs.

As part of its overall planning process, 3M has a multiyear plan to deploy three PeopleSoft modules—Financial Management, Procurement, and Customer Service—throughout its global organization. As part of the development effort, the Network Support and Systems Services Group of the IT Infrastructure organization was charged with determining what network infrastructure would be required to support these new applications. With the help of a consultant, the group implemented a Network Resource Planning (NRP) study to evaluate the network's ability to support the PeopleSoft deployment plan. The NRP project actually looked at only two of the three PeopleSoft applications: the Financial Management and Procurement modules. The modules studied for this project were PeopleSoft version 6.

This case study focuses primarily on the application planning and capacity planning areas of 3M's NRP study, although the baselining activities are also described, because they are requirements for the other two areas. It also describes how 3M created quality-of-service metrics that could be used to evaluate the results obtained during the capacity planning phase of the project.

Project Background

At the time of this NRP study, 3M's network was worldwide and supported a work force of approximately 74,000 employees. Of these, approximately one-half are located within the United States. The enterprise network consisted primarily of Bay Networks routers with some IBM and Cisco routers, all using a combination of OSPF and RIP routing protocols. The main network hub site for the corporation was located in St. Paul (serving the United States and international locations outside of Europe), with a second network hub site located in Bracknell, UK, that served Europe. 3M's enterprise network was a combination of leased-line circuits and Frame Relay PVCs. There was also a metropolitan area network (MAN) serving the St. Paul, Minnesota, area using SMDS.

The 3M enterprise network had two wide area networks: 3MNETXpress and OUS (for "Outside the United States"). 3MNETXpress consisted of over 100 sites located in the continental United States, Alaska, Hawaii, and Mexico. OUS connected sites in Europe, Asia-Pacific, South America, and Canada. These two networks connected in St. Paul through a LAN-based network called the Exchange Network.

3M Information Technology's Objectives

3M's overall objective for the NRP project was to determine what network infrastructure optimization was needed to support the new

PeopleSoft modules with an acceptable quality of service. Specific areas of concern were the locations of the PeopleSoft servers and application-level response times for PeopleSoft clients using the new modules.

3M's objective for the baselining phase was to collect data to create a model of existing WAN usage relevant to the selected set of proposed PeopleSoft server and client sites. 3M initially decided to focus the baselining effort by limiting the scope of the data collection to the first-phase proposed PeopleSoft client sites (approximately 20) and the proposed PeopleSoft server sites within the 3M enterprise network. All analyses within this project were to be focused on these selected locations.

For the application planning phase, 3M's objective was to characterize the traffic behavior of the PeopleSoft version 6 modules and document a set of quality-of-service metrics to be used as a goal within the capacity planning phase. The group wanted to evaluate the behavior of these application modules with and without using the Citrix WinFrame application as a proxy server, as well as running the application modules over several different types of WAN circuits.

The objective for the capacity planning phase was to predict how the network infrastructure would support the quality-of-service goals identified in the application planning phase for the PeopleSoft modules. To do this, 3M needed to create representative models of the network as it was predicted to behave after deployment of the PeopleSoft application modules. The group created "what-if" scenarios using the data collected during the baselining phase along with the PeopleSoft application profiles created during the application planning phase. These "what-if" scenarios also used metrics developed as part of the projected application deployment strategy, such as numbers of users and transaction rates, to represent the proposed deployment of the PeopleSoft application.

Project Tasks

3M's NRP project took place in three phases that corresponded to the three NRP phases as described in this book:

■ The baselining phase consisted of collecting baseline usage-based data from the selected sites (designated as proposed PeopleSoft client

Figure 9-1
3M PeopleSoft
test bed.

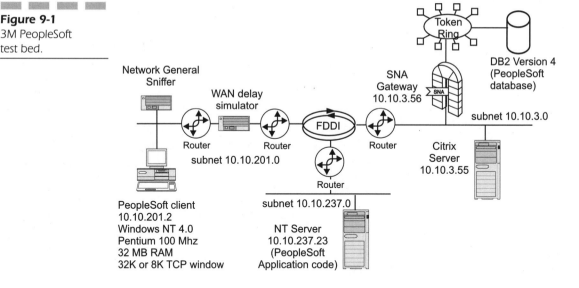

or server sites), using Make Systems' NetMaker XA WAN Baseliner tool. This data was used to model the network as it existed.

- The application planning phase consisted of capturing application traffic data from two of the three PeopleSoft modules (Financial Management and Procurement) in the development lab using a Network General Sniffer. An Adtech Data Channel Simulator was used to simulate the delays that would occur over various wide area circuits. Quality-of-service metrics were developed, and application profiles were created for selected transactions within the PeopleSoft modules studied. The lab test bed environment was set up as shown in Figure 9-1.

- The capacity planning phase consisted of creating "what-if" scenarios that projected throughput and performance of the network when the new PeopleSoft modules were deployed. The data collected during the first two phases was used to create the models. This phase was strictly analytical and did not involve any further data collection.

Specific tasks were identified within each of these three NRP phases. The consultant worked with the 3M staff, guiding them through the following tasks:

Baselining tasks:

- Discover the 3M network, including the sites selected as proposed locations of PeopleSoft clients and servers, using Make Systems' NetMaker XA Discovery tool.

- Collect usage-based traffic for one 24-hour period on the relevant components of the network that include the specific locations of interest for this study, using Make Systems' NetMaker XA Baseliner tool.

- Import the usage-based traffic into Make Systems' NetMaker XA performance management tool, and create relevant reports to document and analyze network utilization.

Application planning tasks:

- Perform the benchmark activities for the two PeopleSoft modules (Procurement and Financial Management) between the native PeopleSoft client and the SNA gateway, with delays introduced using the Adtech Data Channel Simulator to simulate both Frame Relay and leased lines at various speeds. Using a Network General Sniffer, monitor the traffic as a test of the benchmark. Evaluate the application response times to develop quality-of-service metrics. See Figure 9-1.

- Perform the benchmark activities for the two PeopleSoft modules between the Citrix WinFrame client software and the Citrix server, with delays introduced to simulate both Frame Relay and leased lines at various speeds. Evaluate the application response times to develop quality-of-service metrics. See Figure 9-1.

- Using a Network General Sniffer, monitor the traffic between the native PeopleSoft client and the SNA gateway for each of the two PeopleSoft modules to identify application traffic characteristics over a LAN. See Figure 9-1.

- Monitor and collect the traffic for each of the two PeopleSoft modules between the Citrix WinFrame client software and the Citrix server, to identify application traffic characteristics over a LAN. See Figure 9-1.

- Monitor and collect the traffic for each of the two PeopleSoft modules between the native PeopleSoft client and the SNA gateway, with delays introduced to simulate communication over a WAN using the Adtech Data Channel Simulator (see Figure 9-1); simulate both Frame Relay and leased lines at various speeds.

- Monitor and collect the traffic for each of the two PeopleSoft modules between the Citrix WinFrame client software and the Citrix server, with delays introduced to simulate both Frame Relay and leased lines at various speeds. See Figure 9-1.

- Import the application traffic data into Make Systems' NetMaker XA performance management tool, and create application profiles for the specific application transactions (Logon, Procurement—Create Requisition, and General Ledger—Journal Query) to be used to create capacity planning scenarios for "what-if" analysis.

Capacity planning tasks:

- Create a merged-peak baseline model to use as the basis for the "what-if" analyses. The usage-based data from the baselining phase is used to create the baseline models.

- Using a set of assumptions about the application deployment (number of users, locations, and frequency of use), create capacity planning scenarios using NetMaker XA tools to model the network traffic load that will occur when the applications are being used over the network.

- Analyze the results to determine whether quality-of-service goals will be met, and redesign the network if necessary to meet those goals.

Project Activities

The activities within the baselining phase prepared the foundation needed to obtain meaningful results throughout the rest of the project.

The project focus was primarily in the area of application planning and capacity planning. 3M put significant effort into defining the metrics of acceptable quality of service from the user perspective. The group worked closely with knowledgeable PeopleSoft users from 3M's application development group to determine the amount of application response delay that would be acceptable to a "typical" user of the new PeopleSoft modules.

The capacity planning activities were intended to identify changes in the network infrastructure that might be required to deliver acceptable quality of service for all new PeopleSoft application activities under study.

Baselining Activities

The project began with the discovery of the 3M network, including the sites selected as proposed locations of PeopleSoft clients and servers. All the selected PeopleSoft client sites were domestic sites connected directly to routers on the St. Paul MAN through either Frame Relay or leased-line circuits. Although 3M had initially identified five proposed server sites throughout their enterprise network, all the proposed client locations identified for this study were to use a server on a LAN in the St. Paul data center as the PeopleSoft server.

The collection of the usage-based traffic was accomplished using Make Systems' NetMaker XA WAN Baseliner tool. Collection was done for two business days. Data was collected from all of the sites (approximately 20) identified as potential PeopleSoft client sites. The data from all of these sites was analyzed for overall network performance. All the sites where data was captured would potentially have PeopleSoft users, and 3M wanted to include these sites within the capacity planning phase of the project. Six of these sites were identified as being the first to deploy the new PeopleSoft modules; they were chosen for an additional, detailed usage-based analysis during the baselining phase of the project. For purposes of this case study, they will be known as sites A–F.

Discovery Results

The task of discovery and validation for the network model of the approximately 20 potential PeopleSoft client sites and potential PeopleSoft server sites was completed in one day. The results of the discovery are shown in Figure 9-2. Note that the map shows all five potential server sites (four were international), although these were not used in any subsequent analyses.

System Activity Results

Figure 9-3 is a System Volume graph, generated by NetMaker XA, that shows the aggregate traffic volume in kilobytes in half-hour intervals for all the subject domestic sites over one 24-hour period. The System Volume graph allowed the 3M project personnel to identify the busiest time periods for the network very quickly.

Figure 9-2
Results of network discovery. (© Make Systems, Inc.)

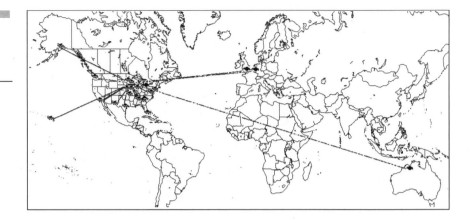

Figure 9-3
System Volume graph, 24 hours. (© Make Systems, Inc.)

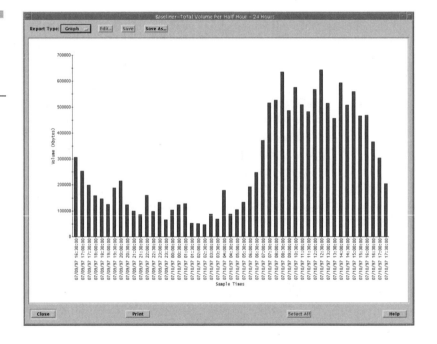

Circuit Utilization Results

Circuit utilization graphs show the percentage of circuit utilization, based on five-minute averages, in both the forward and return directions. The project personnel generated three graphs for each of the six selected sites, covering a 12-hour period (business day) divided into three 4-hour segments between 5:00 A.M. and 5:00 P.M. CDT. Figures 9-4 through

9-10 show one example of these 4-hour graphs for each leased-line or Frame Relay circuit connecting the six sites under study back to St. Paul. The graphs show the four-hour period from 9:00 A.M. to 1:00 P.M., which was chosen for analysis as a "busy" time period.

In the circuit utilization graph in Figure 9-4, the forward direction is Site A to St. Paul and the return direction is St. Paul to Site A. The next three graphs (Figures 9-5, 9-6, and 9-7) show three circuits (forward directions Site B to St. Paul, Site C to St. Paul, and Site B to Site C) together for the 4-hour time period to facilitate comparison of the traffic on the circuits. An examination of the graphs indicates a routing problem. The traffic destined for Site B from St. Paul went through Site C (return traffic in Figures 9-6 and 9-7) instead of over the T1 from St. Paul to Site B (return traffic in Figure 9-5). This problem was temporary and was due to an incomplete rollout of OSPF at the time the baseline data was collected.

In Figure 9-8 the forward direction is Site D to St. Paul, and the return direction is St. Paul to Site D. In Figure 9-9 the forward direction is Site E to St. Paul, and the return direction is St. Paul to Site E. In Figure 9-10 the forward direction is Site F to St. Paul, and the return

Figure 9-4
Circuit utilization,
Site A to St. Paul
(leased 2504K circuit),
9:00 A.M.–1:00 P.M.
(© Make Systems,
Inc.)

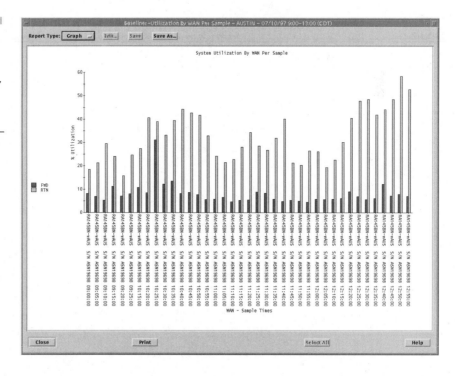

Figure 9-5
Circuit utilization,
Site B to St. Paul
(leased T1 circuit),
9:00 A.M.–1:00 P.M.
(© Make Systems,
Inc.)

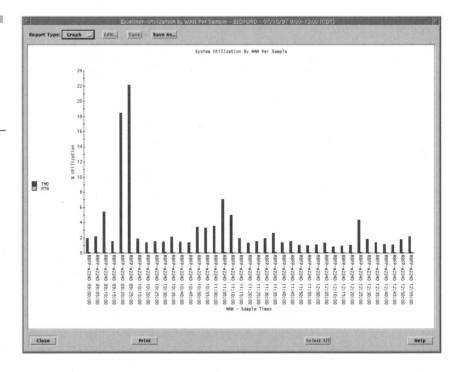

Figure 9-6
Circuit utilization,
Site C to St. Paul
(leased T1 circuit),
9:00 A.M.–1:00 P.M.
(© Make Systems,
Inc.)

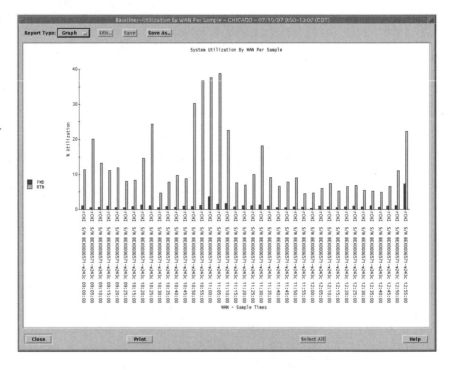

Figure 9-7

Circuit utilization,
Site B to Site C
(leased T1 circuit),
9:00 A.M.–1:00 P.M.
(© Make Systems,
Inc.)

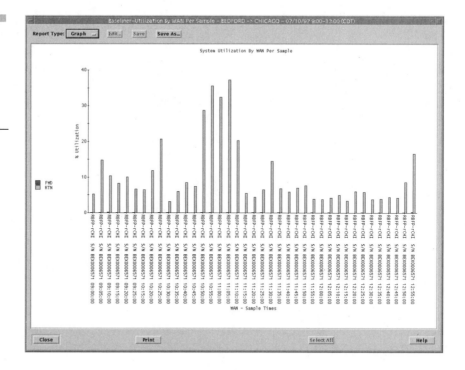

direction is St. Paul to Site F. Based on the results as shown in the circuit utilization graphs, there do not appear to be any utilization problems (saturated circuits), given the existing baseline network usage. There appears to be "headroom" for adding additional traffic on these circuits.

Application Planning Activities

The application planning phase of the project was accomplished in several key steps. First, the hardware (client workstation, Network General Sniffer, and Adtech Data Channel Simulator), the test bed environment, and the benchmark scripts were set up and tested. The activities in the benchmark scripts were representative transactions from two of the three PeopleSoft application modules.

Second, tests were performed to establish quality-of-service goals against which to evaluate the results of the capacity planning phase. The Adtech Data Channel Simulator was used to insert delays in order

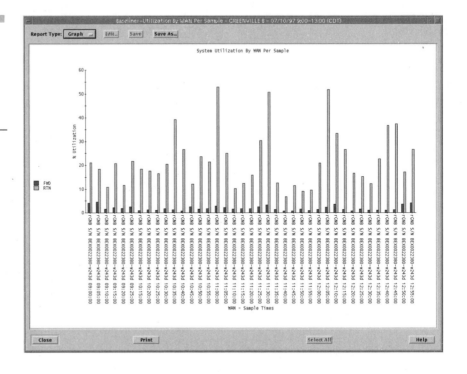

Figure 9-8
Circuit utilization,
Site D to St. Paul
(256K Frame Relay),
9:00 A.M.–1:00 P.M.
(© Make Systems,
Inc.)

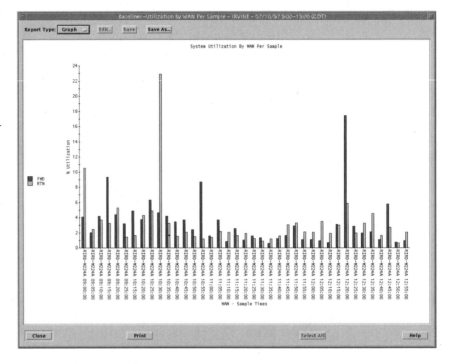

Figure 9-9
Circuit utilization,
Site E to St. Paul
(leased 512K circuit),
9:00 A.M.–1:00 P.M.
(© Make Systems,
Inc.)

Figure 9-10
Circuit utilization,
Site F to St. Paul
(leased 256K circuit),
9:00 A.M.–1:00 P.M.
(© Make Systems,
Inc.)

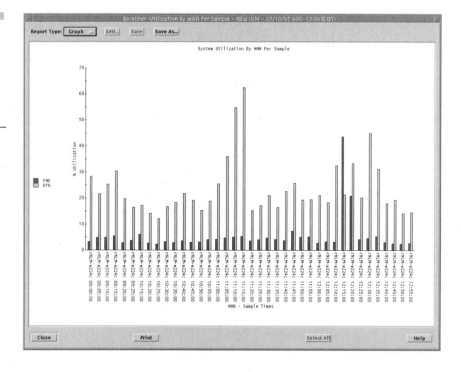

to test the application response time under different types of WAN environments.

Third, application capture activities were performed, using the application transactions defined in the benchmark, for both the native PeopleSoft client and the Citrix WinFrame client. The Adtech Data Channel Simulator was used to simulate different leased-line and Frame Relay circuits. The results of the data capture were then imported into NetMaker XA, and traffic profiles were created for three activities using the Network General Expert Analyzer Output data.

Benchmark Activities

The benchmark script used for this project consisted of three activities: PeopleSoft logon, Create Requisition in the Procurement module, and Journal Query in the General Ledger module. A knowledgeable PeopleSoft user from the application development group performed each of these activities for each client type (native PeopleSoft and Citrix WinFrame client) over four simulated circuit types.

Test Bed Environment

The environment included a standard Pentium client that could run either the native PeopleSoft client software or the Citrix WinFrame client software. The PeopleSoft database was a DB2 database on an IBM mainframe accessed through an IP-to-SNA gateway. The Citrix WinFrame server was located on the same LAN as the SNA gateway. For some PeopleSoft activities, network conversations also occurred between the client and an NT server located on another LAN. To simulate delays experienced on leased-line circuits and Frame Relay circuits, an Adtech Data Channel Simulator was installed between two routers on the LAN where the PeopleSoft client resided, as shown in the diagram in Figure 9-11. The Adtech was used to simulate four types of circuits: a 256K leased line, a T1 leased line, a 512K leased line, and a 256K Frame Relay circuit with a 128K committed information rate (CIR). These circuit types and sizes were chosen because they represent the four most common circuit types within the 3M enterprise network.

Establishing Quality-of-Service Goals

It was important to quantify the level of quality of service needed for the potential 3M PeopleSoft user community in order to be able to

Figure 9-11
3M PeopleSoft
test bed.

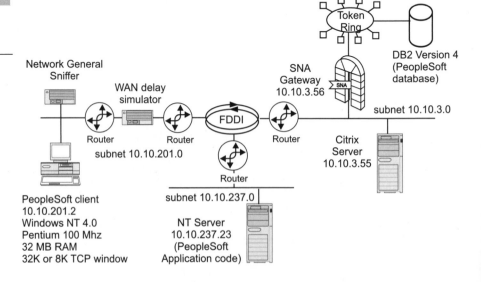

evaluate the results from the capacity planning phase of the NRP project. With the help of a knowledgeable PeopleSoft user from 3M's application development group, the NRP project team tested PeopleSoft activities with a range of delays to determine acceptable quality-ofservice goals. The quality-of-service goals were related to the distance of the circuit as well as circuit type.

3M defined acceptable quality of service based on two criteria. One criterion was the user's *perception* of quality of service, based on how quickly the application responded—that is, was ready for the next input or action. Two knowledgeable users executed the benchmark activities and provided their impressions of the response time. In 3M's case, for both the native PeopleSoft client and the Citrix WinFrame client, the users judged the application to be unusable as the amount of network delay grew from 300 ms to 1 second per packet. In the case of the native PeopleSoft client, the application response became so slow with these amounts of delay that the users felt the application was unacceptably slow. In the case of the Citrix WinFrame client, the screen display and the cursor lost synchronization, making the application physically unusable, with these amounts of delay.

The other criterion was whether the existing enterprise network was capable of supporting the desired response times. In other words, given a simulated application response time that the users deemed acceptable, was the actual enterprise network capable of delivering that response time?

The delays shown in Table 9.1 were found to meet both criteria, providing acceptable response to the user and being within the capabilities of 3M's existing enterprise network infrastructure. These numbers were based on historical data on round-trip delay metrics kept by 3M. The public Frame Relay system inherently has more delay, thus the greater values for the 256K Frame Relay circuit type. These values became the metrics by which the capacity planning results (the delays for each network conversation due to the new application traffic) were evaluated.

TABLE 9.1

Quality-of-Service Goals

Circuit type	Acceptable Round-Trip Delay per Packet
256K leased line	60 ms
256K Frame Relay	140 ms
512K leased line	100 ms
T1 leased line	60 ms

Data Collection

Data was collected for each of three application activities as specified by the benchmark, using each of the two client interfaces under test and varying the circuit size and type as just discussed. This resulted in 24 separate sets of transaction data: 12 for native PeopleSoft and 12 for the Citrix WinFrame client. For each set of tests, the client was set to be either the native PeopleSoft or the Citrix WinFrame client; the Adtech Data Channel Simulator was set to simulate one of the leased-line or Frame Relay circuit types of interest; and then the knowledgeable user would execute the activities specified in the benchmark. The Network General Sniffer was set to capture the resulting traffic on three- to five-minute intervals.

The results of the data capture were then imported into NetMaker XA, and traffic profiles were created.

PeopleSoft Application Profiles

Six application profiles were created using the Network General Expert Analyzer Output data: native PeopleSoft Logon, Citrix PeopleSoft Logon, native PeopleSoft Create Requisition, Citrix PeopleSoft Create Requisition, native PeopleSoft Journal Query, and Citrix PeopleSoft Journal Query. Three used the native PeopleSoft client interface, and three used the Citrix WinFrame client.

Table 9.2 shows the resulting profiles. The profile names correspond to the application transaction. The data reduction and analysis techniques discussed in Chapter 5, "Application Planning," were used to create these profiles. Each profile represents the network activity for a single user. In the case of these application profiles, the transaction rate is 0.0033 per second (1/300 sec). Forward direction is from client to server, and return direction is from server to client. 3M used these profiles in the capacity planning phase of the project.

TABLE 9.2

PeopleSoft
Application Profiles

Profile Name	Source Addr	Destination Addr	Bytes-Fwd	Bytes-Rtn	Trans Rate 1 per 5 min.
Native Peoplesoft Logon	10.10.201.2	10.10.3.56	62000	780000	0.0033
Native Peoplesoft Journal Query	10.10.201.2	10.10.3.56	82450	775811	0.0033
Native Peoplesoft Create Req.	10.10.201.2	10.10.3.56	140399	804532	0.0033
Citrix PeopleSoft Logon	10.10.201.2	10.10.3.55	13069	67887	0.0033
Citrix PeopleSoft Journal Query	10.10.201.2	10.10.3.55	19423	56389	0.0033

Figure 9-12
PeopleSoft application throughput (Citrix vs. native).

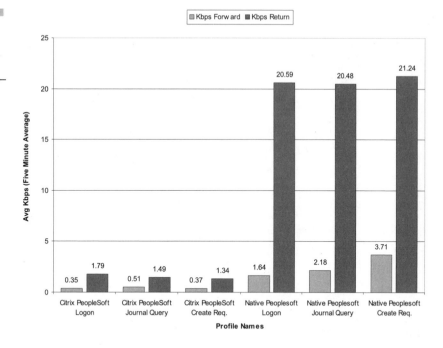

Figure 9-12 shows the average throughput in Kbps for a five-minute data capture interval. The Citrix WinFrame client used considerably less bandwidth than the native PeopleSoft client. In the conclusions section there are more details about the performance and user perceptions for each client type.

PeopleSoft Deployment Projections

When 3M was ready to build a model using the application profiles for capacity planning purposes, projections for the expected number of users at the various sites were needed, as were estimates of the frequency with which those users would execute the specified transactions.

The projected locations and number of users (broken down by module and activity) for the PeopleSoft deployment are listed in Table 9.3. Five of the locations shown were included in the baseline phase of this NRP project. Site G is in Canada, so it is not considered a domestic site and was thus not included in the baselining activities. Site C was included in the baselining phase because of the routing problems

TABLE 9.3

Predicted Number of Users Per Site

Location	Projected Number of Users by Activity
Site F	5 (2 Create Req/3 Journal Query)
Site D	3 (1 Create Req/2 Journal Query)
Site A	42 (14 Create Req/28 Journal Query)
Site B	4 (1 Create Req/3 Journal Query)
Site E	2 (1 Create Req/1 Journal Query)
Site G	37 (12 Create Req/25 Journal Query)

TABLE 9.4

Predicted Frequency of Transactions

Transaction	Frequency
Logon	Once per day (within same five minutes)
Procurement: Create Requisition	Every 5 minutes (12 per hour)
General Ledger: Journal Query	Every 5 minutes (12 per hour)

between it, Site B, and St. Paul; however, Site C was not a proposed PeopleSoft site and is not included in Table 9.3. Table 9.4 shows the estimated frequency per user for the transactions.

Capacity Planning Activities

The capacity planning phase of the project consisted of two capacity planning scenarios. One scenario (the Logon scenario) was created to analyze the impact of adding native PeopleSoft Logon traffic onto the baseline model representing the existing network. The other scenario (the GL/Procurement scenario) was created to show the impact on the existing network (baseline model) of users performing General Ledger and Procurement activities. The baseline model of the existing network was created using a merged-peak-usage strategy, as described later in this case study. The merged-peak-usage strategy creates a conservative network baseline in terms of existing network utilization.

3M built each capacity planning scenario (Logon and GL/Procurement) using the baseline model augmented with traffic data based on the application profiles for these transactions. The new application traffic data was loaded based on the projected number of users and projected frequencies of use as shown in Tables 9.3 and 9.4.

The rest of this section describes in more detail the analysis and results of the capacity planning phase. All results were generated using Make Systems' NetMaker XA suite of tools. In particular, the Net-maker XA Planner tool was used to perform the modeling.

Creating the Baseline Models

For use in the capacity planning "what-if" analyses, a merged-peak-utilization baseline model was created. The baseline data was collected by sampling the appropriate routers every five minutes (12 per hour) over a 24-hour period on each circuit of interest, as discussed previously in this case study. Each sample consisted of the total kilobytes across the circuit of interest during the five-minute interval.

The data was selected for the baseline model by analyzing the baseline data for the 10-hour period between 7:00 A.M. and 5:00 P.M. (120 samples). This period was selected because it represented the busiest period during the 24-hour day (see Figure 9-3). The samples were sorted by size based on total utilization (the sum of forward and return utilization), and the 12 highest samples were averaged to create the baseline usage for each circuit. This merged-peak-utilization baseline provided a conservative utilization model, while minimizing the effects of individual usage spikes that could have represented nonrepeatable anomalies.

For the purposes of this capacity planning phase, two additional assumptions were made and added to the baseline model. One assumption was that there was a 40-ms delay one way through the Frame Relay cloud, resulting in a round-trip delay of 80 ms. The other assumption was that there was 10% utilization on all LANs prior to adding additional application traffic. The assumptions were configured into the baseline model using the NetMaker XA tool.

Figure 9-13 shows a histogram of the baseline bandwidth usage that resulted from the merged-peak-usage calculation for each circuit of interest.

Modeling Analysis Results: Logon Scenario

Using information from Tables 9.3 and 9.4 (number of users, location, and frequency of use) and the baseline model, a modeling analysis of

Figure 9-13
Baseline circuit
utilization results.

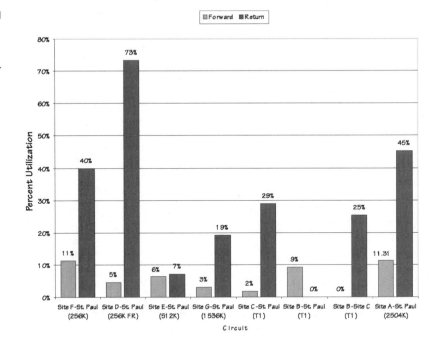

the Logon activity was performed using the NetMaker XA Planner tool.

Figure 9-14 shows the per-packet response times, both forward and return, that resulted from the modeling analysis for each logon. Figure 9-15 shows the calculated bandwidth utilization that led to the delays shown in Figure 9-14. In particular, the utilization for Site D to St. Paul (256K Frame Relay) and Site F to St. Paul (256K leased line) resulted in failure to meet the quality-of-service goals for these circuit types (the quality-of-service goals are shown in Table 9.1). The Site D round trip (forward plus return) per-packet response time is above 600 ms, and the Site F round-trip per-packet response time was greater than 60 ms.

Modeling Analysis Results: General Ledger and Procurement Scenario

Using information from Tables 9.3 and 9.4 (number of users, location, and frequency of use) and the baseline model, a modeling analysis of the General Ledger (Journal Query) and Procurement (Create Requisition) activities was performed using the NetMaker XA Planner tool.

Figure 9-14
Per-packet forward
and return delay in
ms, Logon scenario.

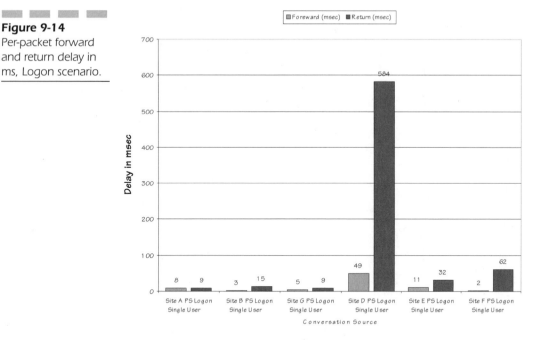

Figure 9-15
Circuit utilization,
Logon scenario.

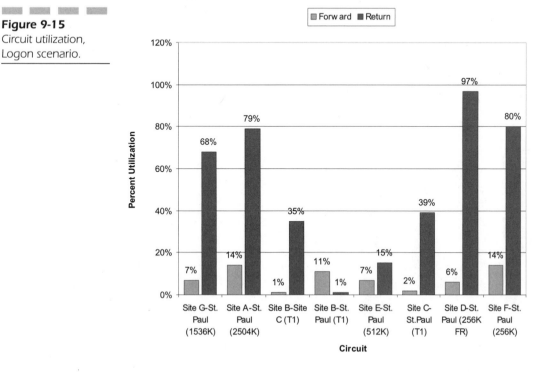

Figure 9-16 shows the per-packet response time, both forward and return, that resulted from the modeling analysis for each activity. Figure 9-17 shows the bandwidth utilization that led to the delays shown in Figure 9-16. In particular, the utilization for Site D to St. Paul (256K Frame Relay) and Site F to St. Paul (256K leased line) resulted in failure to meet the quality-of-service goals for these circuit types (the quality-

Figure 9-16

Per-packet forward and return delay in ms, GL/Procurement scenario.

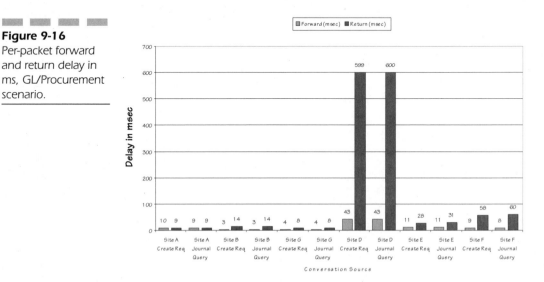

Figure 9-17

Circuit utilization, GL/ Procurement scenario.

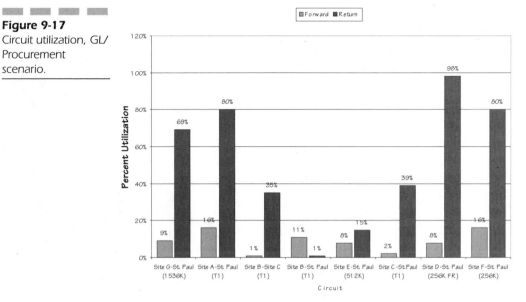

of-service goals are shown in Table 9.1). The Site D round-trip (forward plus return) per-packet response time was above 600 ms, and the Site F round-trip per-packet response time was greater than 60 ms.

Network Redesign Results

The analysis of the modeling results for the two capacity planning scenarios showed circuits that were predicted to be inadequate to support 3M's quality-of-service goals for the new PeopleSoft application. Therefore, the next step was to redesign the network models for the two capacity planning scenarios, adding bandwidth to the models of those circuits.

The network models for both the Logon scenario and the GL/Procurement scenarios were reconfigured with the following two changes, using the NetMaker XA Object Editor:

- The Site D to St. Paul circuit was changed from a 256K Frame Relay circuit with a 128K CIR to a 512K Frame Relay circuit with a 256K CIR.

- The Site F to St. Paul circuit was changed from a 256K leased-line circuit to a 512K leased-line circuit.

Figures 9-18 and 9-19 show the results of running the Logon scenario again using the NetMaker XA Planner tool after the capacity changes were made to the network model. As a result of the changes, the round-trip per-packet response times for all activities on all circuits were within the acceptable range for quality of service as defined in Table 9.1. Figure 9-18 shows the per-packet response times, both forward and return, that resulted from the modeling analysis for each logon after the changes to the circuits connecting Sites D and F to St. Paul. Figure 9-19 shows the bandwidth utilization that led to the amount of delay shown in Figure 9-18.

Figures 9-20 and 9-21 show the results of running the GL/Procurement scenario again using the NetMaker XA Planner tool after the capacity changes were made to the network model. As a result of the changes, the round-trip per-packet response times for all activities on all circuits were within the acceptable range for quality of service as defined in Table 9.1. Figure 9-20 shows the per-packet response times, both forward and return, that resulted from the modeling analysis for each activity. Figure 9-21 shows the bandwidth utilization that led to the delays shown in Figure 9-20.

Figure 9-18
Per-packet forward
and return delays
after circuit changes,
Logon scenario.

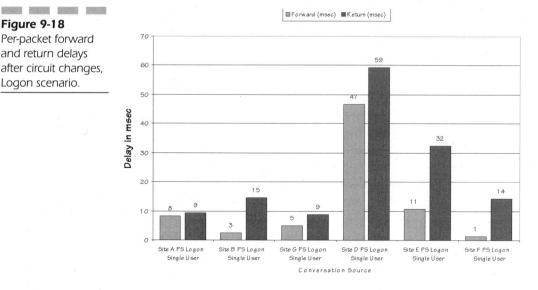

Figure 9-19
Circuit utilization after
circuit changes,
Logon scenario.

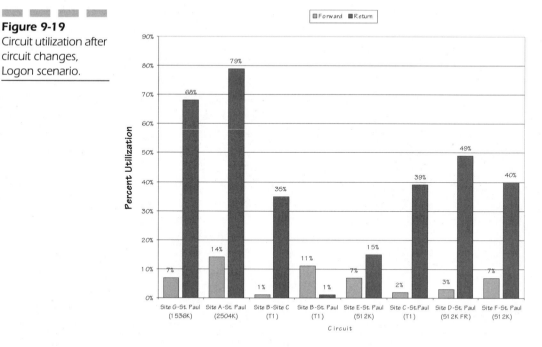

Figure 9-20

Per-packet forward
and return delays
after circuit changes,
GL/Procurement
scenario.

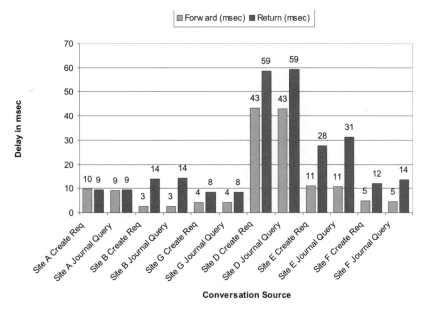

Figure 9-21

Circuit utilization after
circuit changes,
GL/Procurement
scenario.

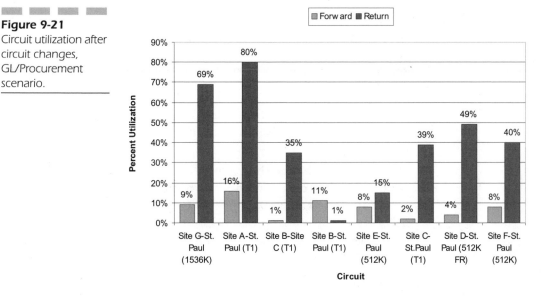

Project Conclusions

The objective of this Network Resource Planning project was to determine what network infrastructure optimization was needed to support the new PeopleSoft version 6 modules with an acceptable quality of service. The objective of the baselining phase was to collect data on the behavior of the existing network, to be used to create a baseline model to which the new PeopleSoft traffic profiles could be added for purposes of capacity planning. The objective of the application planning phase was to characterize the behavior of representative activities from the new PeopleSoft modules in order to create traffic profiles that could be used to simulate the new application traffic. 3M also quantified its quality-of-service goals in this phase. In the capacity planning phase, 3M's objective was to determine how well the existing infrastructure would support the proposed PeopleSoft deployment. Because the results showed that some circuits would not support the quality-of-service goals, they were able to determine what changes would be necessary to support those goals.

The objective for the application planning activities was to characterize the behavior of selected transactions from two PeopleSoft modules, Financial Management (General Ledger) and Procurement, running under two different client interfaces. Based on the results of executing these selected transactions as discussed earlier, the following conclusions were reached:

- The native PeopleSoft client (version 6) used 10 times as much bandwidth as a Citrix WinFrame client executing the same PeopleSoft transaction.

- However, even though the Citrix WinFrame used much less network bandwidth, it became unusable if the network round-trip delay per packet increased above 300 ms (slightly more than the acceptable delay for a 256Kbps frame relay circuit). Under these circumstances the cursor and client display would lose synchronization, making it extremely difficult for the user to select objects on the screen.

Based on the amount of traffic generated by the transactions tested using the benchmark, 3M reached the following conclusions about the adequacy of various circuit types:

- If the native PeopleSoft client was used, smaller circuits such as 64Kbps and 128Kbps circuits would be able to support only 1–2 PeopleSoft users simultaneously, because each native PeopleSoft user required approximately 20Kbps (5-minute average) of network bandwidth.

■ Larger circuits such as 256Kbps would be able to support only 2–3 users simultaneously if the baseline bandwidth usage rose above 50 percent (that is, if half of the circuit capacity was already in use for other types of network traffic prior to the PeopleSoft traffic being added).

■ 512Kbps circuits and above should be able to support quality-of-service goals adequately for this study, but this might not continue to be true if the number of simultaneous users were increased beyond the number tested for this project.

3M's objectives for the capacity planning phase were to evaluate the behavior of the PeopleSoft modules using both native PeopleSoft and the Citrix WinFrame software for client presentation. Two of the "what-if" scenarios (the native PeopleSoft Logon scenario and the native PeopleSoft General Ledger/Procurement scenario) were analyzed for each type of client (native PeopleSoft or Citrix WinFrame), and the results were evaluated relative to the quality-of-service goals to determine whether changes in the network would be needed. 3M, with guidance from the consultant, used the NetMaker XA Planner tool to analyze the models for the two PeopleSoft scenarios. If the quality-of-service goal (in terms of milliseconds of delay) for a particular circuit could not be achieved after the new PeopleSoft traffic was added to the network baseline, the circuit size was increased until the quality-of-service goal was met or exceeded.

Based on the analysis of the two scenarios, 3M arrived at the following conclusions:

■ For the PeopleSoft Logon scenario using a native PeopleSoft client, two circuits needed to be increased in bandwidth to meet the quality-of-service goals: the circuits from Site F to St. Paul and from Site D to St. Paul. The Site F–St. Paul 256Kbps leased line had to be increased to a 512Kbps circuit to meet the quality-of-service goal of not more than 60 ms of network round-trip delay per packet for PeopleSoft Logon traffic. The Site D–St. Paul 256Kbps Frame Relay circuit had to be increased to a 512Kbps Frame Relay circuit with a 256Kbps CIR to meet the quality-of-service goal of not more than 140 ms of network round-trip delay per packet.

■ For the General Ledger/Procurement scenario using the native PeopleSoft client, the circuits from Site F to St. Paul and from Site D to

St. Paul needed to be increased in bandwidth to meet the quality-of-service goals. The Site F—St. Paul 256Kbps leased-line circuit had to be increased to a 512Kbps circuit to meet the quality-of-service goal of not more than 60 ms of network round-trip delay per packet of PeopleSoft General Ledger or Procurement traffic. The Site D—St. Paul 256K Frame Relay circuit had to be increased to a 512K Frame Relay circuit with a 256Kbps CIR to meet the quality-of-service goal of not more than 140 ms of network round-trip delay per packet.

- For both scenarios (Logon scenario and General Ledger/Procurement scenario) using a Citrix WinFrame client, the network bandwidth needed was at least 10 times *less* than that needed by the native PeopleSoft client executing the same PeopleSoft activities.

- Given the numbers of users, locations, and frequencies of use as documented in Tables 9.3 and 9.4, the additional Citrix WinFrame traffic, when modeled using the existing network baseline, met and exceeded all quality-of-service goals as documented in Table 9.1.

- The usability of the Citrix WinFrame client was found to be less than optimal when the network delays were increased. Multiple knowledgeable PeopleSoft users from 3M's application development group found that when the network round-trip delay was increased to above 300 ms, the Citrix client became not merely slow but also difficult to use (the cursor and the screen display lost synchronization). The same users also perceived the native PeopleSoft client to be slow at this level of network delay (the user would have to wait for data to be returned) but the application was still usable.

Based on the results of this NRP project, 3M upgraded the circuit between Site F and St. Paul from a 256K leased line to a 512K leased line, and the circuit between St. Paul and Site D from a 256K Frame Relay permanent virtual circuit (PVC) with a 128K CIR to a 512K PVC with a 256K CIR. 3M also decided not to use PeopleSoft version 6 and the Citrix WinFrame application. Instead, the company decided to evaluate PeopleSoft version 7.0, which uses a three-tier client-server model. 3M did another analysis similar to this project and found that PeopleSoft version 7.0 appeared to provide acceptable quality of service to meet the requirements.

10

AlliedSignal

AlliedSignal is an advanced technology and manufacturing company composed of eleven major business units that serve customers worldwide with aerospace and automotive products, chemicals, fibers, plastics, and advanced materials. Some of AlliedSignal's well-known brand names in the United States include Autolite, Fram, Garrett, ANSO, Spectra, and Bendix. AlliedSignal ranks among the top 100 of the Fortune 500, has 76,000 employees, and is one of the 30 companies comprised in the Dow Jones Industrial Average. Because AlliedSignal has many different customer types, it has an assortment of networking needs.

Project Background

In mid-1991, under new CEO Larry Bossidy, and having new leadership in many key businesses, AlliedSignal began a comprehensive program of transformation. Bold actions were taken to improve cash flow and operating margins, to increase productivity, and to position the company as a global competitive force for the years ahead. As a part of these initiatives, AlliedSignal built and implemented a global multiprotocol network and began looking for ways to understand and document its usage. The network management personnel within the Global Network Services (GNS) began acquiring tools to assist them in analyzing the data they gathered. Today they use several tools in concert to gather and analyze the baselining information needed to determine whether the network is providing the quality of service the AlliedSignal business units require. Providing detailed information about how the network is being utilized is one of the services AlliedSignal GNS performs for the business units.

AlliedSignal has been involved in Network Resource Planning (NRP) for several years. The firm is particularly active in the area of baselining.

Enterprise Network Infrastructure

AlliedSignal's network includes approximately 300 Cisco routers, with both domestic and international sites. Five key network hub sites constitute the backbone of the network. Three of the hub sites are located in the United States, one hub site is located in Europe, and one is located in the Asia-Pacific area. Figure 10-1 (generated in IBM NetView) shows the business units comprised in the AlliedSignal network, with the submap showing the hub sites within the United States. The entire network uses Cisco's EIGRP routing protocol. The most prevalent network protocols in AlliedSignal's WAN environment are TCP/IP and IPX (Novell).

The satellite sites are connected to the network hub sites via Frame Relay in a spoke and wheel fashion. AlliedSignal operates most of its Frame Relay connections at a CIR (committed information rate) of 50% of the PVC (permanent virtual circuit) port speed. The five key hub sites are interconnected using leased lines.

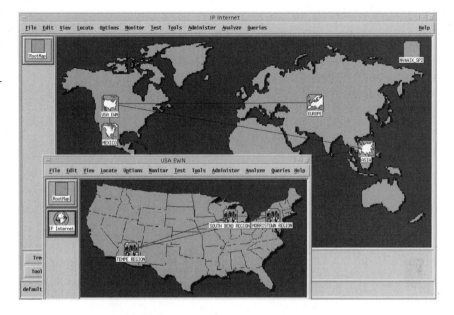

Figure 10-1
AlliedSignal wide area
backbone structure.
(© AlliedSignal)

Support for Business Units

Each AlliedSignal business unit is tasked with managing the costs of
the network resources that support its business functions. In order to
manage the costs of those resources, each business unit must understand how its network is being used. As a business unit's network utilization changes and grows, it also needs to understand what is causing
those changes. When the business units have network performance
questions, they come to AlliedSignal GNS for help.

In addition to supporting specific requests from the business units,
GNS is also responsible for planning, implementing, and maintaining
network resources to provide acceptable quality of service for mission-
critical enterprise applications, such as SAP R/3 and PeopleSoft. Allied-
Signal has found that to support these enterprise applications effectively, it must also understand the day-to-day network usage patterns
caused by miscellaneous departmental applications and Internet access
activity. For example, the day-to-day usage of the network might
include such activity as using a Microsoft Access database to track a
department's call logs or using the Internet for marketing research. In
order to identify and document overall network usage, it is necessary to
understand this unplanned, miscellaneous network activity in addition

to the more predictable planned activity of corporate applications. This understanding is critical in order to develop network usage policy properly (regarding Internet usage, for example) and provision the network resources accordingly.

Monitoring the network activity over time has shown that this miscellaneous network activity continues to grow. A key responsibility of AlliedSignal GNS is to ensure that this network activity does not interfere with the quality of service that is required for the mission-critical applications. AlliedSignal has incorporated baselining techniques into its daily and weekly network management routine to track how well the network is doing at delivering this level of service.

Project Scope

This case study will focus on the baselining techniques that are used at AlliedSignal to monitor and understand all network activity to the level of application usage. These techniques are being used continuously for ongoing network management. This case study will demonstrate the importance of monitoring day-to-day miscellaneous network activity as a key ingredient in ensuring the quality of service provided by the network for mission-critical enterprise applications such as SAP R/3 and PeopleSoft.

AlliedSignal's NRP Objectives

AlliedSignal has two goals for its NRP efforts. One goal is to monitor and document the utilization of the enterprise network on an ongoing basis, thus enabling the firm to identify utilization trends and, ideally, anticipate possible areas where performance problems may arise. The other goal is to be able to respond to reports of performance problems perceived by the business units. AlliedSignal wants to be able to identify the possible causes of these problems and to recommend solutions. To accomplish these goals, GNS needs to be able to document the average utilization for every leased line and Frame Relay PVC in the network. It also needs to identify the applications and network conversations that are responsible for that utilization.

To meet these goals, AlliedSignal GNS developed the following NRP objectives:

- To implement a process that provides bandwidth usage information on a weekly basis for the entire AlliedSignal WAN, including all Frame Relay PVCs and all leased-line circuits

- To implement a process to determine and characterize the applications and users that are the most active on the AlliedSignal enterprise network

AlliedSignal GNS began by collecting only application-based data using strategically placed Network General Distributed Sniffer Servers. GNS wanted to use this data to determine what the overall utilization was for each circuit in the enterprise network. The AlliedSignal network management staff attempted to take the network General Sniffer data they were gathering and compute the utilization on a per-circuit basis. When they compared the information provided by the Sniffers to their router byte counts, they soon realized that they were not getting all the traffic traversing the wide area network. They realized that, without the help of additional tools, the utilization metrics for the circuits would not be accurate and that they would be unable to compute reliable average utilization numbers for the wide area connections in the enterprise network. Going through these steps and attempting to derive average utilization metrics for each circuit led the network management staff to find a way to collect usage-based data from their routers.

To accomplish this, GNS built its own solution developed in-house: an SNMP MIB collection device that allowed GNS network managers to collect data on critical circuits. However, as time went by, the scope of their data collection needs continued to grow, and they realized that Concord's Network Health product would meet their needs better than their own tool did.

AlliedSignal GNS now uses the following performance management tools:

- Network Health from Concord Communications, which AlliedSignal uses to collect and report on SNMP MIB statistics gathered from routers and switches; the key tool that AlliedSignal uses for data collection and that underlies all the baseline analysis it performs

- Network General Distributed Sniffer Servers (DSSs), used to capture application-based data to identify which applications are utilizing the network resources, and to what extent

- Cisco Systems NETSYS Connectivity Service Manager, used to import configuration files and create a map of the network, and Performance Service Manager, used to import and analyze application-based data

▧ NetMaker XA from Make Systems, Inc., used to import application-based data for analysis

The tasks and activities needed to accomplish AlliedSignal's objectives are exactly the activities discussed in Chapter 4, "Baselining the Network." This case study will focus specifically on the specific baselining steps that apply to AlliedSignal's objectives.

Baselining Process Overview

To meet its NRP objectives, AlliedSignal developed a process that included collecting and reporting on both usage-based data and application-based data. Collecting both types of data allows GNS to watch the network traffic behavior trends as well as to provide support to the business units in a reactive manner when needed.

AlliedSignal's baselining process includes the following steps:

▧ Creating a topological inventory
▧ Creating a traffic inventory
▧ Doing a traffic analysis

These steps are a part of AlliedSignal's daily and weekly network management routine to monitor the enterprise network's bandwidth utilization.

AlliedSignal's network management staff collects both usage-based and application-based data at the same time. Usage-based data is collected using Concord Communications' Network Health. Application-based data is collected using Network General DSSs.

The network management staff routinely reviews the usage-based data to identify problem areas. Concord's Network Health tool provides a report, known as an Exception report, that lists circuits that exceed thresholds for various metrics related to utilization, congestion, and network errors. This process helps GNS to identify problems or potential problems proactively before they affect business unit users.

In addition to routine review of the data, GNS also responds to phone calls from personnel within various business units reporting network problems. The network management staff uses the same process of collecting and reviewing usage-based and application-based data (including Concord Network Health's Exception report) to find answers to the specific questions or problems reported by the business units.

Topological Inventory

AlliedSignal GNS performs its network discoveries using both Concord's Network Health and NETSYS Connectivity Service Manager. Each tool has a discovery function, although the discoveries provide different types of information.

Network Health's discovery provides detailed information about individual network components such as servers, switches, routers, leased lines, and Frame Relay PVCs. However, it does not discover network topology or connectivity information.

The NETSYS Connectivity Service Manager discovery process is really an import of Cisco configuration files. This provides both device configuration information and topological information on an enterprisewide basis at the network level. For each router found, subnet local area networks are identified from the routers' interface addressing information. Hosts residing on each of the local area networks are inferred according to the TCP/IP host addresses available within the given subnet. NETSYS presents its discovery results in a graphical view that provides an overall look at the network's topology and connectivity, as shown in Figure 10-2.

Traffic Inventory

AlliedSignal collects and reviews two types of traffic data: usage-based data and application-based data.

AlliedSignal uses Concord's Network Health to collect usage-based traffic data from its wide area network routers, 24 hours a day, seven days a week. The capture periods are five-minute intervals.

AlliedSignal uses Network Health to collect and monitor

- Utilization of circuits (leased lines and Frame Relay PVCs)

- Frame Relay congestion indicators: FECN (Forward Explicit Congestion Notification) and BECN (Backward Explicit Congestion Notification)

- Other network errors

Figure 10-2
NETSYS topology
view. (© Cisco
Systems, Inc.)

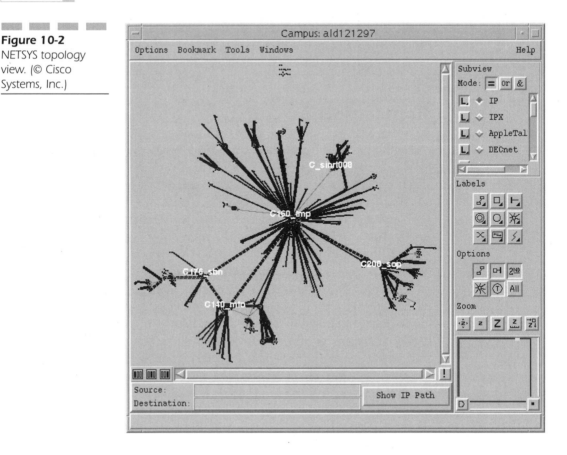

This SNMP MIB data is gathered on all routers of interest. Initially, a set of data was collected for a one-week period and then averaged and documented as the starting point or network "baseline" as defined by Concord's Network Health. In addition to average values, the maximum initial value for each data point was also recorded.

AlliedSignal uses Network Health to collect data seven days a week. Network Health maintains a baseline over the last six weeks of data collection and maintains indexes (or counts of conditions that exceed a threshold) for excessive utilization and errors for each network element it monitors. A Network Health Exception report, generated every day, notes any situations in which a combination of the circuit utilization and error indexes exceeds a set threshold, indicating a potential problem area within the enterprise network.

The second type of traffic data AlliedSignal collects is application-based data from strategically placed Network General Distributed

Sniffer Servers (DSSs). The Network General DSSs are configured with capture intervals that correspond to the Network Health five-minute capture intervals. The AlliedSignal network management staff collects both usage-based and application-based data simultaneously in order to be able to correlate application-based network conversations with specific usage activity on individual leased-line circuits or Frame Relay PVCs. Analysis of both the usage-based and application-based data is performed during the traffic analysis step of the baselining process.

Traffic Analysis

AlliedSignal uses the reports from Concord's Network Health to perform what GNS calls a "peak analysis" of network usage. The network management staff reviews the Network Health reports to identify network components that have an activity level above a set threshold or show abnormally high activity or errors.

Reviewing this data as a whole helps to build a revealing picture of how well the enterprise network is performing. AlliedSignal uses the following Network Health reports:

- Daily report, compared to the previous day's activity
- Weekly report, compared to the previous week's activity
- Exception report, which identifies components that exceed defined thresholds

The Network Health Exception report provides a listing of circuits and other network components where the Congestion Health Index or Error Health Index exceeds AlliedSignal's threshold. The index values are used as a guideline to identify which network components are behaving differently enough to warrant further investigation. The network management staff can then look at a detailed display (such as shown in Figure 10-3 for circuit mtort001-hsf2.tmpprv-S2-dlci-5) for any of the components on the Exception report. They pay particular attention to the Frame Relay congestion indicators (FECNs or BECNs) as well as circuit utilization metrics.

On a daily basis AlliedSignal GNS reviews the usage-based data, especially for the network components that appeared on the Network Health Exception report. When a WAN circuit (leased line or Frame Relay PVC such as mtort001-hsf2.tmpprv-S2-dlci-5 in Figure 10-3) appears on the Exception report, the network management staff reviews the

Figure 10-3

Detail of a daily
Exception report for
an individual circuit.
(© Concord Commu-
nications, Inc.)

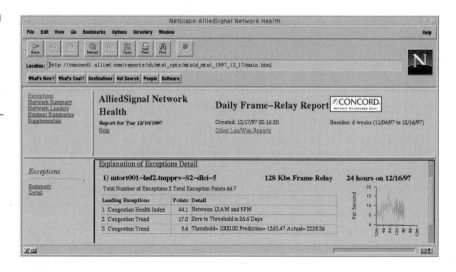

usage-based data over the previous two weeks to identify whether this exception has happened previously (a trend). They match utilization trends with the Frame Relay congestion indicators (FECNs and BECNs) to determine whether the utilization levels are simply high or are responsible for congestion.

For each network component that appears on the Exception report, the AlliedSignal network management staff determines the location of that network component. AlliedSignal keeps the closest watch on its Frame Relay resources. Of all the network components, the Frame Relay PVC bandwidth has the smallest throughput capability and therefore the greatest potential to become a bottleneck. The Frame Relay PVCs are also the most costly of the recurring network infra-structure expenses and should be utilized at an optimal level to be cost-effective.

If an Exception report lists a specific Frame Relay PVC, such as mtort001-hsf2.tmpprv-S2-dlci-5 in Figure 10-3, as having index numbers that indicate possible problems, the AlliedSignal network management staff will investigate the network activity that has caused the high index number in the daily report. Using Network Health's name for the Frame Relay PVC, they can determine which router the PVC is connected to, which then points to the affected location or locations within the enterprise network. Once the network management staff have determined the specific areas of the network that need further analysis, they review the relevant usage-based data, Frame Relay congestion indicators, and other network errors collected by Network Health for that particular PVC. They look at the data from the previous two weeks for that PVC so that they can determine whether to consider this normal activity or an anomaly.

For the circuit in question, the first step is to look at the usage-based data for the 24 hours on 12/16/97—the period when this Frame Relay PVC appeared on the Exception report. The report shown in Figure 10-4 displays the percent of bandwidth utilization over a 24-hour period (12:00 A.M. on 12/16/97 to 12:00 A.M. 12/17/97) for the PVC called mtort001-hsf2.tmpprv-S2-dlci-5. Although there were only a few spikes above 50% utilization, it is noticeable that utilization stayed consistently above 20%.

The report in Figure 10-5, which displays the errors on all the Frame Relay PVCs on physical circuit S2 for router mtort001, shows that congestion was an issue for the PVC in question (mtort001-hsf2.tmpprv-S2-dlci-5). This finding then prompted the network management staff to produce a report on congestion indicators, as shown in Figure 10-6. This report shows that, again, there was a fairly constant level of congestion on this PVC.

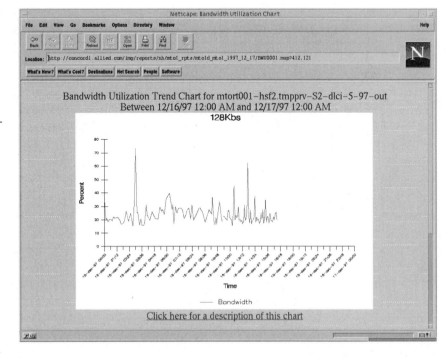

Figure 10-4
Report showing bandwidth utilization on a Frame Relay PVC. (© Concord Communications, Inc.)

Figure 10-5
Report showing
health indexes.
(© Concord Communications, Inc.)

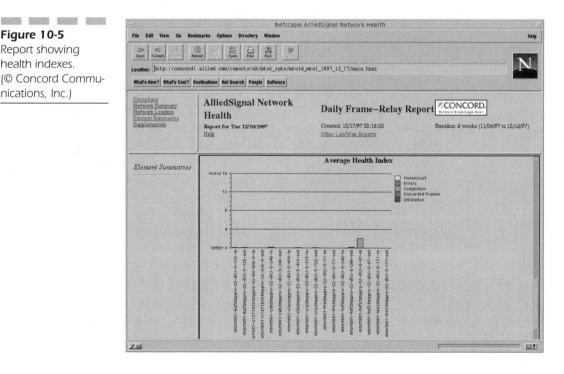

Figure 10-6
Report showing congestion errors on a
Frame Relay circuit.
(© Concord Communications, Inc.)

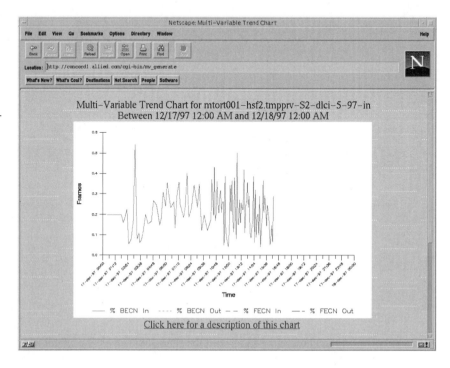

For this particular PVC the congestion turned out to be due to Novell Service Advertising Protocol (SAP) broadcast traffic that should not have been on this circuit at all and was not being filtered correctly at the router mtort001. The solution was to install a filter on the router on the interface for this PVC to remove the broadcast traffic. Once the filter was installed, the congestion problems went away.

If the problem had not been identified as broadcast traffic, the next step would be to review the corresponding application-based traffic data for the same Frame Relay PVC. The network management staff imports the corresponding application-based data (collecting using the Network General DSSs) into Cisco's NETSYS Performance Service Manager. The NETSYS software is used to produce a network conversation report for an individual router: the End-to-End Conversation Breakdown report, which can be sorted by application type or by network user. An example of an End-to-End Conversation Breakdown report is shown in Figure 10-7. This report provides details about each network conversation between any two host pairs. It is also possible to select an individual conversation and see a graphical representation of the route between the two end points (shown in the overlaid window in Figure 10-7). The network management staff uses this report to analyze which application conversations and hosts are responsible for most of the traffic on the Frame Relay PVC of interest.

When an End-to-End Conversation Breakdown report is obtained sorted by application type, it provides a relative measure of the amount of network resources being used by each application type. The application types are sorted in order of the total amount of traffic (conversations) generated by each application type or port during the capture interval. The network management staff then looks for shifts in the type of applications using the network resources or in the types of traffic loading a circuit during a particularly high utilization period. By reviewing the End-to-End Conversation Breakdown report, the Allied-Signal network management staff can determine which network conversations are the most likely cause of high utilization or excessive numbers of errors seen by Network Health.

It sometimes happens that GNS does not have application-based data captured from the area where a potential problem is indicated. In such instances, network management personnel use a LAN Hopper (from LAN Hopper Systems) to switch the Network General Sniffer to target the appropriate wide area network circuit for data capture. They can then capture data on that Frame Relay PVC using a Network General

Figure 10-7
Report showing conversations traversing a router. (© Cisco Systems, Inc.)

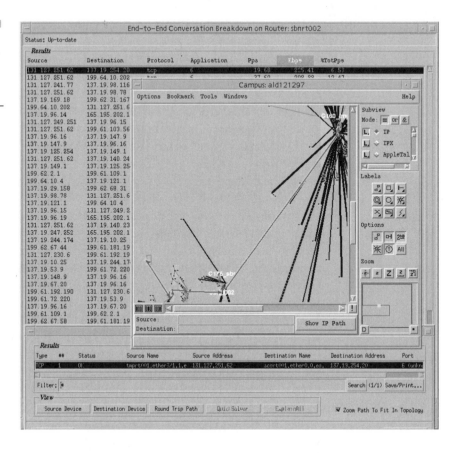

DSS. They capture data for at least one business day and do their analysis with that day's data.

Business Unit Performance Issues

In addition to analyzing network components that show up on the Concord Network Health Exception reports (proactive analysis), AlliedSignal GNS routinely uses the baselining process for investigating network performance complaints from the business units (reactive analysis). Generally, complaints about network performance are extremely vague. For example, when a contact person from the business units calls reporting poor response time, they typically report only that it is taking a long time to open a file or to print a report after running a query. When the network management staff tries to get more details about the perceived problem, their questions usually cannot be answered. Commonly, the only facts that can be determined are the time of day when the problem occurred, which application was being used, and how often the user has noticed the problem.

GNS begins the analysis of a user complaint by looking at the usage-based data collected for the past two-week period and also at the corresponding data on network or congestion errors for the circuits that support the locations reporting the problems. Reviewing this information for a two-week window allows the network management staff to determine whether the problem is a sudden change or has been occurring over time but has gone unnoticed (or unreported) by the end user community.

The next step is to locate and review the corresponding application-based data collected using the Network General Sniffers. The network management staff imports the application-based data into Cisco's NET-SYS Performance Service Manager and performs the analysis as just discussed.

For example, at one particular AlliedSignal site where users had complained about network performance, the network conversation report showed that Internet traffic accounted for 28% of the network traffic activity going to and from the site. Based on prior baselining work, AlliedSignal GNS knew that the average usage for total Internet traffic is usually around 6% per circuit. The level of Internet traffic on the circuit in question was four to five times the average and was therefore causing performance problems. Based on this analysis, the AlliedSignal network management group was able to propose a number of possible solutions to the responsible business unit.

One suggested solution was to increase the bandwidth of the circuit from the remote site to the associated network hub. The network management group was able to provide estimates of the costs of this solution. However, as a first approach, the network management staff recommended filtering on the port number associated with Internet activity at the appropriate routers and setting up a low-priority router queue for Internet traffic. The business unit decided to try both approaches. The router configuration was changed to lower the priority of Internet traffic, and the bandwidth for the circuit was doubled, from 128 to 256Kbps. The network performance for that business unit is now stable. AlliedSignal GNS keeps a close watch on the utilization levels for this site and checks regularly with the site representative on how network performance is being perceived.

Summary

AlliedSignal has implemented Network Resource Planning techniques as an integral part of the way it manages its enterprise network using various network tools. Collecting both usage-based data and application-based data provides GNS with information that allows staff to identify quickly which particular network behaviors are "normal" and which are not. GNS uses this information to manage the recurring costs of the enterprise network and determine when miscellaneous, unplanned network usage could begin to become a problem for their mission-critical applications, such as SAP R/3 and PeopleSoft.

AlliedSignal GNS attempts to alert the business units and make recommendations whenever possible *before* a WAN bandwidth availability problem occurs. The network management staff uses the information provided by the various network tools to identify and document the AlliedSignal enterprise network behavior. GNS network management personnel continue to implement and improve upon these NRP techniques and are always developing new ways to use the information they collect.

APPENDIX A

BASELINE MODEL CREATION STRATEGIES

The following sections discuss five strategies for creating baseline models. A model can be based either on utilization (percentage of capacity used) or on volume of usage (total Kbytes in a given sample period). It can model either peak or worst-case conditions (peak utilization or peak volume), attenuated or averaged peak conditions (merged-peak utilization or merged-peak volume), or average conditions (average utilization or average volume).

Using total volume as the basis for the model will tend to weight the model toward the effects of major or backbone circuits, because the volume on the largest circuits will tend to overwhelm the effects of the volume of the smaller circuits. Using utilization as the basis for the model will tend to give small circuits greater influence in the model, because percent utilization is calculated relative to each circuit's size, and smaller circuits may have a higher percentage of their bandwidth utilized than larger circuits.

Peak Utilization Baseline Model

A peak utilization baseline model is created using the highest-utilization sample from among a given set of consecutive samples (for example, from among the set of five-minute samples taken over a 10-hour business day), for each leased-line circuit or Frame Relay permanent virtual circuit (PVC) in your model. This is the most conservative model and is appropriate to use if you absolutely must guarantee quality of service 100% of the time. This model can be used to answer the question, "How will my network perform if every circuit on my network simultaneously experiences maximum utilization?"

Figure A-1 shows an example of utilization on a single circuit, from 8:00 A.M. to 1:00 P.M. (The full 24 hours of data are not shown here, because of space and visibility constraints.) The peak utilization value for this circuit (based on total utilization, forward plus return) is the sample that occurred at 9:15 A.M. This is the value you would load into your performance management tool for this circuit.

Figure A-1
Circuit utilization in
five-minute samples
for a single circuit.

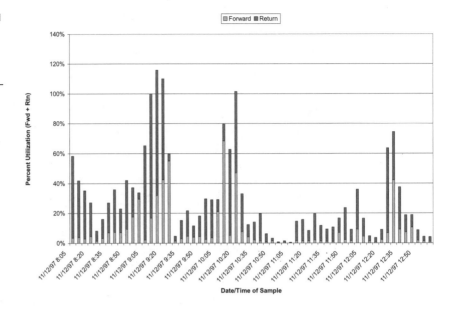

Figure A-1
Circuit utilization in five-minute samples for a single circuit.

Selecting the Sample Values

You can use the sum of the forward and return utilizations as your peak utilization value, or you can pick either the forward or return utilization as your criterion for selecting the highest sample. If you use the highest forward or highest return utilization value, the peak sample you choose may be different than if you use the sum of the two. For example, for the samples shown in Figure A-1, if return traffic is used as the selection criterion, the peak sample still occurs at 9:15 A.M. (as it does with the summed forward and return values). However, if forward utilization is used, the peak sample occurs at 10:10 A.M.

Once you have selected the peak utilization values for each circuit, you need to load these values onto each circuit within your performance management tool. This requires that the performance management tool have the ability to create new traffic within the network model. The end points for the peak utilization sample for each circuit within the model are the two routers that connect to the circuit. This is true for both leased-line circuits and Frame Relay PVCs.

Advantages and Disadvantages of a Peak Utilization Baseline Model

A peak utilization model is a time-independent model—the values used in the model are not necessarily observed at the same time in the real network. For example, the highest utilization on circuit A may occur at midmorning, but the highest utilization on circuit B may occur in the early afternoon. This model is an abstraction of reality, and the enterprise network may never actually be in this state.

The benefit of using this model is that it represents the absolute worst case in terms of network performance, based on actual peak loads observed on the network based on the days and time periods chosen. As a result, you know that if you can achieve acceptable quality of service under this model, you will be able to guarantee acceptable quality of service under any less extreme conditions (meaning virtually all actual situations you would encounter). However, there are two drawbacks to using this strategy for your baseline model.

One is that, by selecting the one highest sample for each circuit, you run the risk that the measured utilization is due to some sort of error condition in the network or to some sort of anomalous, nonrepeatable network activity. To ensure that this is not the case, you should create multiple baseline models, using different sets of usage-based data from different days, and analyze them to see whether the peak utilization results are similar. Otherwise, your analysis and results may be based on a model that is unlikely actually to occur, especially if the cause of the anomalous behavior can be identified and fixed.

The second drawback is that this type of model will always result in a higher network cost solution (if network capacity redesigns are needed), because it ensures that you will provide the largest margin of safety in terms of capacity to allow for peak utilization conditions. If utilization frequently approaches peak utilization on your network, then this investment may be appropriate. It may also be appropriate if you are supporting mission-critical applications in which the consequences of not being able to provide acceptable quality of service, even for a short time, are catastrophic. Otherwise, basing your planning decisions on this baseline model strategy may simply lead you to provide (and pay for) capacity that you rarely use.

Merged-Peak Utilization Baseline Model

The merged-peak utilization baseline model is also a conservative model, good for use in a situation in which guaranteed quality of service is the priority. However, it addresses the first drawback of the previous model (the peak utilization model) in that it creates an "average peak" by averaging several of the highest utilization samples rather than the single highest sample. This lets you control somewhat for anomalous peak samples while still preserving the conservative characteristics of a peak utilization model. This model is probably the best for creating the most cost-efficient network that will still meet quality-of-service objectives.

A merged-peak baseline model is created in much the same way as the peak utilization model. However, instead of selecting a single peak utilization value, you select a number of the highest samples (typically 12 to 24 samples) and average them to get a "merged" or average peak value for each leased-line circuit or Frame Relay PVC. Like the peak utilization model, this model is time-independent. The samples you choose to average do not need to be consecutive in time.

Selecting the Sample Values

Figure A-2 again shows the example of utilization on a single circuit. Figure A-3 shows the top 24 utilization samples for this circuit, sorted according to the sum of forward plus return utilization for each sample. To create a merged-peak baseline model, you would average the top samples—the top 12 or 24, for example. You can see from the chart

Figure A-2

Circuit utilization in five-minute samples for a single circuit.

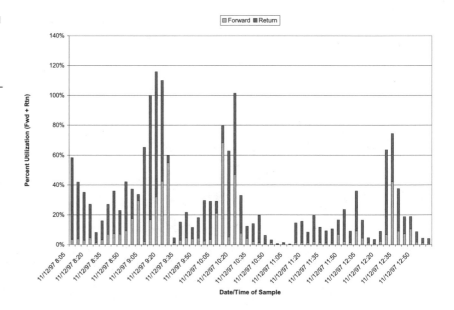

Figure A-3

The top 24 utilization samples from those shown in Figure A-2.

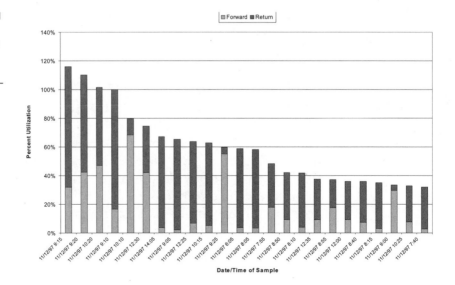

in Figure A-3 that the more samples you include in your average, the more the merged-peak average value will attenuate and approach a regular average value for each circuit.

To create a merged-peak utilization baseline model, you would take the top 12 to 24 samples for each circuit and average the following metrics:

- Packet size in bytes, forward direction (data flowing from source to destination)

- Packet size in bytes, return direction (data flowing from destination to source)

- Number of bytes transferred during sample period (e.g., five minutes) forward

- Number of bytes transferred during sample period (e.g., five minutes) return

The resulting averages are recorded and used to create a "load" within the performance management tool for each circuit. Some performance management tools can create the merged-peak samples for you. If this feature is not available, you can calculate the merged-peak value for each circuit by hand or by creating a script using a scripting language such as Perl.

You load the merged-peak utilization values for each leased-line circuit and Frame Relay PVC into the network model using your performance management software in the same way as for a peak utilization model.

Advantages and Disadvantages of a Merged-Peak Utilization Baseline Model

The number of samples you use to create your merged-peak baseline model will depend on your capacity planning objectives, the characteristics of your network utilization, and how conservative you want to be in creating your model. Typically you would use one or two hours' worth of samples (12 to 24 five-minute samples), which would model the busiest hour or two hours (nonconsecutive) on your network.

Depending on the characteristics of your data, the larger the number of samples you use, the more your merged peak may approach average usage. This property can help you avoid the problem of creating a baseline based on a single, possible anomalous peak sample, which will require capacity that you are unlikely to use in reality. However, creating a merged-peak model from too many samples could also result in a model that is not sufficiently conservative for your needs, based on the characteristics of your data and your need to support application quality of service. For example, suppose your data contains a short spike of traffic (say, a half-hour) that represents repeatable, legitimate activity for which you want to provide adequate capacity on that circuit. In that case, creating a merged peak from two hours' worth of samples would attenuate that peak and could lead to undercapacitation for purposes of supporting that half-hour of peak activity. Thus, it is critical that you have a good understanding of the nature of the activity on your network, and the causes of that activity, before you decide on the strategy you will use to create your baseline model.

Figure A-4 shows the difference between the peak value for a single circuit and a merged-peak value created by averaging the top 12 samples for that same circuit.

As with a peak utilization model, the best strategy is to create several baseline models with data from multiple days, and compare the models to make sure that the resulting usage on the circuit is similar from day to day. The merged-peak utilization would be considered sufficiently similar from one model to the next if it were within a 5–10% variation on most circuits, especially on backbone circuits.

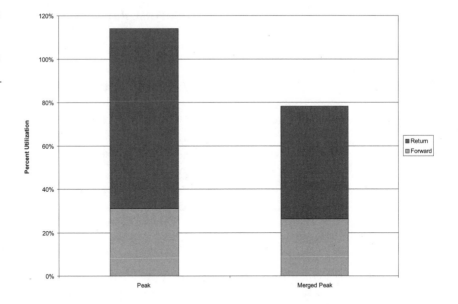

Figure A-4
Peak versus merged-peak utilization values for a single circuit.

Peak Volume Baseline Model

This method provides a baseline model that represents the network at the point in time when the total volume of traffic is the highest. In this method, instead of selecting samples circuit by circuit as in the previously discussed utilization models, you select a complete set of samples for all circuits on the network, measured at the time when the total network volume (measured in bytes) was the highest. This is a time-dependent model, in that all samples represent the same point in time (they were collected during the same sampling period). Like the peak utilization model, this model represents a worst case, letting you answer the question, "How will my network perform under conditions equal to the highest traffic volume measured on the network?"

Selecting the Sample Values

To determine which sample to select for your peak volume baseline model, you must look at the overall system traffic volume over time. The system volume is the sum of the total number of bytes for all circuits that are represented in your network model. Summing the traffic volume for each five-minute sample on every circuit generates a system volume chart like that shown in Figure A-5, showing the total system volume over time. This methodology was discussed in detail in Chapter 4, "Baselining Your Network."

By looking at the system volume chart for the time ranges of interest, you can pick the point in time that represents the highest total activity for the network as a whole. With your performance management tool, you then use the traffic data collected during this time period (the forward and return utilization for each circuit) to load all the circuits in your baseline model. (Note that, although the selection criteria for what samples to include are based on system volume, the actual data you enter into the performance management tool is the same for either a volume-based or a utilization-based model.)

This method is somewhat easier to implement than the two strategies based on utilization, because you do not need to analyze every circuit to find the data for your baseline model. Assuming you already did the system volume analysis during the baselining phase, you simply need to select the one set of samples that represents the peak volume and then load your network model with data from the time period that you select. For example, given the data in Figure A-5, you would pick the five-minute sample data set that was collected at 13:35 and then use the utilization values during that time period for each circuit. This requires that the performance management tool have the ability to create new traffic within the network model. The end points

Figure A-5
Total system volume, five-minute intervals.

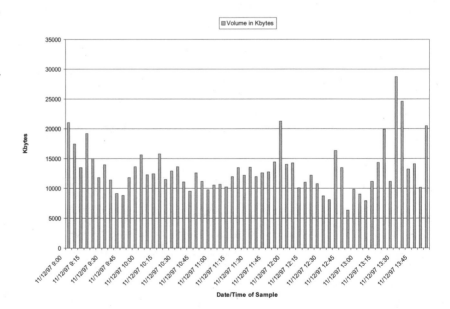

for the utilization samples for each circuit within the model are the two routers that connect to the circuit, for both leased-line circuits and Frame Relay PVCs.

Advantages and Disadvantages of a Peak Volume Baseline Model

Because the peak utilization model is time-independent, it represents a theoretical worst case that might never occur in reality. The peak volume method uses the actual worst case, as determined from the baseline results obtained during the baselining phase of the NRP process, and therefore is time-dependent. Thus you know that this is a "real" worst case that can actually occur on your network.

The peak volume model has the same drawback as the peak utilization model in that if the peak volume samples represents an anomaly in the system's behavior, the resulting model may be too extreme to be a valid representation of your network, and all the results based upon it will then be suspect. On the other hand, depending on the actual data on which it is based, this strategy leaves open the possibility that there could be worse "worst cases" on individual circuits (especially on smaller circuits) that are not reflected in the sample you selected. This is because total system volume will tend to be influenced much more significantly by larger (backbone) circuits, which may overwhelm the effects of smaller circuits. The peak volume baseline model may not be sufficiently conservative if guaranteeing quality of service on *all* circuits is paramount under all conditions. A peak volume model tends to be sufficient if your focus is on backbone circuits, but it may not take into account the needs of smaller circuits.

As with the previous model-building strategies, it is a good idea to create several baseline models using data from different days and compare the resulting models to ensure that the utilization on the various circuits is reasonably consistent.

Merged-Peak Volume Baseline Model

Like the peak volume baseline model, this method lets you model actual worst-case network behavior based on observed traffic volume.

However, this model lets you control for anomalous peaks by using an average created from several samples that represent the highest enterprise network volume measurements observed during the period under study. This method can be either time-dependent or time-independent, depending on whether the samples you use to create your average are consecutive (you average across the enterprise network's "busy hour") or represent the highest total system volume values, regardless of when they occur.

Selecting the Sample Values

As with the peak volume baseline model strategy, you use the system volume information you documented during the baselining phase of the project as the source for determining which sample periods represent the highest total system activity on the network. The total system volume is the sum of the total number of bytes for all circuits represented in your network model. By looking at the system volume chart for the time ranges of interest, you can pick a set of points in time that represents the highest total activity for the network as a whole, based on total system volume values. As with the peak volume baseline model strategy, you select the traffic data sets of interest based on total system volume, but you use the circuit utilization data from those data sets to load the baseline model.

You select some number of traffic data sets (12 or 24, for example) that correspond to the sample periods that show the highest level of system activity based on total system volume. With your performance management tool, you then use the traffic data collected during these time periods (the forward and return utilization for each circuit for each time period) to load all the circuits in your baseline model. This is done in the same way as for the merged-peak utilization baseline model, discussed previously.

For example, the chart shown in Figure A-6 shows the total system volume for an enterprise network in five-minute samples, from 9:00 A.M. to 2:00 P.M. This is the starting point for selecting the sets of traffic data you will use. You will select the sets of traffic data based on the time periods that show the highest system volume values.

If you want to create a time-dependent merged-peak volume baseline, you would select a certain number (12, for example) of consecutive five-minute sets of traffic data, such as the last twelve shown in Figure A-6 or the twelve from 11:30 to 12:30.

Figure A-6
Total system volume,
five-minute intervals.

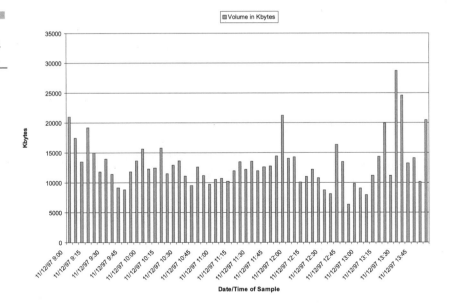

If you want to create a time-independent merged-peak volume baseline model, you would select the traffic data sets that correspond to the highest system volume values shown in Figure A-6. For example, the chart in Figure A-7 shows the 12 highest system volume values that

Figure A-7
Top 12 system vol-
ume measurements
sorted by total system
volume.

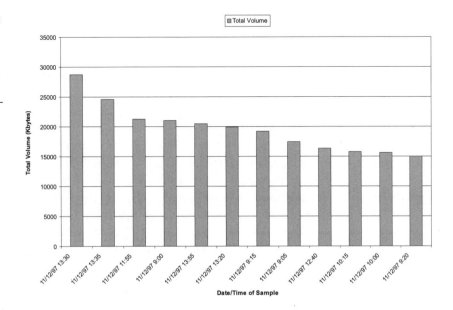

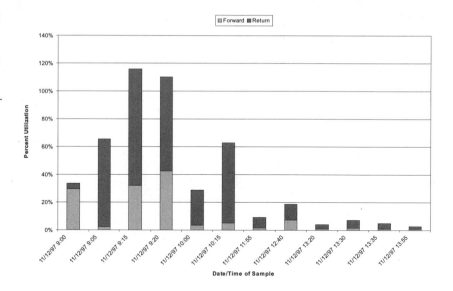

Figure A-8
Utilization on one cir-
cuit corresponding to
periods of highest
system volume.

correspond to the data in Figure A-6, sorted by total volume. You would then use the usage data collected during those twelve sampling periods in creating your merged peak baseline model.

To create the values for an individual circuit in the model, you would take the forward and return utilization values for the circuit from each of the 12 data sets and create an average, just as you did for the merged-peak utilization baseline model. The difference between the merged-peak volume baseline strategy and the merged-peak utilization baseline strategy is that the utilization values used for the merged-peak volume model may not be the highest utilization values that occurred for a given circuit but instead represent the utilization on the circuit during the time periods when the network was showing its highest total volume usage.

For example, Figure A-8 shows the utilization values for one individual circuit, taken from the 12 traffic data sets that correspond to the sampling periods shown in Figure A-7. These are not the 12 highest utilization values for this circuit; rather, they are the utilization values that occurred on this circuit during the 12 time periods when the overall system volume was at its highest levels.

The methodology for creating a merged-peak volume value for each circuit is the same as discussed under the merged-peak utilization baseline model and requires that you average the following metrics from every sample selected for each circuit:

■ Packet size in bytes, forward direction (data flowing from source to destination)

■ Packet size in bytes, return direction (data flowing from destination to source)

■ Number of bytes transferred during sample period (e.g. five minutes) forward

■ Number of bytes transferred during sample period (e.g. five minutes) return

Ideally, you will be able to use your performance management tool to do the calculations for you. If not, you can do the calculations by hand, write a script, or use a spreadsheet to do the manipulations. The resulting average utilization values are recorded for each circuit and used to create a "load" within the performance management tool for each circuit, as discussed previously.

Advantages and Disadvantages of a Merged-Peak Volume Baseline Model

Like the merged-peak utilization baseline model strategy, a merged-peak volume strategy lets you control for anomalous peaks by averaging over multiple peaks. This feature can help you avoid the problem of creating a baseline based on a single, possibly anomalous peak sample, which could lead you to predict a requirement for capacity that you are unlikely to use in reality.

On the other hand, like the peak volume strategy, the merged-peak volume strategy leaves open the possibility that there could be worse "worst cases" on individual circuits (especially on smaller circuits) that are not reflected in the samples you selected, because total system volume will tend to be influenced much more significantly by larger (backbone) circuits, which can overwhelm the effects of smaller circuits. Like the peak volume baseline model, the merged-peak volume baseline model may not be sufficiently conservative if guaranteeing quality of service on *all* circuits is paramount under all conditions.

As with other modeling strategies, it is a good idea to create several baseline models from data collected on different days and compare them to ensure that the usage on the various circuits is reasonably consistent (within a 5–10% variance).

Average Utilization or Average Volume Baseline Model

This method creates the least conservative baseline model. It is based on average network usage (measured either as volume or percent utilization) and, as a result, greatly attenuates the effects of peak periods of network activity. It may be quite sufficient if the usage on most circuits in your network is consistent, with only small ranges in volume or percent utilization over time. You may also choose to use this model if your paramount concern is minimizing the ongoing costs of the enterprise network and the possible sacrifice of application quality of service during periods of peak network activity is tolerable. For example, those conditions might be true if you know that peak activity is always due to batch processing that happens during noncritical periods or that it can be prioritized in such a way that the more time-sensitive user activities are given priority during periods when network resources are limited.

With an average baseline method, you average all the samples across the time period of interest, for each circuit in your network model. This model can be created using either volume or utilization as the basis—the method of averaging is the same.

As with the other methods, you need to make sure that you pick a set of usage-based data that is a good representation of the characteristics of the network you plan to model. You might choose to model normal usage during an average day, or average usage on a specific day of interest, such as the last day of the quarter. You should select a time period that includes the active periods of interest (say, 8:00 A.M. to 6:00 P.M. for a normal business day within a single time zone) but excludes periods when network activities occur that you do not want to model. For example, you might want to exclude periods of low activity during "off" hours in your average, because they would create an average that was too low to represent "normal" network usage during the business day. On the other hand, there might be specific activities such as batch jobs or backups run over the enterprise network during "off" hours that would create an average that was too high for some circuits, and again these time periods should be avoided if your goal is to create a "business day" average baseline model.

Again, however, it must be emphasized that you need to make the decisions about how to create your model based on your understanding of your individual situation. For example, you might elect to create an average over only the four hours during the middle of the day

(11:00 A.M. to 3:00 P.M.) because repeated baselining has shown that the bulk of enterprise network activities occur during those four hours. On the other hand, suppose you are planning to implement a new client/server application across an international network. In that case your model may have to account for the fact that backups running at night over the system backbone in the United States are occurring during the middle of the Asian business day and potentially affecting communication between clients in Asia and the proposed application or database servers centrally located in the United States.

Figure A-9 again shows the circuit utilization from 8:00 A.M. to 2:00 P.M. for an example circuit. Figure A-10 shows volume for the same circuit for the same hours. Note that the two charts show identical patterns for the circuit—for an individual circuit it does not matter which you use to calculate the average. The average usage value will be calculated by averaging all the utilization values or all the volume values across the target number of hours. Figure A-11 shows the resulting average utilization value (calculated using utilization data) compared to the peak and merged-peak utilization values, as calculated previously for this single circuit. As can be seen by referring back to the graph shown in Figure A-9, the average value definitely underestimates the utilization compared to the various periods of high utilization.

The implementation of an average utilization or volume baseline model is similar to that of the other two models that make use of

Figure A-9

Circuit utilization in five-minute samples for a single circuit.

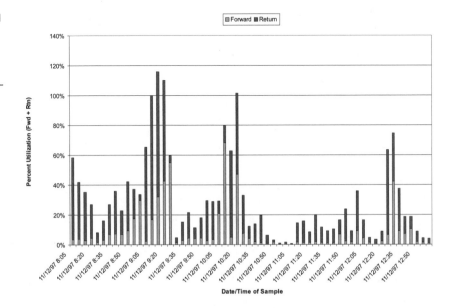

Figure A-10
Total volume over
five-minute samples
for a single circuit.

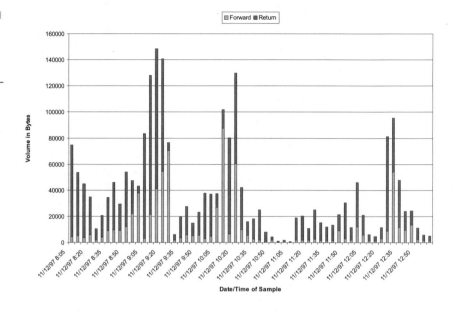

Figure A-11
Comparison of utiliza-
tion values for differ-
ent baseline model
strategies.

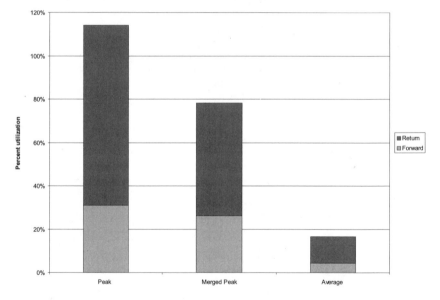

averages. It requires that you average the following metrics from
every sample in the time period, for each circuit:

■ Packet size in bytes, forward direction (data flowing from source to
destination)

■ Packet size in bytes, return direction (data flowing from destination
to source)

- Number of bytes transferred during sample period (e.g., five minutes) forward
- Number of bytes transferred during sample period (e.g., five minutes) return

If possible, you should use your performance management tool to do these calculations. If the software does not have this capability, you can do the calculations by hand, write a script, or use a spreadsheet to do the manipulations for you. Then record the resulting average utilization values and use them to create a "load" within the performance management tool for each circuit, as discussed previously.

The benefit of the average-usage baseline model, when used as the basis for capacity planning analysis, is that it lets you determine capacity requirements necessary to support the application under "average" network load conditions. The drawback is that it can lead to undercapacitation for periods of peak activity if those peaks diverge very much from the average.

As with the previous baseline model strategies, it can be very beneficial to create baseline models from samples taken on different days. Comparing the results of multiple baseline models lets you determine whether the usage on the various circuits is reasonably consistent (within a 5–10% variance).

APPENDIX B

TOOLS FOR NETWORK RESOURCE PLANNING

Data collection and analysis tools and performance management tools are central to the Network Resource Planning (NRP) cycle. These tools are used to collect and report data, generate a traffic baseline description of a network, and model and analyze that network.

One of the key tasks in setting up an NRP project is to determine the set of tools most appropriate for the tasks to be accomplished. Every tool has limitations, an implicit methodology, and set of data characterizations and constraints. These must be taken into account relative to the needs of your planning activities.

This appendix provides an overview of many of the tools currently available for use in an NRP project.

Data Collection and Analysis Tools

Data collection and analysis tools are very important for collecting "live data" from networks for use by performance management tools. For most NRP projects, "live data" will be required, because it is literally impossible to know the traffic flow within a network well enough to enter it into the performance management tool. The data that is collected will be either usage-based data (utilization of WAN circuits or LANs) or application-based data (network conversations).

In Chapter 2, in the section "Tools That Are Available for NRP," data collection and analysis functionality is broken down into two categories: router Management Information Base (MIB) statistical collection tools and traffic analyzers and RMON2 (Remote Monitoring)-compatible probes. The router MIB statistical collection tools collect usage-based data, and the traffic analyzers and RMON2-compatible probes collect application-based data.

Currently available data collection tools will be discussed here in terms of these functional areas. In some cases the data collection and analysis product is also a performance management tool (such as Concord's and NetScout's products), for the baselining processes. The discussion in this area will focus on their ability to provide data to other performance management tools that can do application planning and "what-if" analysis (capacity planning) as well as baselining. Neither Concord's or NetScout's products had any modeling or simulation capability at the time this book was written.

The vendors and tools discussed in this book do not by any means represent an exhaustive list of tools on the market today. The tools described here are those that are market leaders in the data collection and analysis arena at the time of the writing of this book.

Router MIB Statistical Collection Tools

Statistical collection tools extract router MIB data, using Simple Network Management Protocol (SNMP), to create a snapshot of the current traffic load or utilization on a segment (usage-based data). A byte count of traffic transiting through the router is collected by polling each router's MIB at designated time intervals (every five minutes, for example) over several hours/days. This is a quick and efficient, albeit gross, means for determining total network system usage and WAN circuit usage (leased line or Frame Relay PVCs).

Figure B-1 shows an example of a report showing network volume in Gbytes/day over multiple weeks. This particular report was created using Network Health from Concord Communications, Inc.

This type of usage-based data can be very important for understanding the current available capacity of the network. Also, the router MIB statistical collection tool may provide a capability for importing usage-based data into a performance management tool's network model for use in capacity planning. Usage-based data can also help determine where traffic analyzers or RMON2-compatible probes should be placed for a more in-depth analysis of usage-based data.

The following vendors have router MIB statistical collection tools.

Figure B-1
Daily Network
Volume report for
multiple weeks.
(© Concord Communications, Inc.)

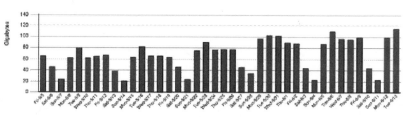

Daily Network Volume

MAKE SYSTEMS, INC. The WAN Traffic Baseliner Plug-In for the NetMaker XA Interpreter tool measures usage patterns and loads on individual WAN circuits (leased lines and Frame Relay PVCs). The WAN Traffic Baseliner Plug-In collects SNMP MIB statistics from each router serial interface. It uses the results from the Discovery Plug-In (an add-on product for the NetMaker XA Visualizer, discussed later in this chapter) to determine which routers have serial connectivity, and then it samples only those routers.

Reports from the WAN Traffic Baseliner tool show usage trends over time, allowing you to pinpoint usage on individual circuits and at various times of day. The tool also provides the usage-based data in a form suitable for importing into a network model created by the Visualizer Discovery tool. The usage-based data loads the WAN circuits in order to perform utilization analysis and capacity planning (Make Systems, Inc., 1996).

CONCORD COMMUNICATIONS, INC. Concord's Network Health is a family of Web-based software applications that automate the collection, analysis, and reporting of critical network data. Network Health discovers and collects SNMP MIB statistics from existing network devices (LAN devices, RMON2 agents, and WAN routers). Figure B-2 shows the architecture, with inputs and outputs, for the Network Health tool.

Like NetMaker XA, the Concord Network Health tool performs a discovery of the network devices to determine which device interfaces to sample. Once the data is collected from the appropriate network devices, the database stores the collected network data and analyzes the historical resource requirements and trends as well as forecasting future resource requirements.

The reporting capability is extensive and includes the categories of baselining reports, bandwidth utilization reports, multivariable reports, and exception reports. The baselining reports compare network activity to an automatically computed baseline for the entire network, including individual segments. The bandwidth utilization reports enable you to view bandwidth usage of each LAN segment and WAN circuit (leased line or Frame Relay PVC) over a specified time period and determine the busiest time of day for the network or for an individual network device. Multivariable reports display values for up to four variables that provide detailed data (such as router CPU or buffer utilization) for particular network devices over a specified time period. Exception reports deliver a concise high-level summary of network locations that require immediate attention.

Figure B-2
Network Health architecture. (© Concord Communications, Inc.)

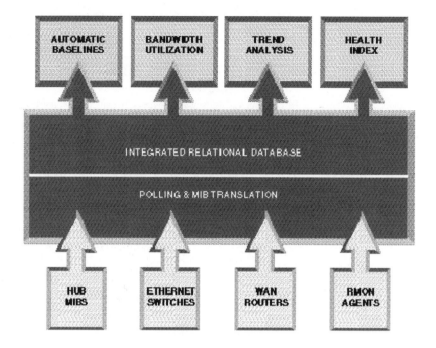

Figure B-2
Network Health architecture. (© Concord Communications, Inc.)

Exporting Network Health data for use with a performance management tool's network model is not currently a function provided directly by the tool. However, it is possible to export the metrics needed for usage-based data from the Network Health database using standard database query capabilities (Concord Communications, 1996).

Traffic Analyzers and RMON2-Compatible Probes

Router MIB data is limited in that it cannot provide information about the type of traffic, application activity, mix of protocols, or other information needed to conduct application planning or capacity planning activities. Traffic analyzers or RMON2-compatible probes monitor network traffic and record detailed application performance parameters about the traffic. This information is usually recorded by the analyzer or probe as network conversations that represent the traffic seen by the collection device. If a performance management tool can support the format of the saved network conversations, the data from the analyzer or probe can be imported into the tool for the purposes of baselining, application planning, and capacity planning ("what-if" analysis).

The following vendors have traffic analyzers or RMON2-compatible probes that work with various performance management tools.

NETWORK GENERAL CORPORATION The Network General Sniffer Network Analyzer (stand-alone or distributed) captures frames and builds a database of network objects from the observed traffic. These network objects will represent global statistics (such as percent utilization of the segment), network stations, network conversations, and so on.

The Sniffer Network Analyzer collects current and historical segment statistics that can be displayed in real time, stored for later display, or exported in Expert Analyzer Output File Format for use by a performance management tool. Many performance management tools use Network General's Expert Analyzer format for import (Network General, 1997).

NETSCOUT SYSTEMS, INC. NetScout Systems' product family consists of intelligent probes and management software that work together to monitor, analyze, and report on distributed enterprise networks. The intelligent probes are based on the RMON and RMON2 (Remote Monitoring) industry standards. The NetScout RMON and RMON2 probes monitor network traffic and can be customized to monitor any application regardless of its protocol. The NetScout Manager collects data from the NetScout probes and provides the depth of performance statistics for use by the NetScout Manager itself as well as for use by other performance management tools.

The performance statistics can be exported from the NetScout Manager's database in the form of network conversations, for use by various performance management tools. This data is used by the performance management tools for doing baselining, application planning, and capacity planning "what-if" analysis (NetScout, Inc., 1997).

Performance Management Tools

Several performance management tools that may play a role in a NRP project are available. One of the key tasks in setting up such a project is to determine the set of tools most appropriate for the tasks to be accomplished. All tools have limits, and each tool is invested with an implicit methodology and set of data characterizations and constraints.

These features must be taken into account relative to the needs of the planning activities. The following sections survey some of the better-known performance management tools available that may be useful in a NRP project.

Performance management involves measuring and predicting the performance of network application traffic, network devices (such as routers and switches), and the network media (WAN circuits and LANs). Examples of measured activities are overall network application throughput (Kbps), utilization of WAN circuits and LANs, error rates, and user response time.

In Chapter 2, in the "Tools for NRP" section, performance management tool functionality is broken down into the following categories: visualization and reporting tools, topology acquisition tools, traffic integrator and consolidator tools, application-profiling tools, and network modeling and simulation tools. Currently available performance management tools will be discussed in terms of these functional areas. The vendors and tools discussed here do not provide an exhaustive list of tools on the market today. The tools described here are ones that, at the time of writing this book, are the market leaders in the performance management arena.

Visualization and Reporting Tools and Topology Acquisition Tools

Visualization (or layout) and reporting tools provide a means to view and report on network resources and traffic and to add to or modify the visualization. The visualization of network devices can be either geographical or logical. These functions usually form the framework of the particular performance management tool—its graphical user interface (GUI). The output of these tools (the map) forms the structure on which other functions depend.

Topology acquisition tools acquire information about the devices on a network in order to record a topological inventory of the network and construct a network topology map. Acquisition can be done by using SNMP queries, by importing data from router configuration files, or by importing data collected from network management platforms or other data collection devices. Topology acquisition tools are necessary because of the extreme difficulty of creating network models manually. Almost all visualization and reporting tools allow you to create network models manually, but it very time-consuming to do this for an entire network, and the resulting model is only as good as the current network documentation (usually outdated). However, this capability can be very useful for modifying the model, such as for adding devices not acquired in the discovery process for one reason or another, or for simulating parts of a network that don't actually exist when the automatic topology collection is done.

Figure B-3 shows an example of a network map, which was created using Optimal Networks' Optimal Surveyor. All of the tools described here can create visualizations similar to this one.

The following vendors have visualization and reporting and topology acquisition tools.

MAKE SYSTEMS, INC. NetMaker XA Visualizer, from Make Systems, Inc., has comprehensive graphical capabilities for viewing, organizing, querying, and reporting on network models. With user-defined network subviews, Visualizer is optimized for dealing with large and complex network models. Because of the fundamental network visualization capabilities it provides, Visualizer is required for implementation of other NetMaker XA tools.

The Visualizer has topology acquisition capability by means of the Discovery Plug-In add-on product. The Discovery Plug-In acquires

Figure B-3

Optimal Surveyor network map. (© Optimal Networks, Inc.)

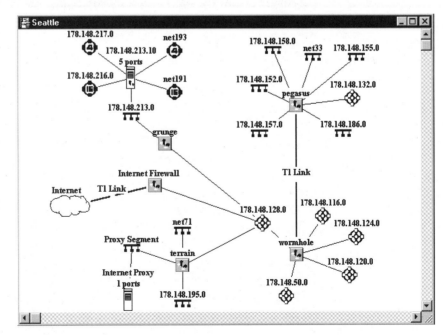

topology data by querying the SNMP agents of routers to identify router configuration assignments and connections within the network. The Discovery Plug-In starts with one seed router (IP address) and SNMP community strings of all the routers. Using the route information provided in the SNMP MIB of each router, all other routers can be found and their information recorded in the NetMaker XA database. Once the discovery process is complete (all routers found), the information is saved as a NetMaker XA network file (model) for use by all NetMaker XA tools. This network model includes all routers (and router configuration), LANs and WAN circuits (leased lines or Frame Relay PVCs). The Visualizer can display the network map in geographical layouts or logical layout (Make Systems, Inc., 1994).

CISCO SYSTEMS   Cisco's NETSYS Connectivity Baseliner provides the dialogs and navigation capabilities needed to visualize all aspects of network connectivity. Connectivity Baseliner can view the network model in campus or flat layouts or view the logical topology by protocol. For example, users can compare an IP network view with an IPX network view. The NETSYS Connectivity Baseliner also lets users troubleshoot router configuration problems in their networks.

The NETSYS Connectivity Baseliner provides topology acquisition capability using Cisco router configuration files, which provide similar information to that gained by querying each router's SNMP agent. The Cisco router configuration files are imported into the Connectivity Baseliner tool and used to construct a network topology map. The resulting graphical representation of the network becomes the "baseline" from which configuration planning and problem solving can be done using the Connectivity Solver tool (Cisco Systems, Inc., 1997a).

OPTIMAL NETWORKS CORPORATION   Optimal Surveyor from Optimal Networks includes a Topology Browser, which displays a variety of views of the network model, such as the example shown in Figure B-3. For example, the Browser allows the selection and viewing of IP or IPX segments, router configurations, and all switches and users on each segment within the model. Graphically based editing capabilities allow changes to be made to a specific network model. The model can be exported for use by the Optimal Performance tool.

Optimal Surveyor provides topology acquisition capability using a multiprotocol topology discovery and analysis tool that creates models of the logical interconnectivity of a network. Using SNMP and IPX to discover the topology of routed networks and the logical connectivity of bridged and switched networks, Optimal Surveyor can build a complete graphical model of the network (see Figure B-3). As with the Net-Maker XA Visualizer Discovery tool, the discovery is started from a seed router and continues until all network information is recorded into the network model (Optimal Networks Corporation, 1997a).

CACI PRODUCTS COMPANY   ComNet Baseliner from CACI Products extracts topology information from popular network management systems such as HP OpenView (and many others) to create a network model. Once the network model is created, ComNet Baseliner allows the combining of multiple network traffic data files, previewing imported traffic patterns through a bird's-eye view of network activity, and the viewing of network conversations between network devices. The network model can be uploaded into ComNet III or ComNet Predictor to perform further analysis (CACI Products Company, 1997a).

Traffic Import and Consolidation Tools and Application-Profiling Tools

Traffic import tools import network data ("live data") captured from Router MIB statistical tools, traffic analyzers, and RMON2-compatible probes into performance management tools for the purpose of baselining, application planning, and capacity planning. Some traffic import tools will import both usage-based data and application data; others import only application-based data.

Traffic consolidation tools integrate multiple files of captured data representing the simultaneous occurrences of traffic seen by multiple analyzers or probes. A consolidation tool purges duplicate, incomplete, or inadequate conversations from the captured data sets during the traffic import process.

Application-profiling tools use imported traffic to create application profiles from the relevant metrics found in the captured data. For example, metrics from 100 captured SAP R/3 GUI sessions could be used to create a profile for a single SAP R/3 user by averaging the relevant statistics for the 100 sessions and recording the averaged numbers into one SAP R/3 single-user profile. The new profile can be used to represent the "average" SAP R/3 user.

The following sections discuss vendors who have traffic import and consolidation tools. Application-profiling tools will not be discussed by vendor, but most vendors that have traffic import capability provide some limited ability to create application profiles, although in some cases the user may have to create the profile manually from the data imported into the tool.

MAKE SYSTEMS, INC. The NetMaker XA Interpreter tool from Make Systems, Inc., imports data from Router MIB statistical tools (such as NetMaker XA WAN Baseliner), traffic analyzers (such as Network General's network traffic analyzers), and RMON2-compatible probes (such as NetScout probes) into a network model created by the NetMaker XA discovery capability. The Interpreter also provides consolidation for data sets collected at the same time from multiple analyzers or probes.

Once the data is imported into the network model, the NetMaker XA Interpreter tool provides many reports for analyzing the usage-based data and the application-based data (network conversations) (Make Systems, Inc., 1994).

Figure B-4 shows the NetMaker XA Interpreter panel for importing either usage-based or application-based data into the discovered network model. In addition, the NetMaker XA Interpreter tool provides a "Generate Profile" capability that automates creating an application profile, as discussed previously, from imported data.

CISCO SYSTEMS   Cisco's NETSYS Performance Baseliner tool imports data from traffic analyzers (such as Network General's network traffic analyzers) and RMON2-compatible probes (such as NetScout probes) into a network model created by the NETSYS Connectivity Baseliner. The Performance Baseliner also provides consolidation for data sets collected at the same time from multiple analyzers or probes.

Once the data is imported into the network model, the NETSYS Performance Baseliner tool provides reports for analyzing the application-based data (network conversations) (Cisco Systems, Inc., 1996b).

CACI PRODUCTS COMPANY   CACI Products' ComNet Baseliner tool imports data from traffic analyzers (such as Network General's network traffic analyzers) and RMON2-compatible probes (such as NetScout probes) into a network model created by the ComNet Baseliner prior to traffic data import. The ComNet Baseliner also provides consolidation for data sets collected at the same time from multiple analyzers or probes.

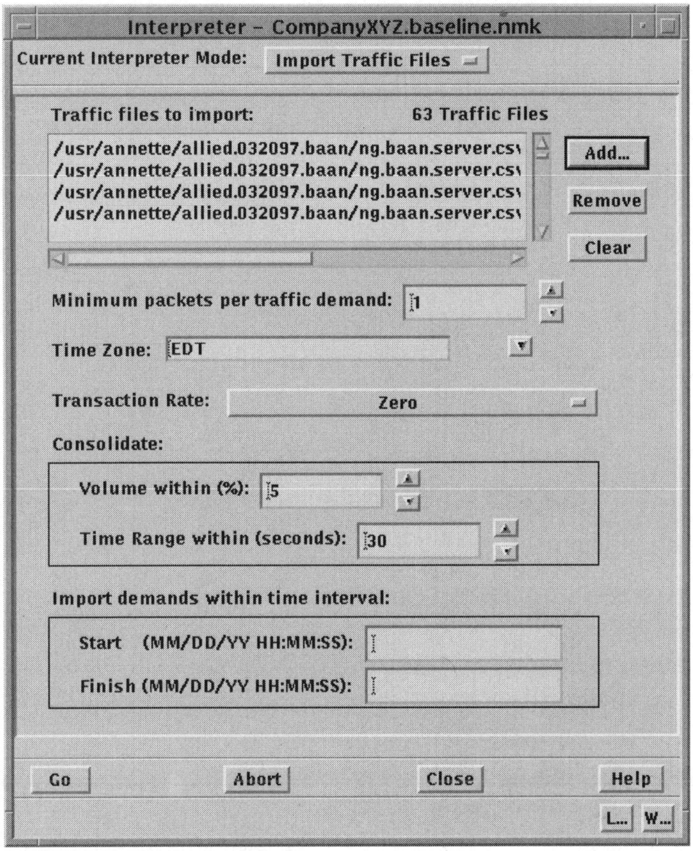

Figure B-4
NetMaker XA Interpreter Import panel.
(© Make Systems, Inc.)

Once the data is imported into the network model, the ComNet Baseliner tool provides reports for analyzing the application-based data (network conversations) (CACI Products Company, 1997a).

OPTIMAL NETWORKS CORPORATION Optimal Networks' Optimal Performance tool imports data from traffic analyzers (such as Network General's network traffic analyzers) into a network model created by the Optimal Surveyor discovery capability. The Optimal Performance tool also provides consolidation for data sets collected at the same time from multiple analyzers.

Once the data is imported into the network model, the Optimal Performance tool provides reports for analyzing the application-based data (network conversations) (Optimal Networks Corporation, 1997b).

Network Modeling and Simulation Tools

Network modeling or simulation is yet another performance management tool function that can be used for doing the "what-if" or capacity planning process. The most difficult part of producing an adequate network simulation is building the network model, which can be accomplished using the tools described in preceding sections according to the process discussed in Chapter 6, "Capacity Planning."

The following vendors provide (analytical) network modeling tools or (discrete) simulation tools. See Chapter 2, "The Network Resource Planning Process," and Chapter 6, "Capacity Planning," for a discussion of analytical modeling versus discrete-event simulation.

MAKE SYSTEMS, INC.   NetMaker XA Planner from Make Systems, Inc., is a device-specific modeling tool (for Cisco, Bay, and 3Com routers) that uses analytical modeling techniques for engineering network changes. Planner can model "what-if" scenarios such as adding users and applications, changing bandwidth or topology, and changing traffic flow patterns. Planner can predict LAN or WAN performance and utilization before and after changes are made to a particular network with a particular set of traffic data.

NetMaker XA Planner is a component in the suite of the NetMaker XA tools. It depends on the NetMaker XA Visualizer and Interpreter tools to build the network model that underlies its analysis (Make Systems, Inc., 1994).

CISCO SYSTEMS   The NETSYS Performance Solver tool is a Cisco-specific modeling tool that uses analytical modeling techniques similar to those of the NetMaker XA Planner product. The Performance Solver performs "what-if" analyses to generate highly quantitative and qualitative estimates of traffic, network resource utilization, and end-to-end transport performance as well as traffic routing analysis. "What-if" analyses can be performed for an existing network to see the results of absorbing new users, relocating resources, or modeling failures of LANs, WAN circuits, or routers.

The network for NETSYS Performance Solver tool is built using the NETSYS Connectivity Baseliner for topology data and the Performance Baseliner for importing traffic data from various analyzers and probes (Cisco Systems, Inc., 1996b).

OPTIMAL NETWORKS CORPORATION Optimal Networks' Optimal Performance's discrete-event simulation capability allows the user to evaluate proposed network designs and changes before they are actually implemented. Starting with a model of an existing network, desired changes to the network can be analyzed to evaluate their effects. LAN segments, workstations, servers, bridges, routers, switches, WAN links, and applications can be added, moved, deleted, and reconfigured. Traffic intensity can be increased and decreased. Simulations of new client/server applications can be designed to evaluate their impact on existing network traffic.

The network is built using other tools, such as the Optimal Surveyor for network discovery and Network General Sniffer Analyzers for collecting traffic data. The data is then imported using the Optimal Performance tool (Optimal Networks Corporation, 1997b).

CACI PRODUCTS COMPANY ComNet III is CACI's discrete-event simulation legacy product. ComNet III accurately predicts LAN, WAN, and enterprise network performance, enabling users to experiment with diverse network alternatives while avoiding costly mistakes. Users describe their proposed networks graphically to obtain immediate views of dynamic animation and reports showing how the network will perform. ComNet III simulates all networking technologies and traffic types including ATM, Frame Relay, TCP/IP, FDDI, client/server, and voice. Using ComNet III's extensive library of objects, you can easily create your network model using the icon drag-and-drop technique or by importing current topology from your network management system and traffic from your data collection devices using the ComNet Baseliner tool (CACI Products Company, 1997b).

CACI PRODUCTS COMPANY ComNet Predictor is more of an analytical modeling product using CACI's Flow Decomposition technique. ComNet Predictor is designed for network managers and planners who need to predict how changes will affect their networks but do not have the time to perform detailed simulation studies. After you use the ComNet Baseliner tool to import current topology and traffic into the model, ComNet Predictor immediately generates graphs and charts illustrating how changes such as adding users or applications, altering equipment, or changing bandwidth affects network performance. Measures of delay and utilization can be analyzed to find network bottlenecks. ComNet Predictor complements CACI's simulation tool, ComNet III, by quickly identifying scenarios that warrant detailed simulation studies. ComNet Predictor can then export network models to ComNet III (CACI Products Company, 1997c).

References

CACI Products Company (1997a), ComNet Baseliner datasheet. Available at http://www.caciasl.com/Baseliner.html.

CACI Products Company (1997b), ComNet III datasheet. Available at http://www.caciasl.com/comnetthree.html.

CACI Products Company (1997c), ComNet Predictor datasheet. Available at http://www.caciasl.com/COMNETPredictor.html.

Cisco Systems, Inc. (1997a), NETSYS Connectivity Tools 3.0 datasheet. Available at http://www.cisco.com/warp/public/734/toolkit/ctols_ds. htm.

Cisco Systems, Inc. (1996b), NETSYS Performance Tools 2.0 datasheet. Available at http://www.cisco.com/warp/public/734/toolkit/perft_ds. htm.

Concord Communications (1996), Network Health datasheet (family.pdf). Available at http://www.concord.com/products.htm.

Make Systems, Inc. (1994), NetMaker XA datasheet.

Make Systems, Inc. (1996), *Technical Bulletin—WAN Traffic Baseliner Plug-In.*

NetScout, Inc. (1997), NetScout Products datasheet. Available at http://www.netscout.com/products/netscout.html.

Network General (1997), Sniffer Network Analyzer datasheet. Available at http://www.networkgeneral.com/product_info/sna/san_intro/portable.html.

Optimal Networks Corporation (1997a), Optimal Surveyor datasheet. Available at http://www.optimal.com/OS.

Optimal Networks Corporation (1997b), Optimal Performance datasheet. Available at http://www.optimal.com/op/about.htm.

APPENDIX C

GLOSSARY

ACK (acknowledgment) A packet sent from destination to source acknowledging that the preceding transmission has been received

agent A component of a network management system that collects defined data points and reports on those data points when queried by the management system

analysis Examination of the elements of something complex and their relationships; *see also* network utilization analysis, sensitivity analysis, survivability analysis.

analytical modeling The use of numeric equations to determine how a given network environment will perform given a set of conditions

application-based data Data that specifically describes a conversation on a network, such as source and destination address, number of packets in each direction, start and end time of transmission, and the type of application that produced the conversation

application planning The analysis of individual application transactions to determine the demands they will make on a given network

ASCII (American Standard Code for Information Interchange) The usual method for representing characters (such as E) by bytes of data (such as 1000101), using seven bits in each octet

asymmetrical In reference to bidirectional communication, not having equal volumes of data flowing in each direction

average usage A method for creating a baseline model in which the usage-based data samples for a given time period are averaged to identify the representative traffic load that will be used

baselining The process of collecting and documenting the physical configuration and the traffic utilization of an existing network

BECN (Backward Explicit Congestion Notification) The mechanism used in Frame Relay to notify a device that there is congestion on the backward path

benchmark A defined or standardized set of steps, together completing a task or tasks that are used as a basis for evaluation of an application's behavior within a given network environment

BGP (Border Gateway Protocol) An interdomain policy routing protocol used to exchange Internet routing information incrementally rather than by sending the entire database

bottleneck The network element that restricts the flow of network traffic from free movement or progress at optimal throughput rates

bps (bits per second) A measurement of the rate at which data travels

browser A graphical user interface typically used to navigate within the Internet

byte A measure of data, usually 8 bits, generally used when discussing an amount or volume of data; *see also* octet

capacitate To allocate and provision bandwidth in order for a network to be capable of supporting network traffic

capacity The amount of bandwidth a network has available

capacity planning Techniques that provide a methodical approach to determine how a network will behave when changes are introduced to the given network environment

capture To collect and record network traffic statistics

CDV (Cell Delay Variation) A measure of the standard deviation of the arrival of cells. This measure may be reported as a certain level of jitter—packets or cells arriving out of synchronization

CIR (Committed Information Rate) The maximum average data rate at which a customer reserves bandwidth and is guaranteed availability on a Frame Relay circuit

client/server Distributes the computing function of an application between the client (or end user) computer and the server

client The end user portion of a client/server application, which makes requests to the server for services

CLR (Cell Loss Ratio) The ratio of lost cells to the total number of transmitted cells (the sum of cells received plus cells lost)

collection device A specially configured device that gathers and stores specified data points

congestion An excessive amount of network traffic so that symptoms of delay and inability to connect begin to appear either within collected traffic data or to the end user

conversation A bidirectional exchange of packets between two hosts

CTD (Cell Transfer Delay) The time from the insertion of the first bit of the cell to the exiting of the last bit of the cell, from source to destination. This time incorporates both propagation delay and processing delay for each ATM device along the route

delay simulator   A device that can mimic or represent a "live" network connection for purposes of measuring throughput and response time

discrete-event simulation   Use of mathematical representations of specific events, such as packets, to predict how the network will perform

encapsulation   A method for enveloping data that is not in the form used by a network's protocol within a packet header and trailer so that it can be routed on the network; for example, TCP/IP encapsulation of SNA traffic allows data to be sent over the Internet between IBM mainframe systems

enterprisewide   In use over an entire organization or network

ERP   (Enterprise Resource Planning) A client/server application that is designed to coordinate and act as an information resource to an entire organization or enterprise

FECN   (Forward Explicit Congestion Notification) The method used in Frame Relay to notify a device that there is congestion on the forward path

Frame Relay   Packet-oriented communication for the transmittal of data, primarily used to interconnect local area networks with wide area networks

FTP   (File Transfer Protocol) The protocol within the TCP/IP family of protocols that supports file transfers or copying from one system to another as well as file delete and renaming

GUI   (Graphical User Interface) The portion of an application that is viewed and used by an end user to make requests to the server or receive and display responses to a request

headroom   Capacity available for future growth within a given network design

host   An individual device or computer on a network

HTTP   (HyperText Transfer Protocol) The protocol used by end users to communicate with a server to access information on the World Wide Web or a similar web on an intranet

IfInOctets   (Interface In Octets) The object within a MIB that counts the number of octets moving into the interface of a device

IfOutOctets   (Interface Out Octets) The object within a MIB that counts the number of octets moving out of the interface of a device

IGRP (Interior Gateway Routing Protocol) A Cisco Systems, Inc., proprietary distance-vector routing protocol

Internet A TCP/IP-based global network of networks

interval An amount of time such as that between the start and stop of a network process; for example, five-minute intervals are commonly used in collecting traffic samples, so that a new collection period begins every five minutes

intranet A TCP/IP-based network that is accessible only to users within a specific organization

IPX (Internetwork Packet Exchange) The peer-to-peer networking protocol used by Novell NetWare

IS (Information Systems) A common name for the group or department that manages a corporate network

IT (Information Technology) A common name for the group or department that manages a corporate network

Kbps (Kilobits per second) A measurement of the rate at which bits are traveling

Kbytes (Kilobytes, 1,024 bytes) A measurement of data in volume

LAN (local area network) Computer systems connected via coaxial cable, twisted-pair, or fiber within a local environment, such as a floor, a building, or a campus

latency The time it takes for packets to traverse a network

MAC (Media Access Control) The protocol that defines how a system will access and communicate data at the datalink layer

MAN (Metropolitan Area Network) Computer systems connected within a metropolitan or city area

media The type of physical network connection, such as Ethernet, Token Ring, or FDDI

merged peak A statistical method for averaging a given number of highest known data points in order to lessen the effect of possible anomalies and yet preserve the peaks

methodology The approach or procedure taken to accomplish a given set of tasks or project

metric A numerical measurement used to determine performance

MIB (Management Information Base) A database of definitions and manageable objects that collect statistics and can be queried for status, configuration information, or specific data points

MIS (Management Information Systems) A common name for the group or department that manages a corporate network

mission-critical Required in order for an organization to succeed in its purpose

model A representation or replica of a given item

modeling *See* analytical modeling

multicast A message addressed to a specific group, one to many

network utilization analysis A study of the available bandwidth and how much of that bandwidth is in regular use

NRP (Network Resource Planning) A set of software-enabled methods for ongoing management and planning of enterprise networks

octet Eight bits of data; *see also* byte

OSPF (Open Shortest Path First) A link-state routing protocol that supports a layered or hierarchical approach to routing

packets The format in which data is transmitted

peak usage A method for selecting the usage-based data sample that represents the peak or highest level of usage known to occur for each connection within the network regardless of time of occurrence

peak volume A method for selecting the usage-based data sample set that represents the largest volume of traffic in bytes to occur during any one interval period

performance management tool A software tool that has been designed to help with the sorting, correlation, and reporting of data in order to determine the type of performance a network is delivering under given conditions

pilot A test scenario

PPS (packets per second) A measurement of the rate at which packets travel

probe A device that collects and records traffic data

profile A statistical representation of an application in terms of the amount of bandwidth needed to complete a given activity successfully

propagation delay The delay that data incurs by transmitting through a network

PVC (permanent virtual circuit) A permanent association between two hosts on a packet-switch network (such as Frame Relay) as though they were directly connected

Quality of service   Application performance (response time and throughput) as perceived by the application user. Quality of service is affected by server performance, network performance, and client performance

QoS   (Quality of Service) The performance or service level provided by the network, and measured in an ATM environment by metrics such as Cell Transfer Delay (CTD), Cell Delay Variation (CDV), and Cell Loss Ratio (CLR)

queue   A buffer within a device to store packets temporarily while waiting to send them to their next destination

redistribution   The process in which a device republishes information to neighbors on the network, such as a router publishing its routing tables

redundancy   A duplicate route to the existing connectivity within a network in order to diminish the effects of a single component failure

response time   The amount of time a user must wait for screens or keyboard to be ready to accept further input

RIP   (Routing Information Protocol) A distance-vector routing protocol within the TCP/IP family that is responsible for exchanging routing information between routers

RMON2   (Remote Monitoring) A standards-based MIB within a network device that collects information and performance statistics about network traffic and responds to SNMP queries to allow monitoring of remote devices

RTD   (round trip delay) The amount of delay or time in milliseconds for a packet to travel to its destination and back again

sensitivity analysis   A study of how the network responds to excessive levels of bandwidth utilization; that is, at what level of utilization the network breaks

SLA   (service level agreement) An agreement that defines the level of service that a network must guarantee

SMDS   (Switched Multimegabit Data Service) A Bellcore data transfer service

SMTP   (Simple Mail Transport Protocol) A protocol within the TCP/IP family used to transfer electronic mail between systems

SNA   (System Network Architecture) A protocol for data communication defined by IBM

SNMP (Simple Network Management Protocol) A protocol used to communicate and request management data from a device's MIB

SPF (Shortest Path First) A routing protocol that uses the network's topology to make routing decisions

SQL (Structured Query Language) A language used with databases to query or request specific information

survivability analysis A study of how the network handles failure conditions

T1 circuit A communication circuit capable of allowing data to pass at 1.544 megabits per second

TCP/IP (Transmission Control Protocol/Internet Protocol) A protocol suite that supports communication between systems from different vendors

Telnet A login and terminal emulation program within the TCP/IP family

test bed Typically an isolated environment that allows for testing of equipment and software

three-tier Having the capability of maintaining an application's database, the application software, and the GUI on separate host computers on a network

throughput An overall measurement of the data transfer rate at which network traffic can move from computer to computer through a network

traffic analyzer A device that collects and reports network traffic statistics

transaction A set of specific activities that, when executed in sequence, complete a task

two-tier Having the capability of maintaining an application's database and the GUI on two different host computers on a network, and the application software on one or the other of the two hosts

usage-based data The number of bytes that have traveled through a given portion of the network during a given period of time

UUCP (UNIX to UNIX Copy Program) A file copying service typically used in electronic mail systems

WAN (wide area network) A network that is connected with either dedicated or public circuits typically provided by telephone companies or public utilities

"**what-if**" **scenario** A set of changes to specifically investigate how a given network environment will perform

WWW (World Wide Web) The collection of interlinked documents stored on servers that are connected via the Internet and can be retrieved using HTTP

INDEX

ABOUT THE AUTHORS

Annette Clewett is a Senior Network Consultant at Make Systems, Inc. (Mountain View, CA) where she specializes in the deployment of SAP R/3 applications in enterprise networks. As Consulting and Education Services Manager at Make Systems, Inc., **Dana Franklin** (Sunnyvale, CA) has maintained intensive network planning courses for a number of Fortune 500 companies. A former writer and network management product manager at Hewlett-Packard and Sun Microsystems, **Ann McCown** is the principal of her own consulting company, Ann McCown & Associates (Menlo Park, CA).